Achieve Your Dreams

Live Each Day With Passion, Success & Happiness

GARY N HANEY

Achieve Your Dreams
Copyright © 2019 by Gary N Haney

Tellwell Talent
www.tellwell.ca

ISBN
978-0-2288-1570-9 (Paperback)

Table of Contents

Acknowledgments

This book would not have been possible without the inspiration, support and guidance of many people. All that I am and all that I offer have been made possible by the grace of God and the many people I have been blessed to encountered during my life journey.

First and most important is the Lord my God and the angel he sent to guide me, my wife and best friend, Linda. Through their inspiration and support, I was able to develop hope and desire to improve my life. When I think of Linda, I think of the song by Alabama *Angel's among Us*. Linda was sent down to me from somewhere up above. She came to me in my darkest hour to show me how to live, to teach me how to give and to guide me by the light of love. To this day, she stands at my side, encouraging and supporting me.

Next, I would like to thank all the people who give of themselves to help others improve their lives. They provide guidance and hope though their writings, workshops and presentations. Their knowledge and experience have been a great help in creating the wonderful life and world I now live in.

A special thank you to Anthony Robbins who, through his book *Awaken the Giant Within* and his self-improvement program Personal Power, gave me the tools and strength I needed to turn my life around and guide me to become the man I now am. Without Tony's inspiration, I would not have found and travelled the path I am now on.

I would also like to thank Jack Canfield for his book *The Success Principles* and his programs that instruct how to learn and teach the success principles. It is through his inspiration and teaching that I am able to pass this important information on to others.

A special thank you to all six of my children. Though I was not a good role model and father to most of you throughout the years, you have continued to call me dad and love me. I know I cannot make up for my past mistakes, but your forgiveness and love are a powerful comfort. I truly believe that in need you will always be there for me. I am proud of you all and am blessed to have you as my children. I pray that I am able to become an inspiration to you on how to live a life of love, giving and happiness. I cannot express enough how happy our family events and dinners together make me feel.

I would also like to thank all the board members and volunteers of the St. Dismas Prison Ministry Society for their commitment of love, care and effort in making our prisoner reintegration and aftercare ministry such a great success. They have truly helped change lives and heal communities.

Finally, I would like to thank all the prisoners and support workers I have met and worked with over the years as a prison chaplain and aftercare provider. Their journeys, stories and commitment to improving their lives and the lives of others around them have been a great inspiration to me. I consider myself blessed to be able to use my life experience and growth to help others who struggle in life discover hope, inspiration, purpose and happiness.

Preface

I am confident that the reason you are looking at this book is because deep inside your heart and mind you truly believe that you can be more than you are now. You believe that there is more to life and you want to experience it. You are searching for answers to questions such as "why is my life the way it is? Why am I not able to live the life I know I am capable of? Why am I being treated this way?"

If this is true and you feel this way, then I know you are no different than I was only a short time ago. Like you, my life was not going according to plan. I found myself doing and saying things that brought misery not only to myself but to those I love. I could not understand why I did what I did. It was not my intention. I truly wanted the best for myself and those around me.

I wrote this book to provide you with hope and show you that our dreams and desires can be attained. I use the lessons and example of my life to show the change from pain and misery to joy and happiness, from disruptive desperation to purpose and passion. Yes, you too can achieve your dreams and live the life you have always desired. It is within your power and no one can stop you if you decide that you will no longer accept the life that you have been experiencing.

Yes, you and you alone have the power to learn and improve if you choose to. Read on and let what I have learned and implemented into my life guide you to be the person you always wanted to be. It is up to you.

I have spent years learning and implementing what it takes to live life on my terms. I give this to you as a gift. If I can help change one life, then all my struggles have been worth it. I believe in you so it is now time to believe in yourself. Read on and let me and the many others I have learned from and the lessons I have experienced in life be a guide to you. I pray that you find purpose and passion and live a joyful and happy life. If I was able to achieve such a life after the things I have done and the life I lived then I know you can do it.

Let the Beatitudes written below (Matthew 5:3–10; *New American Bible*, Saint Joseph Edition) inspire you and may God be with you and guide you towards a life of meaning and happiness.

Blessed are the poor in spirit, for theirs
is the kingdom of heaven.

Blessed are they who mourn, for they will be comforted.

Blessed are the meek, for they will inherit the land.

Blessed are they who hunger and thirst for
righteousness, for they shall be satisfied.

Blessed are the merciful, for they will be shown mercy.

Blessed are the clean of heart, for they will see God.

Blessed are the peacemakers, for they
will be called children of God.

Blessed are they who are persecuted for the sake of
righteousness, for theirs is the kingdom of heaven

Foreword

The Purpose of This Book
What's in it for you?

"In order to change it is important to know who you are, what you believe, and how you became that person. Only then can we live more comfortably in the present and cease unconscious reactions that result in undesired outcomes."

— Paula Heller Garland

We all have dreams and desires and maybe even a vision of how we would like our lives to turn out. Most of us are seeking purpose, acceptance, happiness and fulfillment in our lives. The problem is that life itself tends to get in the way and our dreams become nightmares, desires become shrouded in doubt and hopes become bleak. Our lives have become so overwhelming that we accept or even expect disappointment and failure. We come to believe that we are not worthy or capable of achieving that great vision we once had.

Why is it that we want to act and live one way but our actions and the results are the opposite? Our heart is loving but our endeavours are hurtful. We desire to do the right thing but we end up generating something destructive. Our motivations are well intentioned but the accomplishments are few.

The problem is that our life conditions are not matching our life blueprint. We had a great blueprint of how we wanted to live our life but we stopped following it. We have allowed many years of outside influences and personal experiences to negatively program our minds. This influx of disappointment, pain and suffering has ultimately formed our beliefs and guides our actions today. This negative programming, if not addressed and reversed, will keep us on the path to disappointment and despair.

The good news is that just as we have been affected and guided by negative programming, it is not only a possibility but a certainty that we can effectively reprogram our minds to believe and achieve all that we have ever desired or envisioned.

This book is designed to assist you in doing just that. Below, you will find straightforward, understandable and easily implemented strategies to help you reprogram yourself, create lasting change and live the life you have desired and dreamed of.

We begin by discovering who we are. "Who am I" is a question many of us ask ourselves but never come to understand. It all starts by learning and understanding why we are here, who we are and what we want. The first section of this book is focused on learning our purpose, mission, vision and identity in life.

First, we need to discover our purpose. Knowing your purpose gives meaning to life. What is life all about? Why am I here today and in this place? These are questions we all seek an answer to. When we discover our purpose, we are able to develop references that show us how to live and what will bring happiness and fulfillment into our lives. Living on purpose is a driving force that helps us to overcome many things we endure and may not understand.

By discovering our purpose, we now need to define how we will live our purpose. How we live our purpose becomes our mission. Defining that mission and being able to use it as a guide in what we do and how we live our life become our second task.

When we know and understand our purpose and mission, we are ready for the next step, envisioning our future. It is time to create a compelling future by developing a life vision. A life vision defines who we want to be, how we want to live, what we want to be known for and the set of experiences and accomplishments we aim to achieve. We all have glimpses of the future, small visions of what our perfect life would look like. But what we envision is quickly dispersed by our disempowering beliefs and identity. Over time, the negative experiences of our day-to-day life cause our vision to become distorted, morphed into a vision we neither created nor desired. This morphed vision takes control and leads us to its painful fulfillment. It is time to take back control of our vision and use it to create a plan that will allow us to passionately work towards and achieve our new vision and receive the happiness and fulfillment we have always desired.

The next step of our journey is to discover who we are and how we can become the person we want to be. We need to discover and understand our identity. Who am I as a person? What makes me do what I do? Your identity consists of the qualities, beliefs, values, needs, experiences, personality and expressions that define you as a person. These qualities include those that set you apart from others and the qualities that control all your actions and thoughts. Our identity is the controlling factor of how we act and are perceived. Most of us have never consciously focused on or understood our identity. Our subconscious identity has taken over and our lives become a result of this hidden character.

If your conscious or subconscious identity is that you are an alcoholic, then your actions will be those of an alcoholic. You may be able to change your behaviour for the short term, but eventually your identity will take over and the result will be the behaviours and actions of an alcoholic. Only by understanding your present uniqueness and then developing strategies to develop a new empowering identity will you be able to have a chance at positive life change.

Once we have discovered ourselves, it is time to move on to the second section and understand ourselves by finding out why we do what we do. Have you ever planned to do or not do a certain activity or act in a certain manner only to end up doing the opposite? Have you or anyone else asked why you said something or acted a certain way only to respond "I don't know?" Rest assured that you're not the only one to experience this frustration. Much of what we do, how we act and how we treat others is a result of several factors that subconsciously control us.

In the second section of this book we discuss several concepts that affect why we do what we do and learn how to take back control of these guiding principles.

Everything we have ever done is the result of a decision or choice we have made. Each day we make thousands of decisions and choices, both conscious and subconscious. The first concept we will explore is the power of our decisions and choices, and how we make them.

Have you ever found yourself judging someone new and acting a certain way towards them without references or reasons to back up your reaction? This brings up the next concept, perception and beliefs. There are many situations in our daily lives in which we allow perception to control our behaviour or actions. Just as perception can affect our actions and reactions, our beliefs—whether factual or imagined—make an even larger impact on our lives. Our beliefs can be empowering or limiting, conscious or subconscious. Only when we are able to understand and control our perceptions and beliefs can we start to effect lasting change.

The desire to gain pleasure and avoid pain is inherent in each one of us. Though we all seek pleasure in life, we will do more to avoid pain than to achieve pleasure. This is one of the main controlling factors of our actions and behaviour. Understanding and learning how to use and control pain and pleasure can bring about immediate positive change in our lives.

We all have certain beliefs, values, needs and desires in our lives. Each of us strives to have these areas of our lives met on a daily basis. Most of us do not wholly understand what they are or their priority in our life. This leads to confusion as our life areas compete with each other, resulting in contradictory behaviour.

How about the actions we do regularly without consciously thinking about them, or how we instantly respond to certain situations without reasoning? These are the result of habits and rituals we have formed over the years. We all have good and bad habits and routines. Knowing and controlling these habits and routines are fundamental to living a successful life.

The next important concept to understand is the effect that what we focus on or the mental state we are in while moving through the day will have direct input on our actions. Our focus can become very narrow, not leaving room for other possible thoughts. Our mental state including how we feel is a powerful controlling factor in our lives.

One of the most influential factors that affects the quality of our lives is our environment. Our community, family, friends and work as well as what we see or are involved in have the greatest impact on us. Much of what we have programmed in our minds is the result of life that goes on around us. Most of this programming came over time without our sensing it. To understand how our past and present environment has shaped how we live today is one of the most important steps we can undertake to begin change.

Once we understand ourselves and have learned why and how we function in life, it is time to delve into the third section of this book. We are now ready to create lasting change.

First, we must learn to take absolute responsibility for ourselves and our actions. We no longer let outside situations or influences become a distraction or excuse. Our fears, demons and experiences of the past—whether conscious or suppressed—can and usually do affect how we live our lives. Until we acknowledge and treat those fears and demons, they will be a controlling factor in the progression of our lives. Dealing with the past hurt in our life necessitates us to confront our fears. Fear—whether real or imagined—can prevent even the smallest steps forward.

Developing a healthy attitude is also important. Our attitude towards others and ourselves can both help us along our life journey and become a stumbling block. Our attitude affects how we act and how we treat others; it is how others perceive us and how they act and react toward us. It is also responsible for the effort we instill in what we are planning or doing.

One of the most influential activities we can do is to come up with a plan, a road map as to what we will do on a daily basis to live our vision. It is the power of goal setting that can lead us to success. Without a proper plan and direction, we are like a rudderless ship trying to cross the ocean bouncing from one wave to another. We live our lives aimlessly travelling through life one day to the next.

It is important that we now start to believe in ourselves and our future. We need to search within ourselves to understand and develop a personal faith. By employing faith in ourselves, we are able to overcome most distractions, disappointments and mistakes that happen in our life.

Once we understand how to create change, it is time to take massive action. We are now able to implement the changes we have discovered and start the journey to passion, success and happiness. We begin by understanding and applying the successful life formula. This formula is a process that helps you get from where you are to where you want to be. We need to challenge the limiting and disempowering beliefs we have that impede positive change. Next, we must set ourselves up to win. In this stage we address the many areas of our lives that will frustrate and hinder lasting change. We immediately implement the steps required to attain our vision and goals. Then it is time to raise our standards. No more settling for less as now is the time to become strong. As we move along the journey, we learn to foresee and adjust to the many roadblocks and setbacks that we will encounter along the way. As we manoeuvre through our daily lives, our destination becomes closer, helping our fears and doubt to dissipate.

Finally, in the last section of the book, we learn how to keep our efforts going and experience lasting change. It takes passion and effort to succeed and be happy. There are four easy-to-implement routines that will keep us going even when we are tired, uncertain or discouraged. We see how starting the day right will give us strength both physically as well as mentally. Learning to reflect and humbly acknowledge our faults, learn from them and acknowledge our many blessings helps us to grow, overcome our mistakes and be truly thankful. Effective preparation will aid us along the journey, keep us securely on the path of our life map and ensure we achieve our goals along the way. To ensure this achievement and success, we must access and allow others to assist us along the way through mentorship and personal coaching. This one step is vital as it provides us accountability and support.

At present, your life may seem so unmanageable that you have all but given up and have accepted the fate you are living. If you are still reading at this point, then I commend you. I know that deep down you desire more from your life and that you still have a glimmer of hope.

Similar to you, I was at this point in my life. It took many books and workshops for me to learn how to understand who I was and why my life was opposite to my dreams and desires. Then I was able to learn and use that knowledge to create positive and lasting change. I was a stubborn man of no faith, but I reached out and asked the Lord who I did not believe in to help me find this elusive faith. Slowly, through trust and commitment, a faith grew in me so strong that it gave me the strength I needed when fear and doubt were all around.

I am here now as proof and inspiration that if you truly open yourself, learn and begin to implement the strategies you will discover in this book, your life will start to improve. Over time, you will become stronger and start to believe in yourself as I did. Like a small snowball rolling down a hill, you will grow, pick up speed and finally realize the dreams and desires that for so long seemed impossible.

The purpose of this book is to help you discover and understand who you are, what you truly want from life and how to achieve it. What you will get from the book is the understanding, strategies and tools to create lasting change in your life and live each day with passion, success and happiness. I have included many examples of people just like you who have stepped up and experienced lasting change. They are now living happy and passionate lives that once were only a dream. It is up to you, but rest assured you are not alone. There are many people who want to help and support you if you let them.

Are you ready now to create positive and lasting change in your life? If so, I have three requests of you:

→ First, read through this book and complete the tasks as they are presented.
→ Second, find someone to mentor or coach you. At the end of this book are contact numbers for support or you could try a member of a church or someone you look up to. Step up and ask. Most people would feel blessed to be asked and willing to help you.
→ Third, read an incantation I learned from Anthony Robbins. Repeat this incantation out loud several times a day. Let it sink into your heart and build your passion to start living life on your terms. I encourage you to:

Read it, Believe it, Become it.

I AM THE VOICE.
I WILL LEAD NOT FOLLOW.
I WILL BELIEVE, NOT DOUBT.
I WILL CREATE, NOT DESTROY.
I AM A FORCE FOR GOOD.
I AM A FORCE FOR GOD.
I AM A LEADER.
I DEFY THE ODDS.
I SET A NEW STANDARD.
I WILL STEP UP!
I WILL STEP UP!

I WILL STEP UP!

I was able to create and realize lasting change in my life, and I truly believe you can also experience the passion, desire and fulfillment life has to offer you. We all have the capability if we only access it. Accept responsibility and take charge of your life. I know the Lord will bless you, give you strength and inspire you to become the person you have always dreamed and desired to become.

SECTION ONE

DISCOVERING MYSELF

"Self Knowledge is the beginning of Self Improvement"

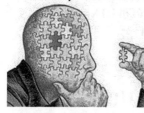

"Discovering who you are is the first step to becoming who you want to be."
— Gary Haney

Quote by: Baltasar Gracian

Who am I?

The search for purpose and meaning has frustrated people since the beginning of creation. Why am I here? What is the meaning of life? Do I have a purpose? These are questions that many ask but few people find the answer to.

Yet the answers are there if you truly want to find them. If someone is to live a happy, successful and fulfilling life, they need to start by discovering who they are. Everybody on this Earth has a unique purpose. To learn this purpose gives them the direction required to find their life mission, envision a powerful future and define who they are as an individual.

In this chapter, we will embark on a journey to discover all that you desire and need to know about yourself. This information is required to enact positive and lasting change in your life. This chapter will be the foundation for the rest of the life-enhancing chapters in this book. Discovering who you are will allow you to become the person you intended to be and allow you to create the life you desire.

CHAPTER ONE

Discover Your Purpose

Why am I here? What is it all about?

"He who has a why to live for, can bear almost any how."
— **Friedrich Nietzsche**

In This Chapter
- ➤ The Search for Meaning
- ➤ The Power of Purpose
- ➤ Discovering Your Purpose
- ➤ Greater Purpose, Individual Purpose and Communal Purpose Exercises
- ➤ Creating Your Life Purpose Statement
- ➤ Life Purpose Statement Exercise
- ➤ Summary

Over the years, one of the biggest struggles I had to face was the question "what is the meaning of life?" I had no idea what my life was about or where I fit in. I could not understand why aspects of my life were not working out in the way I wanted them to. Like most people, I was trying to find purpose and meaning in my life and it was an ongoing battle.

I was never able to properly plan my future because I was always busy trying to discover what it was that I actually wanted. All my focus was centred on finding and experiencing instant gratification. At times, I thought I knew what would bring me happiness based on my past life experiences

At one point in my life, I thought all I needed was the love, respect and attention of others to be happy. But at the time I did not understand what real love and friendship were. I acted out in different ways to get others to notice, respect and love me. Because of my lack of understanding, most of my efforts worked exactly the opposite of my longing and caused more sorrow in my life than the happiness I desired.

I needed direction but had no idea where to get it. I kept struggling to find the answers I needed without really knowing the questions. I was so busy acting and reacting to life around me that I had no focus. I attempted anything that I thought would make me happy so I shifted aimlessly from one situation to the next, thinking I knew what I wanted and how to get it but at the time I had no clue. I journeyed through life attempting different approaches, which brought mixed results. Most of what I tried brought only disappointment or more questions.

Only later in life did I realize that I had no idea what I was doing, and it left me feeling lost and hopeless. I felt there had to be more to life than what I was experiencing. I believed there must be answers to the questions "why am I here, what is it all about, and what is my purpose?" Finally, I decided to stop floating through life and set out to find the answers I so desperately desired.

Only after I was able to humble myself and accept that I did not know as much as I thought I knew about life was I ready to begin an honest search for the answers. Similar to my experience, man's search for meaning and purpose is a question most people strive to answer at some time in their lives. This chapter will help you discover the answer to the most mystifying question: what is the meaning of your life?

The Search for Meaning

Have you ever asked yourself "why am I here, what is it all about, why is my life turning out this way?" These are questions that have been asked by most people at one point in their lives. Often the questions arise when a person is going through a stressful or difficult time in their life and when the pain they are experiencing has become overwhelming. Their life feels unmanageable and not at all as they had imagined or desired it. They feel that their surroundings and other people are controlling the direction of their lives. They are depressed and feel helpless. Had they only been asking themselves these important life questions earlier, a great deal of their stress and difficulties could have been avoided.

The problem is that most people get so caught up in the daily struggle of their lives that they fail to focus on these important questions. The desire to avoid pain and to experience instant pleasure and happiness consume their time and thoughts. The rat race of life keeps them distracted from the true pleasure and happiness that exist in life. They are side-tracked from understanding and living their real purpose and mission in life.

People often give up on their dreams and desires, visibly struggling to get through the day. Only when they are finally forced to confront some of these difficult questions is change possible. These questions suddenly force them to confront their lack of purpose and mission in life. It is only when they realize and come to understand that passion, happiness and fulfillment cannot be achieved without having a mission that positive improvement begins. It is only when they open themselves to candid personal discernment about their present life, relationships, environment, past actions, feelings and desires can they begin to discover their true life purpose. As they learn this purpose, it starts to offer them a meaning for their life and will set them on the mission to live out their purpose and live it passionately. That mission lived passionately is what will bring real happiness and fulfillment into their lives. As for others, once you discover a definite purpose and meaning for your life, you will truly experience a life of passion, pleasure and happiness.

The Power of Purpose

For years I have searched for my purpose, and I have finally come to believe that we are all born with a purpose for our lives. Being on purpose helps guide us along the path of life. If discovered, pursued and applied, an individual life purpose can provide meaning and passion in our daily lives. This meaning and the mission to live it will guide us to the true pleasure and happiness we so desire. It is in seeking, discovering, understanding and living this purpose that we receive the strength needed to overcome the distractions, disappointments and sufferings the world and others place upon us. When life gets difficult, it is purpose and meaning that help us to keep going. Purpose is the "why" that Nietzsche refers to in the quote "He who has a why to live for, can bear almost any how." Purpose provides us power to overcome any difficulty we encounter and to achieve the dreams we have so long desired but pushed aside as unattainable.

Purpose provided the meaning necessary for Victor Frankl to survive several years of abuse, torture and suffering in the Nazi death camp in Auschwitz during the Second World War. In his book *Man's Search for Meaning*, Frankl described the terror and death he overcame by finding a purpose and meaning that allowed him to survive the death camps that took the lives of over six million fellow Jews.

Whereas most prisoners perished because they lost faith in the future and resigned themselves to the fact they had no chance and would die, Frankl did the opposite. He searched and found a purpose that gave him meaning and the will to live. Frankl envisioned being with his loving wife again and lecturing to the world about the lessons learned from his experiences to ensure that this atrocity would never happen again to anyone.

Numerous other examples show people overcoming insurmountable odds by finding a purpose and meaning to their lives while suffering. Once they had discovered a purpose and meaning, they were able to focus within themselves and draw the strength required to develop and implement a plan that brought about a solution to their problems and helped them achieve their dreams. Once they discovered their purpose, everything began to fall into place. Passion entered their lives and powered them to success. Being on purpose means you are doing what you love to do and are good at. You have a goal and will not stop until you reach it. Accomplishments pile up because you are doing what is important to you and you have a reason for it.

Like so many others in the world, I had no defined purpose in my life. My only purpose was to find and experience a pleasure that would make me feel happy and fulfilled. I spent my days trying to find this pleasure and happiness. As the years went by, I experienced far more suffering than pleasure from my many attempts. Because of my results and perceived shortcomings, I started to believe I did not deserve happiness and began to seek out selfish pleasure to overcome the pain I was experiencing. I had no plan for my life and I merely lived day to day hoping something would change.

After years of failed relationships and parenting, deceit, incarceration, self-pity and frustration, I was given the book *Awaken the Giant Within* by Anthony Robbins. Because of my life experiences and lack of self-esteem, I was very skeptical of the notion that you can do it if you want to, but I read the book anyway. I quickly discovered that not only was I responsible for my current situation but I was capable of becoming more than I was.

There was hope if I would only accept my responsibility, open up, bear down and take action.

Tony talked about finding your purpose and developing a compelling future. Finally, I started to ask myself the right questions, became honest with myself and looked for the tools to help me overcome myself. I reached out to others and over time it all started to come together. I discovered my purpose and developed meaning in my life. It happened because I began to humble myself, asked questions and discovered who I truly was, what I wanted and how I could get it. I discovered it was up to me and only me. I had the power to become happy and achieve my dreams if I would only decide and commit myself with no excuses nor blaming others or the world. I was the only one who could choose how I felt or take the actions I needed to succeed.

This led me to read many more self-development and biographical books by various authors. I learned with an open mind through principles and experiences of others throughout the years. Their successes and failures all led to one main requirement. They all found that the road to success and happiness necessitated discovering your purpose and developing a meaning in your life.

I then asked myself several questions about the many areas of my life. I even began to investigate my spirituality. To this point in my life, I did not believe in a spiritual life and thought that religion was for weak-minded people. Thus, I began to honestly explore deeper into my personal beliefs. I was introduced to the understanding of what faith genuinely is and how it works. By digging down and asking myself the intimate and difficult questions I had always avoided, I overcame the fear of opening myself up to faith and blind trust, and I discovered I did have a purpose. This purpose brought meaning and passion to my life.

My purpose was to welcome and develop a committed relationship with God, to continually strive at becoming the best version of myself and to help others become better versions of themselves. This immediately sparked hope, promise and enthusiasm into my dismal existence. I began to believe I could succeed at anything I put my mind to and become happy. I could become a better version of myself while at the same time I could help others who were struggling. This brought an incredible blessing and relief into my life.

In the past, I was selfish and ignored the hurt I inflicted on others. Though I pretended that my actions did not bother me, they weighed heavily on my heart. I started to use the tools and concepts I was learning to stop hurting myself and others. Over time, I was able to come to terms with my past, let it go and start to move forward.

I quickly began to look within myself and introduce the badly needed changes in my life. I began to seek out ways to help others. These changes came surprisingly easy as I discovered passion and began enjoying life more. With purpose and meaning, I started to grow and this strengthened my faith and belief that I could and would achieve my dreams and desires. I mattered, was loved and could be happy and fulfilled.

Charles Colson reinvented himself when he discovered a compelling purpose for his life. Colson was the special counsel to President Nixon during the Watergate scandal in the early 1970s and the second most hated man in America next to Nixon himself. He served time in a federal prison for his crimes while with the Nixon administration.

At the lowest time in his life during his incarceration, he discovered his purpose. During his incarceration, he witnessed many injustices in the prison system and in many inmates' lives. Colson was convinced that he was being called by God to develop a ministry to prisoners with an emphasis on promoting changes in the justice system and improving inmates' lives.

He formed an organization called Prison Fellowship, which grew to become a successful and influential worldwide prison ministry. His newly discovered purpose was responsible not only for many changes to the prison system but for bringing positive change to many prisoners and their families' lives. Colson overcame his past, allowing him to live a happy, contributing and fulfilling life full of passion.

Some of the actions during our life may bring us financial rewards, status, fame, power or an abundance of possessions, even all the earthly rewards we could imagine. Though we may think these things will make us happy, they do not provide everlasting happiness or fulfillment in our life. In many cases, this type of perceived happiness is short lived and could be taken away in an instant.

There are many examples of people who tried to find happiness through this method only to end up lonely and miserable or even die by suicide. NFL football player Jovan Belcher, age 25; musician Kurt Cobain, 27; professional wrestler Chris Benoit, 40; comedian Freddie Prinze, 22; actor Robin Williams, 63; and so many more celebrities had it all but in a state of despair died by suicide.

They had lives envied by so many others who believed that a life with fame and wealth would bring them happiness. These famous people were successful and wealthy people but they were not happy; they were lonely and depressed and died by suicide. It is not wealth, popularity, or status that will bring you happiness and fulfillment. It is only when you have a purpose and meaning in your life that you can move on to happiness and fulfillment. By discovering a purpose and meaning for their life, many people who struggled for most of their lives were able to implement massive positive change and realize happiness they have desired.

Many people experience negative programming over the years that includes negative comments and self-talk, and they come to believe and finally consent that it is too late to change. They have done and experienced so much wrong during their lives that they believe they are not deserving of or capable of ever changing.

As a prison chaplain, I have met hundreds of inmates and addicts who have lived their lives inflicting pain on themselves and others. However, through intervention they came to realize that only they were responsible for where they were in their lives. This revelation was instrumental in them finally accepting responsibility for their lives. They then made a conscious decision to commence the needed changes and transform themselves into a productive, loving and happy member of society. Family, friends and community members who have lived with, worked with or known these people would all have sworn they had no chance of changing. Yet by accepting responsibility, making a decision and learning their true purpose, they were able to overcome the most difficult of situations they had put themselves in. By taking action, they were able to discover meaning and find true happiness in their lives.

Serge LeClerc was a child born of teenage rape in an abandoned building. His life of crime began at eight years old and escalated until he became one of Canada's most violent and notorious criminals. LeClerc served many years in several of Canada's maximum prisons. After years of violent behaviour behind bars, LeClerc had a conversion and found a purpose and meaning for his life. He wanted to help young people avoid the pain and mistakes he had made in life. Armed with his new purpose, LeClerc started changing his attitude and behaviour until he was finally able to secure his release from prison on parole. He graduated from the University of Waterloo with an honours degree in sociology with a minor and diploma in social work. He spent many years helping youth change their lives by sharing his life experiences. He not only helped many others improve their lives but continued to grow personally and was elected as a representative to the Saskatchewan government in 2007.

Serge LeClerc is only one of many examples of how finding and living your purpose and mission in life can help you overcome even the most negative background and life situation to become a successful and respected individual living a happy, passionate and fulfilling life. If someone of LeClerc's upbringing and destructive lifestyle can transform their life and situation, then what is stopping you? You have no excuse. All you have to do is accept that you and only you are responsible for how you feel and act. Only you can implement the positive change required. You can find your true purpose and bring meaning and direction into your life if you truly want it.

You too can also breathe passion and happiness back into your life if you open yourself up to seek and find your purpose. You will then develop meaning and passion in your life. With purpose to guide you, you will be on your way to discovering and implementing the many principles and strategies in this book to create lasting change and achieve your dreams. Once you have discovered what your purpose is, you can plan all of your activities around it. Everything you do will be in line with your purpose. If something doesn't move you towards your purpose, then you simply do not do it.

Discovering Your Purpose

Now that you are ready, committed and believe that transformation and happiness are possible, what's next? Now, we move forward and learn how to discover your purpose and bring meaning and hope into your life. Let the transformation begin!

For years, I questioned what my purpose was and what it was all about. I was waiting for a clear answer, nicely presented and easy to understand and accomplish, such as your purpose is to go and build homes for struggling families in Mexico. This is a purpose I can relate to, straightforward and easy to measure. It's something that felt good. Wouldn't it be nice if our purpose were this easy to define? The problem is our purpose is not always that easy and clear. Our purpose is not a task we can complete or something that makes us feel good—it is a way of life.

Our lives involve several elements, and to be happy and fulfilled we need to balance all of the elements in our life. Our relationships, health, career, finances, leisure, personal development and contribution are all ingredients of our life and purpose. Like anything in life, you need the proper balance of ingredients to arrive at a successful outcome.

The hardest part of my transformation and the most rewarding was when I finally found a method to discover my purpose and meaning. During my search, I read over 100 books and attended many workshops and seminars trying to find the answer before I came across the method I will explain below. It was like an "ah ha" moment and became crystal clear to me.

As I struggled to discover my purpose and create meaning in my life, I learned that there are three areas of purpose that I needed to investigate. Most people believe that they have only one life purpose and they would be right. You have one purpose but it actually contains three parts. When you understand your purpose in each of these areas and how they work together, you will be able to understand how your purpose will bring balance to the different aspects of your life.

I will now introduce you to each of these three areas and how they combine to define your life purpose.

1. First, we start with your greater or spiritual purpose, that is, your purpose to a greater power or entity, your God, your source or to the universe.
2. Next is your individual purpose, that is, your personal purpose towards self.
3. Finally, we discuss your communal purpose, that is, your purpose towards others or mankind.

Your Greater Purpose

In determining my purpose, I found this first part was the hardest to get my head around as I had no spiritual beliefs. I thought religion was for weak-minded people and there was no greater power. How could I come up with a purpose to something I did not believe in? If there is no God, then how could there be a greater purpose? I started asking questions and searching for answers that I could accept as the logical person I was and for answers that required proof before I would be able to accept a certain way of thinking. This search was painstaking and eventually lead me to the Lord and my Catholic faith.

After investigation and discerning my greater purpose based on my new spirituality, I determined that my spiritual or greater purpose was determined by God. It is given in Matthew (22:36-40): I am to love the Lord with all my heart, soul and mind and to love others as I love myself. As I investigated more thoroughly and began to accept Christianity into my life, I came to believe that I was born a child of God and that God had a mission for my life. God loved me and wanted me to love Him. He had a loving plan for my life. If I truly believed this, then I needed to find what God's plan was for me.

My purpose became to find this plan and then implement it into my life. I inquired, researched and came to understand that God's purpose and plan for me was to be in a loving and growing relationship with Him and others in my life. Many people have different ways of explaining this purpose but to me it was love, honour and obey God. Loving God means keeping His commandments and honouring God means keeping Him first in my life. Once I knew this, I needed to learn how He wanted me to live and to discover what His mission for me was.

This worked for me as a Christian, but what if you are of a different faith or have no faith at all? I can assure you it works the same, and you can use the same tools and strategy that I did. You must investigate what you believe in and what it means to have this belief. This same way of discovering your spiritual purpose is used no matter which faith you identify with. We all have some sort of faith. It could be a God, a way of life or the universe itself. Even atheism is a form of faith.

No matter what your faith is, you must search within yourself and define it. It is important to question and investigate this faith thoroughly as there are many deceivers or well-meaning people out there who do not fully understand their faith or who hold mistaken beliefs about it. Whether you believe in Christianity, Islam, Buddhism, Judaism or any other religious faith, you need to question, learn and understand the true meaning of your faith and how you are to celebrate and live it. Doing this will lead you to your greater purpose.

If you believe you have no spiritual beliefs, then you need to ask yourself what that means to you. If you deeply question yourself, you will discover there is some kind of a greater entity out there for you to believe in and you need to define it. It could be nature, but even nature has rules. Review your life. Have you ever had a feeling that an outside force has affected your life, saved you or guided you?

I have worked with many inmates who do not believe in a force greater than themselves. However, when we talk, they begin to remember events in the past they could not explain. It may have been how they escaped death when they shouldn't have or how they were the beneficiary of an unexplained event. For some, it was an unexplained mental warning. It is up to you to diligently question and search for what you do or do not believe in.

The problem is that most people try to avoid this difficult topic in their life. Fear of the unknown is usually the reason. Many people say they have certain faith beliefs but have no deep understanding or they misunderstand how that faith is to be implemented in their life.

One obstacle many people have to overcome is the idea that most people who profess to be faithful are hypocrites when they say one thing and do the opposite. This observation is true. Living your faith can be a struggle and sometimes people do the wrong thing. We are born sinners and we are inclined to sin many times when we do not plan or want to. As for churches being full of hypocrites, that is what churches are there for. If everyone were able to live their lives 100 per cent faithfully, then they would be saints. If everyone were a saint, then there would be no reason for churches. Churches are for sinners to help them learn and find the strength to overcome their sinning ways.

Let's now begin the search to better understand ourselves. Use the exercise below to help you find your greater or spiritual purpose. If you find it difficult, reach out to someone you can trust and is living a life you respect.

Greater Purpose Exercise

Ask yourself "what are my greater or spiritual beliefs? How did my life and world come to be? What happens when I die? Who do I answer to?"

_____

_____

_____

_____

_____

Once you have defined your greater or spiritual beliefs, then ask yourself "how do these greater or spiritual beliefs define how I am supposed to act and live my earthly life?"

_____

_____

_____

_____

Once you have answered these questions, write a statement that defines what your greater or spiritual purpose is while alive on Earth.

Example: My greater purpose is to love the Lord with all my heart, soul and mind.

_____

———————————————————————

———————————————————————

———————————————————————

———————————————————————

Your Individual Purpose

Once we have discovered our greater purpose, then we are able to ask ourselves the following important questions. First, we need to ask ourselves "what does my greater purpose ask of me as an individual?" Second, we need to ask "what do I really want from this life? How do I want to live it?" It is vital that we understand our individual purpose, including what is expected of us and what we desire.

After I found that my greater purpose was to love the Lord with all my heart, soul and mind, I needed to define what that meant to me. I started by questioning and determining what a loving relationship with the Lord entails. I was able to determine that a loving and growing relationship was a two-way process. Both the Lord and I are responsible to each other. I have expectations of Him and He has expectations of me.

The Lord's expectations of me were clear: to be in a loving and growing relationship with Him and to love and serve others in the same way. A loving relationship means we both strive to meet each other's expectations. His expectations are for me to follow His commandments and become the best version of myself possible. Another part of a loving relationship is that no matter what, we will always be there for the other. A loving and growing relationship means we will be there especially in the difficult times even if one disappoints or harms the other. Knowing that someone is always there to love you, forgive you and help you is a powerful way to live. Thus, my role for my greater purpose became clear.

Once I knew my role in my greater purpose, I was able to focus on what I wanted out of life. This took time as there were many thoughts that distracted me from focusing on or understanding what I genuinely wanted. Such thoughts included what others expect of me and whether I was worthy or capable. Did I even know what I wanted? I had to take some time alone where there were no distractions and contemplate and accept what I truly wanted. I needed to discern what happiness and fulfillment looked like for me. What would ultimately bring me that happiness and fulfillment I desired? I was then able to reflect on and understand myself. What were my talents and gifts? What did I enjoy doing and what brought me pleasure? It was only then that I was able to understand that to be happy I needed to respect and love myself and others. I needed to live my life doing something I enjoyed. It all came down to this: I needed to work at improving my self-worth and becoming a better person.

By understanding my individual purpose in relation to my greater purpose and to myself, I was able to define my individual life purpose and thus to become the best version of myself possible.

Use the exercise below to help you determine your individual purpose.

Individual Purpose Exercise

Reflect on the question "what does my greater purpose request of me as an individual?" Write your findings in a short descriptive sentence.

_____

_____

_____

_____

_____

Reflect on what you want from life. What will bring happiness and fulfillment into your life? Write a short sentence describing your findings.

_____

_____

_____

_____

_____

Incorporate both answers into a short statement that describes your personal purpose.

Example: My individual purpose is to grow and become the best version of myself possible.

_____

_____

_____

_____

_____

Your Communal Purpose

In this third part of our overall purpose quest, we look at our purpose to others or how we fit in and our overall role in the world. We all need relationships and have a desire to be with and acknowledged by others.

In the movie *Cast Away*, Tom Hanks survives a plane crash and is stranded on a deserted island. He starts to become lonely and to meet his need for relationship with others he draws a face on a basketball and names it Wilson. Wilson becomes his one and only companion. This companionship helps him mentally survive his ordeal.

Some people can appear to be loners, but even they still desire companionship and acknowledgment. Many find a replacement for human interaction through pets, inanimate objects like Wilson, or nature and animals. Though they may believe they do not need anyone else, they subconsciously crave companionship, which is part of their identity, and use the replacement to meet their need.

We do not like to see others hurt or suffering. All people, unless they have a mental disorder, feel sorrow when their actions cause pain in others' lives, whether by accident or in revenge. Most of the time their guilt or the mental anguish they are feeling is disguised and they cover up this sorrow, but deep inside they are hurting and remorseful. Even though we as a society have become desensitized to the pain of others around us through movies, television and music, a deep pain and sorrow exist within us. The reason is that we are all born to be in community and when one hurts we all hurt. When we were created, we were created to be in relationship with God and with each other.

We have all heard about The Golden Rule: do unto others as you would have them do unto you. This is the premise of community—to love one another as we love ourselves. As we live our lives, we have all experienced a time when suddenly we were able to step out and help someone in need. On many occasions, this was someone we had never met. We did it willingly and without expectation. When this happened, we experienced a powerful feeling of exhilaration that only comes when we have unselfishly given of ourselves to another. Helping someone else without benefit will always bring a sense of joy and happiness into our lives.

A great example is the aftermath of the turmoil and devastation of 9/11, the series of terrorist attacks on the United States in 2001. On that day, people by the thousands came together in one common effort to help each other in a time of need. Race, religion, culture and many more dividers were put aside for the good of each other. This is the result of the deep need to care for each other that is within each one of us.

As I reflected on my role in community and again in Matthew (22:36-40) that I am to love others as I love myself, it became clear that my communal purpose is part of my spiritual purpose. I am to love others as I love myself. Therefore, if my individual purpose is to become the best version of myself, would it not make sense that my communal purpose would be to help others become the best versions of themselves possible?

Like the other two examples of purpose, our communal purpose originates from deep within our soul. It is God-given and intricately related with the other two sections.

Let us now use the exercise below to discover our communal purpose.

Communal Purpose Exercise

Ask yourself "what is your role in your community, nation and the world?" Make a list of your answers.

_____

_____

_____

_____

_____

What is your community's, your nation's and the world's role in your life? Make a list of your answers.

_____

_____

_____

_____

_____

Now write a short communal purpose statement that incorporates your findings.

Example: My communal role is to help others become the best versions of themselves possible.

_____

_____

_____

_____

As we went through the three sections of our life purpose and completed the exercises, I am sure it became apparent that though there are three separate life areas, they are all related to each other and in essence one life purpose. I believe that as you completed each exercise, your eyes opened a little and you felt a piece of meaning and hope enter your life. We will now go on to bring it all together and define our life purpose.

Creating Your Life Purpose Statement

Having a clear and meaningful life purpose is the key to developing the life we have dreamed of and desire. To do this, we will now write a clear and concise life purpose statement with which we will draw from as we move forward. This life purpose statement will provide the power to overcome obstacles we are sure to encounter along the way. It will help us to live a life of vision and passion.

Life Purpose Statement Exercise

Take your three life area purpose statements and combine them to become one all-encompassing life purpose statement.

Example: My life purpose is to be in a loving and growing relationship with the Lord, to become the best version of myself possible and to help others to become the best versions of themselves possible.

_____

_____

_____

_____

_____

Summary

As discussed earlier in this chapter, it is only when you have defined a life purpose that you can develop a mission and create goals that will bring meaning, passion and happiness into your life. By completing the exercises above, you should now have discovered and written your life purpose statement.

This statement will be the force that will bring all the other parts of your life together. You will start to experience and come to believe that if you live your life using your purpose as a guide, then you are destined to achieve happiness and fulfillment. Every decision and choice you make, every task you do should coincide with your purpose or you simply should not do it. If you are living on purpose, then everything you do will be done with confidence, passion and enjoyment. Even the difficult times and tasks in your life will be easier to handle if you are truly living your life on purpose.

I pray that you were able to fully discover your purpose and bring meaning into your life. Your purpose is the foundation upon which you will build the life you have always desired.

Now that you have discovered your definite purpose, it is time to incorporate it into your life. Discovering how you incorporate your purpose into daily living becomes the task by turning your purpose into a mission and then envisioning what this will look like. You are now ready to define what you want from life and how you want to live it. This will become apparent as we move through the next three chapters.

CHAPTER TWO

Define Your Mission

What am I supposed to do?

"Every person's mission is to live a passionate, contributing, and joyful life that is guided by and fulfills their greater purpose."
— **Gary Haney**

- -

In This Chapter
> ➢ What Is a Personal Mission?
> ➢ How a Personal Mission Works
> ➢ How To Form Your Purpose Mission
> ➢ Personal Mission Statement Exercise
> ➢ Summary

- -

After some deep soul searching, insight and inspiration, you should now have a clearly defined and written life purpose statement. Your life purpose becomes the why. It is your purpose that will provide meaning for all you do and the power to overcome any setback, disappointment or roadblock you will encounter along your life journey.

Your mission now is to live out your purpose. It is all the things you must consider and do to live on purpose every day of your life. If someone does not fully understand their mission and work towards its success, they are merely floating meaninglessly along in any direction they are pushed. Without a clearly defined mission, you have no goals to guide you to be able to live the purpose you have discovered in your life.

Understanding that having a personal mission is a must, it is now time to explore and define your mission, specifically a personal mission that will guide you to live your life according to your purpose. In this chapter, we will explore what a personal mission entails and how to define your own personal mission.

What Is a Personal Mission?

A mission statement is defined as a written declaration of a person's core purpose and focus that normally remains unchanged over time. Properly crafted mission statements serve as filters to separate what is important from what is not. They clearly state which life areas will be served and how, and communicate a sense of intended direction to your whole being. A personal mission statement contains the core values you live by, what you expect from people and what they can expect of you.

A well-defined personal mission is created around your life purpose and helps to focus your thoughts and actions so you can live according to your purpose. Living your life on purpose and having meaning to what you do are the key and process to living a passionate, happy and successful life. Creating a personal mission statement is a powerful tool because it provides you with a path to success and it gives you permission to say no to the things that are negative distractions.

Oprah Winfrey, the founder of OWN (the Oprah Winfrey Network), had a personal mission statement: "To be a teacher. And to be known for inspiring my students to be more than they thought they could be." In an issue of *O* magazine, Winfrey recalled watching her grandmother churn butter and wash clothes in a cast-iron pot in the yard. A small voice inside of her told her that her life would be more than hanging clothes on a line. She eventually realized she wanted to be a teacher, but "I never imagined it would be on TV," she wrote.

A personal mission statement is a powerful tool because it provides you with a path for success, and it gives you permission to say no to the things that are distractions. It also changes over time. As we get older, we have more life experiences and acquire new skills. If your mission statement doesn't change over time, you risk not being relevant anymore.

While you write a personal mission statement for yourself, there is power in sharing it. The more you share, the more support you get to achieve your mission. Friends and mentors can support you or call you out if you're doing something counterproductive.

For years, I struggled through life seeking happiness and fulfillment. Without having any direction, I simply moved from one mistake and failure to another. I was on a mission, a mission I was unaware of. My mission had no definition or direction; it had no insight or the guidance of a purpose. It was an aimless mission to find and achieve a dream or goal I could not define. I was like a ship in the ocean with no rudder to guide it, just drifting from one current to another hoping that it would end up on the shore of paradise. Many people today struggle through life with the same undefined mission. They push on aimlessly, hoping to find joy and happiness only to experience failure and grief.

Even after I finally discovered my purpose in life, I continued to struggle. I had no idea how to live this newfound purpose. I had not yet heard of the concept of a defined mission statement, a tool that would guide me to live on purpose and direct my life to where I wanted it to be. After a great deal of searching, I discovered that my mission was to define and seek out positive ways to live my life according to my purpose.

This forced me to spend many days questioning myself. I asked myself questions like "how do I want to live? What do I want to do? Why do I want to do it? How will I feel and what will I get if I do it? And what will happen if I don't do it? Are my thoughts, decisions and actions in line with my purpose?"

It was only after truly contemplating those questions that my life started to make sense. I was able to define what I needed to do to live according to my purpose. I slowly began to transform my life from failure and grief to hope and achievement. Having a defined mission brought me the clarity I needed to move my life in a positive direction. My mission still guides all areas of my life today.

How a Personal Mission Works

Businesses create mission statements to provide purpose and direction for the organization. But it is as vital for individuals to have a mission and a vision for themselves as it is for any business. A personal mission statement is:

- A tool for making difficult decisions
- A framework for how you want to live your life and express your life purpose
- A beacon to those around you about the kind of person you are
- A declaration that motivates and inspires you to stay the course
- A statement of your values and life priorities.

Creating a personal mission statement forces clarity, helps you define a purpose and serves as the foundation for your life goals. It also helps you identify the underlying reasons for your choices and behaviours and what truly motivates you to make positive change.

As the author of *The 7 Habits of Highly Effective People*, Stephen Covey said your mission statement is about "defining the personal, moral and ethical guidelines within which you can most happily express and fulfill yourself."

Writing down your mission statement on paper makes it real. It becomes your own personal constitution, the basis for life-directing decisions and a guide for making daily choices that impact you and those around you.

Creating your personal mission may seem like a daunting task, but let me assure you it is not all that difficult. Companies and individuals have been developing and following mission statements for years. It helps guide them by defining who they are and why they do what they do.

I am sure at one time or another you have seen a company's mission statement hung prestigiously on the wall for all to see. This mission statement helps guide each and every employee as they perform their job responsibilities.

Here are a few examples. Coca-Cola's mission statement is "To refresh the world. To inspire moments of optimism and happiness. To create value and make a difference." For Google it's "to organize the world's information and make it universally accessible and useful." Both of these companies have used their mission statement to help propel them to great success.

Just as a mission statement guides a company, they are also effective for guiding our personal endeavours. A personal mission statement is a bit different from a company mission statement, but the fundamental principles are the same. Writing a personal mission statement offers the opportunity to find ways to live your purpose, establish what's important to you and guide you as you make decisions and choices during your life journey.

Here are examples of a few personal mission statements. For Denise Morrison, CEO of Campbell Soup Company, it is "To serve as a leader, live a balanced life, and apply ethical principles to make a significant difference." In an interview, Morrison said,

"The personal mission statement was important for me because I believe that you can't lead others unless you have a strong sense of who you are and what you stand for. For me, living a balanced life means nurturing the academic, physical, and spiritual aspects of my life so I can maintain a sense of well-being and self-esteem."

Joel Manby, CEO of Herschend Family Entertainment, said, "I define personal success as being consistent to my own personal mission statement: to love God and love others." Herschend Family Entertainment owns and operates 26 family-oriented theme parks and attractions across the United States, including Dollywood and the Harlem Globetrotters. Manby said that he achieves his personal mission statement in his own endeavours but feels blessed to be able to achieve it in a growing, profitable business.

Both of these individuals have drawn on their personal mission statements to live their purpose achieving a successful life as they battled through the rough waters of life in our ever-changing and tumultuous world.

We can see that a well-defined mission statement has guided and propelled these companies and individuals to success. Let us now move forward to discover and write our own personal mission statement.

How To Form Your Personal Mission

The first step is to understand what the mission statement should entail. It is important to understand that this is what we are to do to live on purpose. Learning how we do it comes later. A properly defined mission should be directed by your purpose. Every thought, decision and action you do is guided by your mission and should move you along the direction of your purpose.

Here are four steps to help you create a personal mission statement:

Step 1: Examine the lives of others

Think of a person in history or in your life whom you admire. What are the qualities of that person that you would like to emulate? These qualities can relate to their character, values, achievements, personality or simply the way they live their lives. Consider the specific reasons you admire the person and list those qualities in detail.

Step 2: Determine your ideal self

Define the type of person you want to become, not just what you want to have or achieve. This ideal should reflect your core values and your definition of living with integrity. Consider all areas of your life as a spouse, friend, employee, parent, etc. and consider who you want to be in each of those roles. I find it helpful to write down this phrase: "As an ideal spouse (or friend, parent, etc.), I want to . . . ." Then fill in the end of the sentence with as many outcomes as you wish to become. For example, you might write: As an ideal spouse, I want to:

- Express my love daily in words, affection and action
- Be supportive and attentive to my spouse's needs
- Work through conflict calmly and in the spirit of compromise
- Be fully present and emotionally intimate.

This exercise may take some time, but it is well worth the effort beyond its usefulness for your mission statement. It helps you clarify your personal operating system and reminds you of what you are capable of becoming.

Step 3: Consider your legacy

Determine all of your life roles (career, family, community, etc.), and write down a short statement of how you would like to be described in each of those roles. Think about how you would like the important people in your life to remember you and talk about you.

For example, you might want your boss to say, "He was a man of character and integrity who was a compassionate and inspiring leader and a visionary for our organization." This exercise may feel awkward, but no one else has to see it. It is to help you decide how you want to step into each of the roles in your life and to clarify in concise words how you want others to perceive you.

Step 4: Clarify your aptitudes

What are the talents and skills you possess that are most important to you and that you actually enjoy? Part of your mission statement should reflect your best aptitudes and strengths; these are what create joy and energy in our lives. When we spend our time on what we do well and enjoy, our lives not only have meaning but also have vibrancy.

Make a list of all of your personal and professional talents, aptitudes and skills, even those you may take for granted, such as being a good friend or having the ability to organize well. Then circle the skills you enjoy or find fulfilling. Focus on these.

You want a statement that will guide you in your day-to-day actions and decisions, as well as your long-term goals. Try to keep your words positive and affirmative. Focus on what you want rather than what you don't want. Your mission needs to include your enthusiasms for life. If you have no passion for your mission, then it isn't truly your mission.

Once you have completed the four steps above, you are ready to formulate your mission statement. Start by reviewing your purpose statement. Break the whole statement down into individual sections. If your greater purpose has three parts, then your mission should have three parts. I will use how I formulated my own personal purpose statement as an example.

My purpose statement is "To be in a devoted and growing relationship with God, endeavouring to become a happy and better version of myself while helping others to become happy and better versions of themselves."

To understand the first part of this statement better, we must ask what it means to be in a devoted and growing relationship with God. Let's start with the word devoted. To be devoted can mean several things. Upon review, I was able to come up with committed, faithful and persistent as a few of the traits one must display to be devoted. Next, we have the word growing, which means to learn, advance or improve. Finally, relationship entails partnership, reciprocity, trust, respect, openness and commitment. These are all traits that I must develop to produce a devoted and growing relationship with God. I have experienced that if I reach out to God for guidance, He will help me to develop and hone these traits. By reaching out to God, I am becoming closer to Him. Hence, the first part of my mission is to reach out and become closer to God each and every day.

The next phrase is "endeavouring to become a happier and better version of myself." Reflecting on these words, I have come to understand that to become happy and improve myself, I need to know what God has planned for my life and how He wants me to live it. By living my life the way God wants me to live it, I will experience happiness and joy. I also know that if I am truly attempting to do His will, with love He will guide and support me. Therefore, my mission is to learn and live according to the plan God has for my life and to accept the love, guidance and support He provides me along the way.

The final part reads "while helping others to become happy and better versions of themselves." It is now time for me to contribute. I have learned from experience that helping others brings me joy and happiness. We are all made to live as community, helping and loving one another, especially when someone is in distress or hurting. I now understand that by loving and helping others, I become a better version of myself. It becomes obvious that if loving and assisting others helps me to become a better person, then I should find ways to not only help them but teach them that helping others will help them to become better people. Thus, my mission is to continually seek out new concepts and opportunities that will help others to become happy and better versions of themselves.

Now we have taken my purpose statement apart and defined the mission that I need to follow in order to live my purpose. We can now write it out as a single personal mission statement. Taking what I have discovered I wrote this: "My mission in life is to reach out and become closer to God each and every day. To learn and live according to the plan God has for my life and accept His love, guidance and support along the way. To continually seek out new concepts and opportunities that will help to accomplish this as well as help others to become happier and improved versions of themselves."

I now have a mission statement that will help guide me in all my decisions, choices and the direction I choose to follow in my life. I can use this statement to know if my thoughts, decisions and actions are on purpose or not. I need to simply ask myself "is what I am about to do in line with my mission and purpose?" The answer comes quickly. I have found this process to be an extremely valuable tool over the past few years and within a short time I have created the habit of using this process effectively several times on a daily basis. It has greatly reduced the amount of quick or bad decisions I have made.

You have just now witnessed how I was able to define my life mission by taking my purpose and the information I was able to come up with to create a mission I can use to live on purpose. Now it is time for you to create your own personal mission statement.

Personal Mission Statement Exercise

Take out the written copy of your purpose statement. Write the first part below and complete the questions that follow. Do the same with the other parts of your life purpose statement.

First part:

_____
_____
_____

What does the statement mean to you?

_____
_____
_____

What could you do to live this purpose?

_____
_____
_____

Turn what you could do into a short statement:

_____
_____
_____

Second part:

_____
_____
_____

What does the statement mean to you?

_____
_____
_____

What could you do to live this purpose?

_____

_____

_____

Turn what you could do into a short statement:

_____

_____

_____

Third part:

_____

_____

_____

What does the statement mean to you?

_____

_____

_____

What could you do to live this purpose?

_____

_____

_____

Turn what you could do into a short statement:

_____

_____

_____

Now take your individual mission statements and write an all-encompassing personal mission statement:

_____

_____

_____

Summary

You now have your own personal mission statement to guide you in your decisions and help you plan your goals and future endeavours. Decisions and choices will start to become much easier for you, bringing about more success and happiness in your life. By following your life mission, you have a personal life GPS system that will keep you living on purpose. This system will provide direction and meaning to your everyday decisions in everything you do.

By understanding your purpose and defining what you need to do to live your purpose, your new mission, you are now ready to envision how you will live out your mission and purpose. In the next chapter, we will create a clear and inspiring vision of how you will approach your mission in each area of your life. This will be a personal vision of how you want to—and will—live your life. If lived as envisioned, this vision is guaranteed to bring happiness, joy, satisfaction and fulfillment into your life. The vision will help you set many goals and live your life passionately as you accomplish one goal after another.

CHAPTER THREE

Envision Your Future

How do I accomplish it?

"Vision without action is merely a dream. Action without vision just passes the time. Vision with action can change the world."
— **Joel A. Barker**

- -

In This Chapter

- -

Many people set goals at the beginning of the year without projecting their imaginations into the future and thinking about how these goals fit into the big picture. Are you one of those people? If you want to set goals that you're excited to achieve, they need to be in alignment with your purpose and what you want to happen in your life. Your first step is to get clear about your vision.

Your vision is essential to your success, not optional. You set the stage for your desired outcome based on how hard you're willing to work and it starts with being able to clearly see yourself achieving your goal.

A vision is a picture or idea you have in your mind of yourself, your business or anything that is going to happen. A clear vision helps you pursue dreams and achieve goals as it is an idea of or a strong wish for the future. A vision that is clear will open your mind to the endless possibilities of the future.

A vision will help you overcome obstacles in the way and helps you hold on when times are tough. A vision that is well defined helps you focus on your purpose and that becomes the measurement for your success. If you do not have a vision of who you want to be, how you want to succeed or what you want out of life, you begin to lack drive and your life becomes merely an order of events.

A strong and current vision connects with your passions and greatest potentials. Regardless of what is going on in the world or challenges that present themselves, a vision helps you know what and why you are doing the things you are doing. Having a vision is most important in the path of your success in life. You feel much more valuable as a person when you set and achieve visions and goals.

A vision can be used in two different ways: inspiration and prediction. It is first used to inspire you in reaching something that you are wanting. It is also used in prediction for changes in the future and interests you have.

A vision might be the most powerful way to keep you focused on what you want in life while keeping you motivated in achieving it. A vision will open up your mind to many possibilities and a brighter and bigger future. When you can envision a future that is better, happier and more productive, you are more likely to make the changes that are necessary for you to reach that type of life.

When a person has a vision, they have the ability to see today as it is and calculate a future that grows and improves. A successful person can see the future and still stay focused in the present. For a successful person, a vision is not seen as a dream but as a reality that has not yet come into existence. A vision is easily perceived by such people because their dedication and confidence are extremely strong. People are able to spend hours upon hours to bring their visions into reality. Their vision acts as a force within them, driving them to action.

We are now about to embark on one of the most influential phases in transforming your life. It is time to create a compelling future that will provide direction, passion and initiative into your life. Now that you have defined a purpose and understand what is required to live a happy and fulfilling life, you can devise a plan to accomplish it. This is the opportunity for you to discern and create a vision of how you will follow your mission and live the life you have always desired. You will now start to design a future that will inspire you, a future that will drive you, a future that you will live with passion and a future that offers you a life of joy and fulfillment.

You Get To Decide What the Future Will Look Like

Until now, a lack of understanding about yourself has probably had you living a life of trial and error. If your life has been anything like mine was, it has been mostly error and regret. I assure you it does not have to continue that way. There is hope for your future if you decide to accept it. I promise that you can and will live a healthy, productive and happy life if you choose to. All that is required is to make the choice and then step up and commit to your decision. You no longer have to be a slave to the ups and downs of the world and others around you. No longer do you have to go aimlessly searching for an undefined ideal. How your life transpires from this point on is totally up to you. You are in control, and you have the capability to create the life you want and have it become a reality if you truly want it. You are in control of your destiny.

By stepping up, choosing and committing to learn what is required of you to implement positive change in your life, you will become empowered to design and live your own future. You will gain the ability to dream what your perfect life will look like and sculpt it into reality. The rest of your life is now in your hands. Start to dream and open your imagination. Ask yourself "what would I like to do for a living, how and where would I like to live, who would I have in my life?" These are only a few of the questions that will help you design a compelling future and life, a life you can't wait to get up for in the morning and start living. It's a life of passion, success, happiness and fulfillment.

You Can Have the Future You Have Always Desired

I know you are now thinking this is far-fetched. I have dreamed in the past only to be let down, disappointed and hurt. You can't simply dream up a perfect life and expect it to happen. I understand your pain and skepticism. I may make it sound simple, but let me assure you if it were that simple, then everybody would be happy and the world would be whole. It starts by letting yourself dream, but it takes a lot more than just dreaming. You must follow up your dreams with action.

Let me assure you the concept is not difficult, only the process can be a little challenging. Once you have created your perfect life, you have to start living it. Old beliefs, habits and fears will appear and pull you off course. However, the concepts and tools you will learn throughout this book will help you to overcome these distractions.

I assure you that as long as your vision is in harmony with your purpose and you take the appropriate action, you will find the strength, insight and support required to overcome any disappointment, setback or mistake you encounter along your life journey.

The following story is about Heidi Horsley, whose life was changed when her brother and cousin were tragically killed in an automobile accident. Through all her loss and pain, Heidi was able to find a purpose that changed and powered her life. She is now a successful licensed clinical psychologist and social worker. Heidi is also the executive director of the Open to Hope Foundation, providing hope for those grieving a death.

> "It was a long journey out of the darkness,
> but once I found what my purpose was,
> I began to heal." — Heidi Horsley

In her own words, here is Heidi's story from April 2017 as presented in *The Compassionate Friends* February 2019 newsletter:

"When I was 20 years old, my 17-year-old brother, Scott, and cousin were killed in a car accident. This tragic event turned my world upside down and put everything I ever believed into question. I didn't know how I was going to survive, or even if I wanted to. This was not the life I had planned, it was not the life I had signed up for, and it was not the life I wanted.

None of my friends had ever had a sibling die and they couldn't relate. They wanted me to get over it and find closure. I hid my grief from my parents because I was trying to be a good daughter and didn't want to cause them more pain. I felt lost and alone and didn't know how I was going to make it without my brother in my life.

Several months after Scott's death I went on an Outward Bound survival program in the Colorado mountains, a program Scott had done the year before. Prior to boarding the plane my father handed me Victor Frankl's book *Man's Search for Meaning*. This book had a profound effect on my healing journey.

It was a long journey out of the darkness, but once I discovered what my purpose was I began to heal. I realize that I am on this earth to help others who have experienced loss, and to give a voice to the bereaved. I have found hope and joy again. Though my brother is no longer on this earth, he continues to have a profound influence on my life.

Today my life is filled with joy and I have met so many incredible people in my grief journey. I once again have passion, meaning, and purpose in my life. Scott's death has defined my life, but in no way has it destroyed my life. Although I am poorer for having lost Scott, I am so much richer for knowing him for seventeen years."

Heidi found the one thing that could lift her out of her suffering and pain: purpose. From her purpose, Heidi discovered her mission and then formed a vision to live her purpose and mission. Her vision was to become a psychologist and create a foundation to provide hope for those grieving a death.

Your life can also change if you seek, find and then take action to follow and live your purpose by following your vision. All that is required is for you to commit yourself to the concepts, principles and exercises throughout this book.

It Starts by Dreaming

The future begins now by asking yourself "what would my dream life look like? What would a good day look like?" Be sure when you start to dream that you contemplate all the areas of your life: job, career or business, financial status, lifestyle, relationships, personal development, health and fitness, and contribution to others.

Create a vison of this perfect life in your head. Live it in your mind. How does it make you feel? Ask yourself "is the vision in line with my purpose? Does this vision excite me? What would I be willing to do to experience this vision?" These questions will help you focus on what is truly important to you and will make you happy.

What first happens in your mind will most often happen in the future. All things are created twice, first in your mind and then in your life. Successful people think about what they want until they achieve it. Let's get to the details so you can envision that desired future you have always wanted.

If at the moment you are having difficulty and unable to completely create and envision this dream life, do not worry. You are now about to complete an exercise designed to assist you in opening your inner self and envisioning the life you have always subconsciously desired.

Life Vision Exercise

What does your ideal life look like? It is time to step away from the doubt and fear that have been holding you back. I would like you to close your eyes and start to dream. For each of the life areas below, I want you to ask yourself "if I had no worries in my life and I had all the money, health, knowledge and support I needed, what would I do? What would my dream life look like? What would inspire me? What would drive me to get up in the morning and what would I look forward to accomplishing? What would bring me happiness and fulfillment? If nothing could stop you, what would you desire? How would you see your life?"

As you do this exercise, write a description of what you discover in each of the sections below. For example, I would be an addictions counselor helping addicts overcome their addiction and become contributing and happy members of the community.

Follow this up with why this would make you happy. For example, as a past addict I have experienced the pain and hopelessness of addiction and the effect it had on my life and the lives of those I love. Being able to help other addicts will help me feel fulfilled because I was able to help another person escape the pain and find happiness.

Career/Business

What would you like to do for a living? What would your dream job or business look like? What would make you look forward to getting out of bed in the morning?

_____

_____

_____

Why would this make you happy?

_____

_____

_____

Financial

What would your financial situation look like? How much money do you want to earn or have? What does financial freedom look like to you?

_____

_____

_____

Why would this make you happy?

_____

_____

_____

Lifestyle

How and where would you like to live? What would you spend your leisure time doing? What would you like to own? Where would you like to visit?

_____

_____

_____

Why would this make you happy?

_____

_____

_____

Relationships

What would your relationships look like? Would you like to be married or have children? What does your relationship with your parents and siblings look like? Would you like to belong to a certain organization or group? What would your friendships look like?

_____

_____

_____

Why would this make you happy?

_____

_____

_____

Personal Development

What would you like to improve on? Where are you spiritually? What would you like to learn or become better at? Is there something you have always wanted to do?

_____

_____

_____

Why would this make you happy?

_____

_____

_____

Health and Fitness

What kind of physical and mental condition are you in? How do you look after yourself physically and mentally? What would your appearance look like?

_____

_____

_____

Why would this make you happy?

_____

_____

_____

Contribution

How would you give back to the world? What would you be doing for others? Is there a certain cause that would drive you?

_____

_____

_____

Why would this make you happy?

_____

_____

_____

You should now have created a vision that inspires and excites you. This vision would compel you to implement the changes in your life required to change your vision into reality.

How To Write a Life Vision Statement

Next, you will write a life vision statement that brings together all the areas of your life to describe a well-balanced and inspiring life vision that will lead to fulfilling all your dreams and desires. A life vision statement simply brings together all the individual areas of your life in a balanced way to provide a single inspiring and guiding statement.

Life Vision Statement Exercise

I would like you to take the life area statements you wrote and combine them into one single life statement. The statement should flow to describe what your total life will look like. It should give a clear description of how you are going to accomplish your mission and fulfill your life purpose.

I will again use my personal life vision statement as an example:

I am personally and financially independent, living in abundance through my successful and profitable business as a personal development author, trainer, speaker and coach. My career inspires and allows me to help others improve their lives to become better individuals. I enjoy my leisure time travelling, cooking, entertaining and playing competitive pool. I constantly seek out new insight and methods to improve personally and spiritually. I am happily married to an exceptional woman and have excellent relationships with my children, family and friends. I am always striving to be in peak physical and mental health.

Write your Life Vision Statement below.

_____

_____

_____

_____

_____

You should now have a life vision statement that inspires and directs you into action. You will view this statement many times a day. You will memorize it and live it. This statement will be the fuel you require to help overcome any difficulty, setback or disappointment you will encounter in your future life journey.

Creating a Life Statement

I have found that I am more grounded if every day I review my written life statement that describes my life purpose, mission and vision. I view my life purpose statement every morning before I prepare or review my daily action plan. I truly believe this helps me start the day in the right frame of mind and gives me the strength I need when I am facing a difficult or stressful day ahead. As I have mentioned earlier, as we strive to achieve our life vision, we will encounter difficult times. This is one of the tools you can use to help you through those times and not lose focus or become discouraged. I would suggest you prepare a life statement for yourself and then get in the habit of reviewing it every morning. You can also draw upon this uplifting and directing statement during those times you require a little encouragement. In sequence, you write your life purpose statement first, then your life mission statement and follow up with your life vision statement. I provide mine as an example:

My Life Statement

My Life Purpose
To be in a devoted and growing relationship with
God, endeavouring to become a happy and better

version of myself while helping others to become happy and better versions of themselves.

My Life Mission

To reach out and become closer to God each and every day. To learn and live according to the plan God has for my life and accept His love, guidance and support along the way. To continually seek out new concepts and opportunities that will help others to become a happier and improved version of themselves.

My Life Vision

I am personally and financially independent, living in abundance through my successful and profitable business as a personal development author, trainer, speaker and coach. My career inspires and allows me to help others improve their lives and become better individuals. I enjoy my leisure time travelling, cooking, entertaining and playing competitive pool. I constantly seek out new insight and methods to improve personally and spiritually. I am happily married to an exceptional woman and have excellent relationships with my children, family and friends. I always striving to be in peak physical and mental health.

Write your own life statement now, keep it accessible and remember to make it a habit of reviewing your statement every morning, before you go to sleep and when you require a little extra drive or inspiration.

The Power of Visualization

Now that you have a statement that describes how you desire your life to unfold, it is important to put the power of visualization to work and help your vision become a reality.

Visualization is simply a mental rehearsal. You create images in your mind of having or doing whatever it is that you want. You then repeat these images over and over again, programming your mind for success. You use your imagination to see yourself being successful in whatever you desire.

The key to visualizing is to always visualize that you already have what it is you desire. Rather than hoping you will achieve it or building confidence that one day it will happen, you live and feel it as if it is happening to you now. Many successful people have used visualization to overcome adversity and go on to achieve great success. Morris E. Goodman used visualization to overcome what most thought was impossible. Goodman proved that by the power of the human mind and dedication, one can do the impossible.

His story starts in 1981 when the plane he was flying crashed. The impact was devastating. He wound up in the hospital completely paralyzed. The doctors' prognosis was poor, and they told him that he would be a paralyzed for the rest of his life. They told him that he'd never breathe on his own, talk or walk ever again in his life.

Many people in his condition would have listened to the doctors and given up. Goodman wasn't most people. He believed with all his heart and soul that he would one day be normal—not hooked to machines, not silent, not fed through tubes and not pushed in a wheelchair.

At the time, all he could do was blink his eyes. But being the fighter that he is, Goodman summoned all his strength and courage and, through the use of the alphabet and eye blinking, told the nurse that he would walk out of the hospital on Christmas Day.

While the medical team commended his fighting spirit, they did not believe that he could do it. Day in and day out, Goodman visualized how he would be walking out of the hospital on his own two feet. He vividly imagined the details and the shocked faces of the people in the hospital, medical practitioners and patients alike.

One day, Goodman felt the sudden urge to breathe on his own. With all his might, he inhaled deeply. From then on, his progress amazed the people who knew his story. His full recovery was splashed on every tabloid and newspaper in town.

Today, he is a highly sought-after speaker who travels around the world sharing his success story. He encourages people to believe that no matter what hand life deals them, they can still accomplish their goals, achieve happiness and have contentment in their hearts. His favourite saying, "Man becomes what he thinks about," is the final comment he leaves his audience to ponder before leaving the stage.

Many athletes use visualization to become the best in their sport. Lindsey Vonn was one of the most successful female skiers in history. The gold medalist uses her mental practice to give her a competitive advantage on the course. "I always visualize the run before I do it," Vonn said. "By the time I get to the start gate, I've run that race 100 times already in my head, picturing how I'll take the turns."

However, she doesn't solely keep the images in her head. While visualizing a run, she physically simulates the path by literally shifting her weight back and forth as if she were on skis, as well as practises the specific breathing patterns she'll use during the race. "I love that exercise," Vonn said. "Once I visualize a course, I never forget it. So I get on those lines and go through exactly the run that I want to have."

Visualization works in three ways. First, it activates the creative mind. The subconscious mind cannot distinguish between what is real and what is imagined. Your subconscious will act upon the images you create within, whether they reflect your current reality or not. In essence, the subconscious mind is continually looking for ways to make the vision become reality.

Second, visualization activates your reticular activating system (RAS). The RAS is the portal through which nearly all information enters the brain. (Smells are the exception; they go directly into your brain's emotional area.) The RAS filters the incoming information and affects what you pay attention to, how aroused you are and what is important to you. Your RAS tells your brain to become aware of anything that will help you achieve your goal.

Third, visualization attracts you to people, resources and opportunities that you require to achieve your goal through the Law of Attraction. We will discuss the Law of Attraction in Chapter Twelve.

By creating your life vision, you have already set these three advantages into action. We are now going to learn another tool that provides more instruction to our brain by setting up a vision board.

The Vision Board

A vision board is a personally created picture and word collage that displays what you want in life. When you hang your vision board in a place where you can see it daily, your vision board brings your goals and aspirations to life. For anyone who has never heard of a vision board, it is a collage of desired items and results that are meant to kick-start your imagination and help you visualize and achieve what it is you desire.

Creating a vision board helps you to take the time to dream and seriously think about what it is you want from life. The reason that vision boards work so well is because you visually see, think about and feel your desires every day. Visualization is one of the most popular and effective mind workouts that you can do. When you see and experience the feel of something that inspires you on a daily basis, you stay on track. Even when you face setbacks, that vision board will still be there ready to motivate you all over again.

Seeing your vision board will help you passionately connect with your dreams and desires. It can help you notice opportunities or simply make you imagine what something may feel like. If you get fired up and passionate about something, it will spur you into action.

One of the most amazing and inspiring vision board success stories comes from Lucinda Cross. As a young college student, Lucinda made a bad choice that landed her in prison. Instead of becoming another sad statistic, she chose to learn from her mistake, take control of her life and build a better future for herself. She envisioned a different life and created a vision board to guide her. Today, she is a successful entrepreneur, bestselling author, speaker and life coach. She has been featured on such prestigious media outlets as ABC, NBC, Black Enterprise, Essence Magazine and many more. She attributes all her success to vision boards and has literally built her business around them.

Vision Board Exercise

Your vision board can be as simple as placing a few photos on a piece of paper or you can go all out artistically and prepared a display board with photos, quotes and affirmations. When I prepared my first vision board, I downloaded some photos that expressed my desires and placed them on a piece of 8.5- by 11-inch piece of paper along with some text affirming what I wanted. I made several copies and placed one by my bed, one on the bathroom mirror, one by the computer screen in my office and one in my car.

All you need to do is find some photos, magazine clippings or pictures that visualize the different vision areas you have in your life vision statement. Add some positive or affirming text above or below the photo. When your vision board is complete, you should be able to look at it and see as well as feel yourself living the reality of the present.

Place copies of your vision board in areas you frequent. Review and feel their influence on you daily or even several times a day, if possible. View them until they attach themselves into your mind so that at any moment you can recall and feel that you are currently living them today. This vision and feeling will feed and strengthen the mind and its ability to assist you in achieving them.

Please do not take this exercise or concept lightly. The power of envisioning and feeling your life the way you desire it to be will help you achieve your dreams and provide the power required to overcome any setback, disappointment or tragedy you meet along the way.

Using Affirmations

Another great tool that will inspire you to greatness is the use of positive affirmations. Affirmations are short statements that, in the simple terms, are positive sentences that you repeat to yourself. When you first start saying these phrases, they are spoken as if you have already achieved the benefit you are seeking. Often, they are designed to reflect what you want to become a reality in all its glory.

Over time, the consistent repetition of daily positive affirmations helps to reshape your beliefs and assumptions about yourself and the world around you. This reshaping gives you a more positive perception of who you are and where you are headed. The daily use of positive affirmations will interrupt and eventually replace the negative thoughts and limiting beliefs that stop you from succeeding. To use this powerful tool, you must continually fill your subconscious mind with thoughts and images of the new reality you wish to create.

Here are the eight guidelines for creating effective affirming statements from Jack Canfield's book *The Success Principles*:

1. Start with the words *"I am."* These are the two most powerful words in the English language.
2. Use the present tense.

3. State it in the positive. Affirm what you want, not what you don't want.
4. Keep it brief.
5. Make it specific.
6. Include an action word ending with –ing.
7. Include at least one dynamic emotion or feeling word.
8. Make affirmations for yourself, not others.

Once I completed my life vision statement, I wrote affirmations using Jack's guidelines to help me strive for, achieve and live my vision. I have found these affirmations give me the passion and power to continue even on those days I do not feel like doing anything. Here are a few of the affirmations I repeat every morning, throughout the day and before I go to sleep at night:

> I am cheerfully enjoying the financial freedom I receive from my business.
> I am happily helping people to become better versions of themselves.
> I am joyfully travelling and walking the beach with my wife.
> I am proudly winning my pool matches.
> I am triumphantly seeing my weight below 175 pounds on the scale.
> I am excitedly learning new self-improvement tools and techniques.

As I repeat the affirmations out loud, I visualize and feel as if these desires are real and I am living them now. The results are that many of my visions are close to becoming a complete reality. I have seen such a big improvement in my life and how I feel about it. I have built up a confidence so strong that I not only believe I will achieve all my goals soon but am already working on where to go from here.

I have also added positive motivational and belief affirmations while I am running on the treadmill each day:

> I am getting better and better each and every day.
> I am growing stronger and stronger each and every day.
> I am learning more and more each and every day.
> I am loving more and more each and every day.
> I am becoming more and more patient each and every day.

I also listen to music and repeat these affirmations out loud, stepping in time with the music and the words. It is surprising how quickly the 45-minute workouts disappear, and I am amazed at the energy and determination I have after the workout.

As life continues, every thought you think and every word you speak is an affirmation. All of our self-talk, our internal dialogue, is a stream of affirmations. You're using affirmations every moment whether you know it or not. You're affirming and creating your life experiences with every word and thought. Your beliefs are merely habitual thinking patterns that you learned as a child. Many of them work very well for you. Other beliefs may be limiting your ability to create the very things you say you want. What you want and what you believe you deserve may be very different. You need to pay attention to your thoughts so that you can begin to eliminate the ones that are creating experiences you do not want in your life.

Today is a new day. Today is a day for you to begin creating a joyous, fulfilling life. Today is the day to begin to release all your limitations. An affirmation opens the door. It's a beginning point on the path to change. In essence, you're saying to your subconscious mind "I am taking responsibility. I am aware that there is something I can do to change."

Affirmation Exercise

Start today. Write out several new positive affirmations below. Remember to structure them using Jack Canfield's guidelines you read earlier. Take your life vision statement and break it into different visions and write a positive affirmation for each one.

_____

_____

_____

_____

_____

Make copies of your affirmations and place them where you will see them and be reminded to repeat them. Repeat them out loud several times a day. Memorize them deep within yourself. Let your affirmations become a part of your life and replace your old negative thoughts. Follow this life-enhancing gift and you will lead yourself down a path to all the blessings and happiness you desire and deserve.

Summary

In this chapter, we have discussed the power that a clear and defined vision provides to your future and its importance to your ongoing happiness and fulfillment. You have learned how to create a vision that will empower you to live according to your life mission in harmony with your greater purpose. You now have the three pillars of a successful life: a reason to do what you do, what it is you need to do and how you are going to do it. We will now move on to the next chapter and discover if you are programmed to do it.

CHAPTER FOUR

Know Your Identity

Am I programmed to succeed?

"The deeper I go into myself the more I
realize that I am my own enemy."
— **Floriano Martins**

- -

In This Chapter
- ➤ Do You Know Your Identity?
- ➤ How Your Identity Affects Your Life
- ➤ The Power of Self Identity
- ➤ Outside Forces Can Control Your Identity
- ➤ How To Shift Your Identity for Success
- ➤ My Identity Exercise
- ➤ Summary

- -

Personal identity is the concept you develop about yourself that evolves over the course of your life. This may include aspects of your life that you have no control over, such as where you grew up or the colour of your skin, as well as choices you make in life, such as how you spend your time and what you believe. You demonstrate portions of your personal identity outwardly through what you wear and how you interact with other people. You may also keep some elements of your personal identity to yourself, even when these parts of yourself are very important.

We all have a personal identity, whether conscious or subconscious, that influences all our thoughts and actions. Our personal identity defines how we should act and live our life. Each person's identity is formed by many influences. The environment we live in, our family, what we experience as we grow, our relationships, our culture and media are a few of the influences that help form our identity. If we are not aware of or in control of our identity, it can cause great pain in our lives. If understood and implemented properly, our identity will be one of the most important factors and tools available to assist use in living a happy and fulfilling life.

Do You Know Your Identity?

Have you ever taken the time to understand who you are or what influences your thoughts and actions? How would you describe yourself? Are you a writer? A winner? An addict? A free spirit? A criminal? An accountant? A teacher? A parent? A leader? A lover? A football fan? An entrepreneur? A failure? An independent thinker? Do you care about others? Are you good at what you do? These are a few examples of how people identify themselves.

You are not the only one who identifies you by a definition or description. The people you have come in contact with have their own definition or description of how they would identify your character. How would your family, co-workers, neighbours and friends describe you?

Through my experience, I have come to understand that most people answer the question "who are you?" in one of three ways. First, some people simply look at you with a blank stare, unsure of how to answer the question. They have never put any deep thought into who they are. They just let life dictate who they are and how their lives will be lived. Others answer quickly with what Anthony Robbins refers to as the Popeye Principle: "I am who I am." This is a great way to avoid accepting responsibility for your thoughts and behaviours.

The most common response is a definition. People will describe themselves by their profession (I am a lawyer or I am a truck driver), their title (I am a manager or I am a CEO), their financial status (I am a millionaire), their emotions (I am loving or I am forgiving), their behaviours (I am a drug addict or I am a gambler), their spiritual beliefs (I am a Christian, I am a Muslim or I am free-spirited), their accomplishments (I am the prom queen or I am the heavy-weight champion) or their looks (I am handsome or I am ugly). Each of these descriptions has its own definition, which changes from person to person. There are many other ways people use to describe themselves, including what they are not (I am not a quitter).

Take a moment to reflect and consider who you actually believe you are and how you think others describe you. How would you answer this revealing question? Don't let shame or disappointment cause you to cover up how you truly feel about yourself. Dig down deeply and honestly to establish how you would describe yourself and how you think others who know you would describe you? It might be difficult but it will be very enlightening.

Understanding who you are is foundational to your life. The words you use to describe yourself are a big part of who you truly believe you are; it's your identity and how you define yourself. Your identity is the combination of your interests and your values, what you have experienced and learned over the years, what you do and what you enjoy. It is also what you do to avoid discomfort and pain. Your identity is one of the most powerful and controlling factors in your life, more powerful than you might realize. You see, your identity is more than a convenient way of summing yourself up. It is who you subconsciously believe you are. It is how you present yourself to the world. It controls how you act and interact with the people around you, the way you believe you should behave and how others expect you to behave. It is also instrumental in how others react to and treat you.

For many people, the exercise of looking deeply within themselves leads to shock and confusion over what they discover about themselves. Parts of their identity have been hidden within their subconscious. As they reflect on their findings, they discover why events have transpired in their life. Their role in these events becomes clearer. But one question remains: how did they come to possess certain parts of their identity?

A person's identity is formed from many factors. Our upbringing as children has the greatest impact on how we form our identity. As children, we are exposed to all sorts of influences and experiences. Loving and attentive parents will instill a different identity than will broken and abusive parents. Coming from wealth or poverty can mould your identity. The environment you live in affects your identity. How other people treat and talk to you will affect what you believe about yourself. The responses you receive from your own actions can affect your self-esteem.

How Your Identity Affects Your Life

Our identity is responsible for most of the actions we take, the responses we provide and the direction we move in our lives. Our identity also creates the boundaries and limits we have in our lives. It is responsible for controlling what we can or will do, what we can't or will not do, and how we expect others to think and act. We act consistently with the view of our identity, whether that view is valid or not. A negative self-identity is usually responsible for the actions or reactions a person commits that end up causing them unrest, pain or even death.

A great example of this is illustrated in a story I once heard about a frog and a scorpion. One day a scorpion found himself in a dilemma. His family was waiting for him across the river but he was unable to find a safe place to cross. He spotted a frog ready to cross to the other side and called to him. "Mr. Frog, would you do me a great favour and let me ride on your back across the river so I can join my family?" Surprised, the frog thought for a second and replied, "Certainly not, Mr. Scorpion. You are a scorpion and scorpions sting frogs. If I let you on my back, you would surely sting me and I would die."

The scorpion looked at the frog and replied, "No, no, Mr. Frog, you have it wrong. I could not sting you as that would be suicide. If I stung you while we were crossing the river, you would die and sink to the bottom of the river, which would cause me to drown and die also. Surely I would not do something that foolish." The frog thought for a minute and said, "I guess you are right. Climb on my back and I will carry you across the river to your family."

When they were about half way across the river, the scorpion suddenly stung the frog. As the frog was going down and taking his last breath, he asked the scorpion, "Why did you sting me? I am dying and now you are going to die too." The scorpion just smiled and replied, "I am a scorpion and that is what scorpions do. They sting frogs."

Even when faced with severe and drastic consequences, people commit unthinkable acts because of their identity. All reasoning and accountability are overpowered by our subconscious identity programming. Over the years, we have on occasion said something or acted in a certain way that was negative towards ourselves or someone else. Upon reflecting on the event, we are unable to come up with a clear reason for why we had acted this way. This event was the result of our subconscious identity taking control.

Another great illustration of how your identity can affect your life is from Victor Hugo's classic *Les Misérables*. We will look at two of the story's main characters, Jean Valjean and Monsieur Javert, and how their identities controlled their thoughts and actions.

Jean Valjean was imprisoned in the early 1800s in France for stealing a loaf of bread to feed his sister and her children. Throughout his many years in prison, Valjean refused to accept the identity of criminal as he believed he was merely trying to help save his family the only way possible.

Upon his release, Valjean was unable to find an honest day's work. He was continually ridiculed and rejected everywhere he went because of his status as an ex-convict. Feeling helpless and unable to support himself, he finally accepted the identity society had given him and considered himself a criminal. As such, he began to act like a criminal.

Now freezing and starving, he came across a kind bishop who takes him in, feeds him and provides him a warm bed to sleep in. He fulfills his new criminal identity by getting up during the night and stealing the bishop's silverware. The next day, the police stop Valjean and discover that not only is he an ex-convict but he has the bishop's silverware, a crime punishable by a life of hard labour in prison. He is taken to face the bishop who accused him of stealing. Knowing what would happen to Valjean, the bishop, in an act of mercy, told the police that he had given the silverware to Valjean. The bishop went on to give Valjean two silver candlesticks, saying Valjean forgot to take them with him. After the police left, the bishop told Valjean that God loved him and his transgression was forgiven and to go use the silver to live an honest and contributing life.

Valjean was stunned and tried to process what had happened. Why had the bishop forgiven him and not sent him away in chains? The bishop had called him his brother and told him he no longer belonged to evil. The bishop told Valjean he was to become an honest man, as he was a child of God. Again, Valjean's identity is interrupted and changed. He was told he was no longer a criminal but to become an honest and caring man. It is at this point that Valjean decides to take control and define his own identity. He rips up his parole papers, shredding the identity of a criminal, creates his own identity and goes on to become a respected leader and help others in his community.

Monsieur Javert was a prison guard who supervised Valjean while he was in prison. Javert believed in the supremacy of the law and that one had to live by the law and no way other. He believed that if someone broke the law, they were a criminal and would always be a criminal. He had a belief that people could not change. If they did something evil, he would always identify them as evil. Many years later, Javert was promoted to an inspector and posted to the city where Valjean was the mayor.

After reporting to the mayor, Javert soon realized that he was in fact Valjean, the convict who broke parole many years earlier. Javert could not accept that Valjean had changed and had become a good and honest man who was helping so many others in the community. Ignoring all the worthy and sacrificial measures Valjean had achieved, Javert still considered him an evil fugitive. While Javert was trying to prove the mayor was Valjean, an innocent man was mistakenly arrested and accused of being Valjean. This was Valjean's chance; he could let this innocent man go to jail as him and be free forever. However, Valjean's new identity could not let this injustice happen, and he confessed, ready to return to prison before an innocent man was unjustly punished.

During the same time, Valjean was helping a dying woman and promised to care for her infant daughter. Before Javert could arrest him, Valjean kept his promise and took the girl to Paris where he cared for the daughter and again lived a respectable and contributing life. Several years later, Javert again came across Valjean during a revolution. Circumstances led to Javert being captured and his life was in the hands of Valjean, who had been instructed to kill Javert. Instead, Valjean in compassion spared Javert and let him go.

Javert could not understand why Valjean did not kill him and ensure his own freedom forever, even though Javert told Valjean that if he spared him nothing would change and he would hunt him down. After his release, Javert began to question his belief that no one could change, and Valjean's actions were confounding his beliefs and identity. Believing his life was a lie, rather than change his beliefs and identity, Javert chose to let limiting beliefs and not himself define his identity. The result is Javert decided to end his life by jumping off a bridge.

In summary, Valjean had learned the power of identity and that it can be affected by outside forces unless controlled by the individual. He was able to decide what he wanted out of life and define his own identity, which helped him to achieve and live a fulfilling life. On the other hand, Javert let his identity control him and bring about his demise.

We all have a personal identity. The question is "will we define it or will we let other influences define it?" We have the power to define and live our own identity. Are you ready to choose to define your personal identity and use it to live a purposeful and fulfilling life?

The Power of Self Identity

Over the years, I have worked with many people who have attended meetings during which they would introduce themselves by saying, "Hi, I am Bill, and I am a drug addict." They were unknowingly defining their identity. Even though they were courageously trying to break their addiction to become clean and sober, there was a serious problem. They were both consciously and subconsciously identifying themselves as someone they were trying not to be.

When you identify yourself in a certain way, your subconscious mind is always looking for and finding ways to achieve your identity. If you identify as a drug addict, you will end up doing what an addict does—use drugs. For a period of time, you may use self-control to act opposite to your identity but sooner or later your actions will reflect that identity. An addict uses drugs and to live your identity you must use drugs. This is why so many people end up using drugs after long periods of sobriety.

When asked why, after all that time of sobriety, they chose to use drugs, they seem confused and cannot explain it. It happens so frequently that it has even been given a name: a slip. Their subconscious desire to live the identity overpowers the willpower needed to stay sober. The only real way to stop being a drug addict is to change your identity.

A positive new identity would be "I am a person who would not even consider using drugs." If this is programmed into your subconscious, then even when you are faced with a tempting situation, your subconscious would set in motion whatever was needed to not desire or consume drugs.

Throughout my life, I had several identities that affected my life. Just like the example above about the drug addict, this identity was affecting all my thoughts and actions without my knowing it. During my youth, I heard from different people that I was an overactive child and a troublemaker. This negative identity became the motivation for many of the selfish, irresponsible and dangerous actions I did while growing up. My identity was also responsible for giving me lots of attention from the people around me and that fed my need for significance (which we will discuss later in Chapter Nine).

As the years went on, I discovered many new self-definitions for my identity that controlled all my thoughts and actions. I defined myself as selfish, a thief, a drug addict, a manipulator, an outcast and so on. I did not care about the consequences of my actions. It was this identity that brought about behaviours that caused such pain and heartache to myself and people I knew, all to live up to who I identified myself as.

This destructive identity caused me to act opposite to the life I truly desired. I attended many programs designed to help change my behaviour. I would do well for a while only to fall back into old behaviours. Though I was able to change my behaviour in the short term, I would fail because my identity had not changed.

After learning about the power of one's identity, I was able to reflect on my life and became aware of who I truly believed I was. I came to understand the negative identities that were affecting my life. Only then was I able to shift the negative and limiting identities I had of myself to more positive and empowering ones. I shifted the definition of who I was to that of a positive, loving and contributing person, one with a defined and fulfilling future. I was then able to implement the strategies and actions that led me to a path that guided me and allowed me to start living a passionate, successful and happy life.

Outside Forces Can Control Your Identity

Most people mistakenly believe they know who they are and find it difficult to understand how others can take control of their identity. Let me assure you that it is not difficult and that outside forces are influencing people's identity daily. If you are not in control of your identity, then others are. How you see yourself is how you will act. If you are not consciously defining how you see yourself, then other factors are. This may be intentional or by accident.

Robert Rosenthal and Lenore Jacobson undertook a study about the Pygmalion effect, a phenomenon whereby higher expectations lead to an increase in performance and lower expectations lead to lower performance. The study showed that if teachers were led to expect enhanced performance from children, then the children's performance was enhanced. This study supported the hypothesis that reality can be positively or negatively influenced by the expectations of others.

In this study, teachers were told that certain students in their class were gifted and should be treated as such and challenged to help them expand. As a result, these students became the top achievers in the class. In fact, these students were not gifted but were previously labelled poor students. Rosenthal argued that biased expectancies could affect reality and create self-fulfilling prophecies.

The teachers believed these students had a certain identity so they treated the students according to how they were identified. The students began to adopt this new identity and thus acted and achieved as they should according to their new identity. The Pygmalion effect can work in reverse, causing someone to take on a negative identity and live that identity.

Today, if you are not consciously working at defining and forming your own identity, then you can rest assured outside factors are. It could be positive or negative, depending on the environment you are exposed to. For many people, their identity changes several times as their environment changes. Around one group of people a person may take on a different identity than when around a different group of people. They are defined by who they are with.

Your culture, faith background, relationships, living conditions, the media you consume or the music you listen to are only a few of the forces that can shape your identity. Do not leave it up to chance. One of the most important lessons you can learn in your life will be to understand and take control of your identity.

How To Shift Your Identity for Success

It is time to take back your identity and define who you are. Just by asking yourself "who am I?" you are moving forward. The question starts the thinking process, and your mind starts to establish not only who you are but who you want to be and who you do not want to be. This is very beneficial because the mind sets into motion what our identity determines we should be thinking and doing to meet its definition, and also what we should not be thinking or doing.

My Identity Exercise

In this exercise, you are requested to contemplate and define what you want your identity to be. As you complete this exercise, make it yours. Decide what you want and don't want. Do not consider what you think others think you should or should not be.

When I completed this exercise, I remembered to include my purpose, mission and vision. I came up with this: I am a committed child of God, striving to live each day loving and serving the Lord and His people in the same way He loves me.

Let's begin.

Who am I?

List below all the values, talents, attributes, knowledge and beliefs that you require or want to have in your life.

_____

_____

_____

_____

_____

Now write a detailed statement that describes who you are as a person.

I am: _____

_____

_____

_____

_____

Who am I not?

List below all the values, talents, attributes, knowledge and beliefs that you do not want to have in your life.

_____

_____

_____

_____

_____

Now write a detailed statement that describes who you do not want to be as a person.

I am not: _____

_____

_____

_____

_____

You now have a written description of your identity, who you want to be in life and a description of who you want no part of being. Review these statements daily and repeat them out loud. Do this until they are so engrained into your subconscious that all your daily thoughts, decisions and actions are guided by them. As you grow, these statements will become strong beliefs that cannot be overpowered by other influences and forces in the world. You will find that you will be accomplishing more and your confidence will increase, giving you the power to overcome any obstacle or setback you encounter along your life journey.

Summary

In this chapter, I pray that you have come to understand the importance your identity has in your life. By defining your own personal identity, you will be given the direction and confidence required to implement the strategies and tools you will learn throughout this book.

Have you ever wondered how two people from the same upbringing and background in life can go on to have such different lives? An example is two brothers one year apart who grow up in a drug-infested and abusive home. One becomes a successful business owner and family man while the other spends most of his life in and out of prison. There are many examples of this occurring throughout the world.

Then you look at people who have suffered life-changing events, such as losing their sight or use of their extremities. Why do some simply give up and live a life of misery and pity while others go on to achieve wonderful results in life? It all comes down to how they identify themselves. They are either a victim or a person who is willing to do what is required to help them overcome any obstacle or setback they encounter as they journey through their lives.

Your identity is a choice. Either you can define yourself with an empowering identity or you can relinquish the responsibility and live an identity provided by the world. I cannot emphasize enough that you have the power to define your identity. You have the ability to live life on your terms and you have the power to decide if you will be happy and fulfilled each day. You make the choice. Choose and commit to controlling your identity and I assure you that you will achieve all your dreams and desires.

"I know, Therefore I am"
— Gary Haney

SECTION TWO

UNDERSTANDING MYSELF

"At the heart of everything we do is a driving force. Understanding and managing that force is the key to lasting success."
— Gary Haney

Why do I do what I do?

Have you ever asked yourself "why did I do that?" Did you promise yourself you would never do something but yet did it? Why? These are questions that have puzzled many people throughout their lives.

If you ever hope to understand why you do what you do and want to learn how to influence your behavior to live a better life, one where you're in control, then you need to learn and understand what principles and conditions influence your thoughts and actions.

In this section, I will describe several patterns and processes that are influencing your life and how you can reframe them, empowering yourself to do what you want and not the actions that are detrimental to you.

CHAPTER FIVE

Your Decisions

The source of what you feel, believe and do

"It is in your moments of decision that your destiny is shaped."
— Tony Robbins

- -

In This Chapter
> Everything You Are Experiencing Is the Result of Past Decisions
> Control Your Decisions and Control Your Destiny
> Your Life Conditions Are Not Responsible for Your Destiny
> Making a True Decision
> Principles That Influence Our Decisions
> Summary

- -

The purpose of this chapter is to help you learn and come to accept that the most important principle that will affect the direction and results in your life are the decisions you make. In its simplest sense, decision-making is the act of choosing between two or more courses of action. People often say that they find it hard to make decisions. Unfortunately, we all have to make decisions all the time, ranging from trivial issues like what to have for lunch, right up to life-changing decisions like where and what to study, and whom to marry. Some people put off making decisions by endlessly searching for more information or getting other people to offer their recommendations. Others resort to decision-making by taking a vote, sticking a pin in a list or tossing a coin.

How you make daily decisions and the quality of those decisions impact every facet of your existence. You and you alone are responsible for your decisions and the influence they have on you, others and the world.

How many times have you done or said something only to end up regretting it and asking yourself "why did I do that? I know better, and that was not my intention." Maybe you had promised yourself you wouldn't do it again and yet you did. You go on to ask yourself "why does this keep happening to me?"

These are a few of the questions and thoughts we have right after we say or do something we know will negatively impact ourselves or others. A relationship is damaged, physical health is put at risk, a trust or law is broken, or some occurrence happens with irreversible consequences. Though you had no intention of doing it and, in fact, may have wanted the opposite result, it still happened. You are left pondering how this will affect the future and what this means to you personally. Your guilt becomes overwhelming, and a feeling of hopelessness starts to take over. Because of this incident, how you live, feel and act were forever changed.

Fundamentally, you want to know the cause of this reoccurring event and all the resulting despair and hopelessness you are experiencing in life. It all comes down to one reason: a decision you made along the way. The decision may have been conscious or subconscious, but either way you made a decision to do or say what you did or to feel the way you do. In life, we do not act, speak or feel without making a decision to act, speak or feel that way.

In today's society, many people are living lives of quiet desperation. Life is not working out the way they had envisioned. Circumstances and events beyond their control have caused them to except a lifestyle different from the one they have desired. They have come to believe this is their lot in life. For many, their feelings of sadness, loss and helplessness are overpowering as they blame their life situation on outside forces. Their outlook on life has become so jaded that they fail to notice and understand their part in all that has happened to them. They are unable to recognize or accept that their decisions along the way are what has led them to where they are today.

In this chapter, I will help you to understand the effect your decisions truly have on your daily living and that you have the control to make empowering decisions that will enhance your life. You will discover what has been causing you to make limiting and destructive decisions in the past.

Everything You Are Experiencing Is the Result of Past Decisions

Everything that has happened to you throughout your life— all the successes and memorable events and all the challenges and setbacks you have experienced—began with a decision or a choice you made. The choices you make in life are really decisions. It is not the life conditions around us or the influence that others place upon us that decide our destiny; our own personal decisions determine our destiny. Only we have the power to control how we think, feel and act. Others and external forces will try to influence our lives and decisions. But it is how we choose to respond to their input and the decisions we make afterwards that bring about our destiny. Your moments of decision have shaped your life until now and in the same way your future decisions will decide how the rest of your life will unfold.

Where each of us is in our life today is the result of decisions we have made along our life journey. Whether we are happy, sad, grateful or depressed, whether we are successful or floundering, our current situation and feelings are a result of past decisions we have made. Whether our decisions were conscious or subconscious, they have produced a cause and effect that has placed us in the situation we are currently experiencing. Even when we have been wronged by someone or an external situation, it is how we have decided to respond to that event that has resulted in where we are, what we believe and how we feel.

Each day we are making hundreds of conscious and subconscious decisions: what to focus on, what actions to take, what things mean to us, how to interpret events and the people around us, how to react, and most importantly how to feel. Most of these decisions are made in a moment without taking the time to consider the circumstances or whether we have all the information to make a proper decision.

Many of our decisions are made because of fear—the fear of pain, fear of loss or fear of the unknown. Our quick and thoughtless interpretation of events is also a leading factor in our poor decisions and negative responses. Without the time to consider and understand the whole situation, our interpretation is usually defensive and leads to a defensive and negative response.

Let's say you are having a heated discussion with someone and they look away from you. Without knowing that they have a sore neck, you interpret it as a sign of disrespect because they are looking away from you during a serious moment. In a split second, you become defensive and angry and escalate the situation needlessly by your words or actions. This quick and usually subconscious decision-making is the cause of many of our griefs in life.

I remember a woman I was coaching who said that her partner would make gulping sounds while she was talking during meaningful discussions. She interpreted these sounds as a sign of disrespect and her opinion was not important to him. She became defensive and aggressive, which led to a blow up between them. When I asked her if she ever talked to him about this behaviour and how it bothered her, she said that she hadn't. She felt that he knew what he was doing and was doing it on purpose to upset and belittle her.

At our next session, I invited her partner to attend and had her explain her concern. At first, he did not understand what she was talking about, and then he realized that often when he was focusing on a serious conversation his throat became moist so he would swallow. He had no idea she even noticed the swallowing let alone that it bothered her or that she considered it offensive and a purposeful attack on her. After further discussing the situation, they both laughed at the misunderstanding. The lesson here is that much needless stress, anger and suffering could have been avoided if she had mentioned how she felt about the sounds when they first bothered her. See how one decision could have changed the course of their relationship?

Each decision we make usually leads to many more decisions. Here is another example. Let say you arrive home from work tired and expecting to simply relax and sit by the television. You walk in the door only to find your partner unexpectedly entertaining guests. You decide this is not what you wanted and become angry, shown by your attitude and body language. Your partner pulls you aside and explains the guests dropped in unannounced and so she invited them in.

You decide not to accept your partner's explanation nor to care how the guests feel. In your anger, you say something hurtful to them. After saying it, you realize your mistake but decide your inconvenience was huge, they did not meet your expectations, and therefore you do not apologize. Now your partner is feeling hurt and wronged and becomes upset with you. You chastise your partner because you were the one inconvenienced by the situation.

A scene erupts and your partner goes off upset and the guests leave feeling hurt and disappointed. Now everyone involved has been negativity affected because of a series of decisions you made. You are frustrated and cannot understand what happened and why that outcome resulted. You were simply tired and wanted time to yourself.

Everything you experienced was the result of a series of decisions you made without taking the time to think things through. You had several opportunities to change the outcome by making a different decision somewhere along the way. Maybe after realizing you made a hurtful comment, you could have decided to apologize instead of deciding to continue in the way you did. Think of how that one different decision could have changed the whole outcome of the situation.

Because we are usually unaware of the many decisions we have made around a situation, we end up placing the blame for the outcome on others, truly believing we were the one wronged. I am sure if you think about a recent negative outcome you experienced, you can find parts where you could have decided to interpret, feel or act differently, which would have led to a better outcome.

Many of our daily decisions can lead to hopelessness and despair if not focused on and controlled. If you become aware and find a way to make informed decisions, they can produce a life of joy, fulfillment and happiness.

In the real-life example below, recognize the decisions that were made and how a different decision at any time could have changed the outcome.

George was in his last year of high school and wanted to become a teacher. He was preparing for his graduation exams. One night his friends encouraged him to go out to the bar for his buddy's birthday. He was reluctant because he needed to study for the diploma exam he was writing in the morning. His friends convinced him to go out with them, and he stayed out partying into the early morning. Because George was tired and hungover the next morning, he flunked the exam and did not graduate with his class.

Because George did not graduate high school, he ended up taking a job at Walmart to support himself. One night he met Betty at a party. They began dating and started to have unprotected sex. A few months later Betty became pregnant. They both decided not to end the pregnancy, moved in together and had a healthy baby boy. Though their intentions were good, they were not truly in love, and the stress of the relationship and parenting was becoming too much for George. He started to spend time drinking and doing drugs with some unemployed friends that Betty did not like. Because he was constantly late and missed shifts, George was fired from his job. He continued to spend late nights out with friends and was not looking for a job. The couple had several fights, and tired of having to answer for himself, George moved out leaving Betty and his son alone to rely on welfare to survive.

George would visit Betty and his son occasionally and always promised to get his act together and come back to them. To support his drug habit, George eventually committed some petty crimes and ended up in jail. While in jail, he was having a rough time and Betty came to visit him. He again promised when he got out he would seek help for his addiction, get a job and return to his family. While inside prison, George became involved with some gang members and joined the gang. One day he was asked to collect a drug debt from an inmate. When the inmate refused to pay, George hit him harder than he intended and severely hurt the inmate. As a result, he ended up receiving a longer sentence and became bitter with the institution staff. George served the maximum time for his negative behaviour. Betty finally did not believe him anymore and stopped visiting.

Finally, George had enough and when he was released he became involved with a church group that supported him and helped him change his attitude and behaviour. He was able to upgrade his education and get a good job. Though he was clean and doing well, Betty could not believe him and refused to see him or let him see his son for three years.

In this story, George and Betty made many decisions, both good and bad ones. Can you list the various times when a decision changed the direction of their lives and how those decisions impacted their lives? If you think about it, even one decision made differently by George or Betty along the journey could have changed the total course of their story. Whether at the beginning or along the way, one different decision by either one would have changed the whole direction of the story. Even after several bad decisions, one positive decision could have changed the trajectory of their lives. This shows you that no matter where you are in your life, you can make a decision to alter your direction and change your destiny.

That is why the many decisions we make hundreds of times a day are the leading factor in how our lives will transpire. Each day, we decide over and over what to do, how to react, what to feel. Most of this is done subconsciously. Using the power of decision is the most important tool we can use to control our lives and achieve the dreams we so desperately desire. It is never too late to make an educated, controlled and life-changing decision.

Control Your Decisions and Control Your Destiny

The first and most important step to control our decisions and thus our lives is to understand and accept that we are 100 per cent responsible for all the decisions and choices we make from today forward. We cannot change past decisions during our lifetime but we can learn from our past decisions. We may fool ourselves into believing that others can direct and control our decision-making process but no one has control over our decisions unless we decide to let them. Sometimes we do this so that when things do not work out right, we have someone else to blame. But that stops here. When you understand and accept the fact that only you have the power to control your decisions, you will be able to realize positive change.

Often, when things do not go our way or we are wronged, our inclination is to blame others for the results we are experiencing. "He started it" or "I was here first" and many similar excuses are applied to justify our poor decisions. Much of this blame is subconscious. When we are not in total control of our decisions and are hurt, the last thing we want to do is increase our pain by looking at or placing any of the blame on ourselves.

A real-life example of this is when a person is unexpectedly laid off from the job they have worked at for years. Until then, they have lived a happy and extravagant lifestyle enjoying the moment. This sudden loss of income, combined with a large personal loss of esteem, resulted in them scrambling and feeling stressed. Unable to find quick employment due to a downturned economy, they feel the financial pinch. Finally, all their efforts to stay afloat fall short and they are forced into bankruptcy, causing them to lose most of their possessions and their home. They now have to live in a small apartment and need to scrape to survive. Even when they finally find employment, it is not the same and the job pays a lot less. Their lifestyle is not back to what they are accustomed to. This leaves them frustrated, angry and bitter. They put all the blame on the company they worked for and on the government for allowing the economy to slip. This anger leads to tension in their relationships. Depressed and not enjoying life, they start to drink as a way to cope with the pain. This causes more family stress, leading to separation and unemployment. As a result, they give up and blame everyone except themselves for their troubles. They become convinced that the failure and suffering they are experiencing is their destiny and it becomes a reality.

As all this transpired, they never once considered their part in the situation. At no time did they take responsibility for and control of their decisions. It was easier to blame others than to accept their part in the situation. It did not occur to them that had they made different decisions along the way, the situation may have turned out differently. They could have lived within their means and prepared themselves for this type of situation. They could have become proactive rather than simply let things happen. But instead, they considered themselves poor innocent victims of others and life in general.

I heard the following examples frequently as a prison chaplain: "I keep coming back to prison because the system is corrupt and uses people like me. The cops abused me and my lawyer lied to me and sold me out. My family doesn't trust me and will not help me anymore. I am an addict and nobody will help me. The guards treat me like crap and my parole officer is against me. With everyone against me, how am I supposed to succeed on the street?"

These types of responses keep people on the path to failure. People have the power within them to effect real change. It may be hard and it may bring about fear, but only you have the power to decide what to do next or how to react to others and situations that seem unfair. If we had made better decisions in the past, we possibly could have avoided the situation we are currently in. We could have made more informed and empowering decisions. In the example above, the person laid off could have chosen to place some of their income over the years into an emergency savings account rather spend all their income on instant gratification and possessions they wanted but did not need. By making that decision, they would have been prepared to handle this unexpected turn of events. If the prisoner had decided not to commit a crime nor place themselves in a situation where they could be blamed or taken advantage of, they would have avoided the opportunity for the system to wrong them or for their lawyer to make a mistake.

The reality is that we are all responsible for where we are today. The decisions we make on how to act or react in a situation determine our outcomes. If we decide to take a chance, we should not be surprised if the outcome is negative. The same goes with how we react to a situation where someone wrongs us. We can decide to become angry and let that decision cause us to do something that results in a negative outcome or we can decide to step back and learn from what happened, let it go and become stronger from the experience. It is truly our decisions of the moment that will lead to the life we desire or to a life of despair and pain.

Every minute of our life, we are making decisions and choices. Even in our sleep, our mind is busy making decisions for us. These decisions determine our destiny. We can experience the life we desire by learning to become conscious of our decisions and making empowering decisions with thought and foresight, or we can let thoughtless decisions drive us uncontrollably along the road of life to despair and suffering. It is our choice.

Your Life Conditions Are Not Responsible for Your Destiny

Have you ever wondered why two people with the same upbringing and life situation can grow up with lives so totally different? Two brothers both come from the same abusive father, drug-addicted mother, impoverished upbringing and crime-ridden community. One becomes a drug-addicted criminal regularly in and out of jail and the other goes on to become a successful businessman and community leader. What was the difference? Did one have an advantage over the other? No! It was the decisions they each made. One brother decided that society had determined his destiny to become just like his father and mother. He was angry and bitter and blamed everyone else including his family, God and the community for his suffering. On the other hand, the other brother decided this situation was not right and would not accept failure and pain. He could do better. He was going to prove that your current life situation does not determine your future. He wanted to be an example. He made a decision to overcome life's obstacles, no matter how difficult and impossible it appeared. That is the difference—a decision to succeed or a decision to give up.

Sometimes, you make the right decisions to succeed but life suddenly throws you a curve ball. Out of nowhere, a car runs the light and hits your car, sending you into a coma. You awake weeks later only to learn that you will never walk again. How would you react to this setback?

Many would simply decide to give up and become victims, allowing grief, despair and self-pity to overtake them. They would live the rest of their lives bitter, angry and unhappy, blaming others, God or the world for their situation. They have decided to ignore their power to overcome any misfortune that passes their way.

But yet many others facing the same circumstances would make a completely different decision. They would decide to overcome the situation, let the resentment go and move on to make the best of it.

Let's look at Bethany Hamilton as an example of someone who decided to overcome adversity. Bethany first tried to surf at age five. She could catch a wave and stand up on the board without help by age seven. She entered and won her first competition the following year. Before long, the Hawaii native had snagged her own sponsor and was being home-schooled to accommodate her training schedule. She was barely a teenager, yet her dream of becoming a pro surfer seemed not only possible but almost inevitable.

Then, on Halloween morning in 2003, the unthinkable happened. The day started like any other. At 5 a.m., the 13-year-old surfer rolled out of bed to hit the beach. The wave report for that morning was fairly uninspiring, as there was no good surf spotted around the island. But Bethany wanted to go anyway, so her mom dropped her off at one of her usual spots. She joined a group of fellow surfers and they all paddled out to wait for a few good waves.

As Bethany rested on her board, a tiger shark came out of nowhere and bit off her left arm, which had been dangling in the water. "I never saw the shark closing in on me," she said. "[If I had] I'm not sure I'd be able to live with the nightmares or ever go back in the water." She also believes that not seeing the shark coming helped her remain calm immediately after the bite, a reaction that probably saved her life. As it was, she lost over 60 per cent of her blood volume during the attack. Had she thrashed and panicked, she would likely have lost even more blood and died.

The next several days were a blur of surgeries, but as time passed and she began to heal, her anxiety shot up. She began to worry about the future: will I have to forget about surfing forever? What am I going to do? She also fretted about being defined by the attack for the rest of her life. She didn't want people to pity her or think of her as a person whose life had been ruined.

Within a week, she made two decisions: she would never wallow or walk around moaning "woe is me," and she would get back on her surfboard. She implemented the second decision just 26 days after the accident.

When Bethany first returned to surfing, she was extremely afraid of sharks. The attack that happened to her was such a rare occurrence, but she still thought about it. To fight that fear, she would get in the water and focus on catching the waves. She refused to dwell on "what-ifs."

The physical reality of surfing with only one arm was also an adjustment, and she had tremendously frustrating days. Some days she would go into the water and then come out of the water crying, but she kept at it. Her determination paid off. By the following year, she was again participating in national competitions, and within five years she was a staple on the professional surfing circuit. Today, she is ranked 48th among female surfers worldwide with the Association of Surfing Professionals.

While the accident wasn't something she would have wished for, she has embraced it as part of her life and discovered many unexpected silver linings. One of the most beautiful things that came from the accident is how it has allowed her to see that she can overcome difficulties. It taught her that she has the ability to overcome her fear in scary situations.

Bethany also finds joy in being a role model for other young amputees and for girls in general. She created the charitable organization Friends of Bethany, a non-profit that donates money to child amputees around the world. She cherishes being a role model for girls who are going through body changes and adjusting to how they look in the mirror. And she continues to surf daily.

Bethany's story is similar to those of many people who have decided to overcome obstacles and setbacks in their lives through no fault of their own. On the other hand, I can also provide many examples of people who have decided to feel sorry for themselves, blame others and live a life of anger, resentment and complete failure. Which of these two scenarios would you prefer to live your life by? It is up to you to decide. No one else can make the decision for you. Maybe it's time to step up and accept the responsibility, challenge and hard work that goes with it. It's time to decide that you know you can be better, you know your life can be better and you decide to make it that way.

It is your choice. No one can make it for you. You are the only one who can decide to raise yourself up and live life or suffer in self-pity. No one promises life will be fair. It can hurt us at the most inconvenient time. But it is you as a person who decides whether to strive ahead with purpose and passion or fold and live a life of despair.

Making a True Decision

Now you understand how important your decisions are and that you are making many of them each day without any structured thought. First, you need to become aware when you are making decisions. When someone asks you a question, of course you are aware that a decision is required and, using information you have at the moment, you make that decision. But what about those many decisions you make each day without a thought? At any given moment, you are deciding what to focus on, how you feel about it and how you are going to act or react to it.

When you get up in the morning and start your day, it is the result of many decisions. How many of those decisions did you consciously make? I am sure if you think about it, most of them were habit. You did not debate whether or how you would brush your teeth; you simply did it. Thus, you first need to become aware of these decisions, not just act or react but think about the positive and negative consequences your decision may produce. By becoming more aware of your decisions, you will be able to make ones that empower you and not hurt you. At first, it may seem silly thinking about such simple things like brushing your teeth, but the benefit of this practice is that you will build your decision-making muscles. You will start to notice when you need to reason before simply deciding based on habit or unintended mental programming.

Here are a couple of tools you could use to help slow down the decision-making process and allow you to start making positive and informed decisions. The first is a formula I learned from Jack Canfield in his *Success Principles* teachings. The formula is E (Event) + R (Response) = O (Outcome). Everything starts with an (E) event. Waking up in the morning, listening to someone talk to you, noticing the light change to red, receiving an insult and sitting down to dinner are all events. It is your (R) response to these events that produce the (O) outcome you experience. Your response is the result of a decision.

When you wake up, you might decide to be grumpy, raising your voice to your child or partner. You decide the person speaking to you is boring and look away from them while they are speaking. You decide you have enough time to beat the traffic light and drive on through. You decide to retaliate and hit them in the face. You decide an extra piece of pie won't hurt and eat it and the extra calories with it. The response to each event is the result of your decision. The outcomes of these decisions should not come as a surprise. Your child or partner feels hurt, the person speaking is offended and calls you out in front of our friends, a car strikes your car causing extensive damage and you are sued, you break their nose and the police are called and charge you, and your doctor puts you on medication because your blood test result is poor. Based on the above responses to events, one can easily understand why they experienced the outcome they did. Many people will say after the fact that it was a reaction, slip or someone else's fault but remember there can be no action without a decision to act. Blaming it on a reaction, slip or someone else is merely an excuse, deflecting the responsibility for not taking the time to make an informed decision.

I have changed the equation to assist in the decision process. I have added M (Meaning) to the equation: $E + M + R = O$. Meaning is how we perceive the event. If someone is looking at you with a smile, you can perceive it to mean they are happy, are laughing at you or are not taking you seriously. Each of these meanings would probably induce a different response from you. Thus, the first decision you need to focus on is the meaning of the event to you. When used correctly, this valuable tool can change impending disaster to victory.

Let's now examine how you can use this formula to help improve your decision-making and your life experience for the better. In front of your friends, Bob walks up, gets in your face and accuses you of something you did not do. You are upset because you did not do what he accused you of and he is doing this in front of others and embarrassing you. You demand he stop but he becomes more aggressive. In frustration, you punch him in the face and break his nose. The police are called, and you end up with a criminal record for assault.

In this example, the event (E) is Bob's actions. (M) is the meaning you placed on the event. You perceived his actions to be an unprovoked attack on you and your response (R) is to strike him. The outcome (O) is a criminal record. This scenario plays out quite often in today's world because many people do not understand the power of and the responsibility for their decisions. Instead, their decisions are made for them by their subconscious programming. They have not learned how to overcome this by using the above tool to help them.

If you were to use the E + M + R = O formula as a tool, you could change your response and the outcome experienced. When Bob starts to accuse you, you realize this is an event and that you need to decide what it really means. At this point, instead of relying on your subconscious programming to make that decision for you, you can take charge and ask yourself "why is he doing this?" This would allow you to consider that maybe he has a reason, and this would allow you to change your response from becoming defensive and striking him to asking him why he is accusing you. The outcome of that response could clear up a misunderstanding, leading to a positive outcome to the event.

This tool can help you recognize when you are about to make a subconscious decision and change it into a conscious one. It is also a great tool to use when making everyday decisions because it helps you to think through your decision and respond in a more positive way.

A second tool is to decide if a response is even required. I found this tool greatly helped me avoid needless negative outcomes in my life by simply helping me realize that no response was better than any response I could come up with. It works this way. Someone tells you something offensive that you do not agree with or find unintelligent. Your subconscious decision would be to call the person out, which usually leads to negative outcomes. Have you ever thought that the best outcome would be achieved by not responding to the person and simply letting it go? This takes a lot of courage, especially if your pride is on the line. But in most cases, no response is far better than a defensive or condescending one.

The tool here is to ask yourself three questions. First: does anything need to be said in this situation, and would there be any benefit to saying it? Or could commenting cause me or anyone else problems? Second, does a response need to be said by me? Maybe it would be better to let someone else handle it. And finally, does a response need to be said right now? Now might not be the best time to deal with it. By asking yourself these three questions, you are able to think about and make an informed decision rather than rely on your subconscious to decide for the wrong reason.

Here is an example of using this tool. You are at a party and someone in your group is talking about a subject they know little about and are way off base. Your subconscious response would be to set them straight and at the same time show how much more you know about the subject than they do. You may be right, but at the same time you would embarrass the other person and probably offend others in the group by your actions. Surely you were right, but there is a time to be right and a time to be humble. In many cases, the wrong information provided by the other person is causing no harm and they are merely trying to make conversation to fit in. By contradicting them, your ego is the only beneficiary, and at the same time you have managed to emotionally hurt another person, upsetting them and probably others.

If you had asked yourself "does my response need to be said?" you would have realized that there was no real benefit and possible harm in saying something and decided not to say anything. Maybe what they were saying did need to be addressed, but by asking yourself "do I need to say it?" you realized that you did not have to say anything and someone else could be the one to speak up. Or you determine that you are the one who needs to say something, but now you ask yourself "is this the right time to say it?" After reflecting, you realize that it does not have to be now and that you can do this later in private.

By using this three-question process, you were able to make an informed decision and end up with a better outcome. You are still going to make wrong decisions as you travel through life, but at least you will now be able to accept that you are responsible for that decision and learn from it. This is taking responsibility for your decisions by becoming aware and trying to make an informed decision and not leaving it to your subconscious programming. With a little effort and practice, you will find that the outcomes you are experiencing are becoming more positive and life-enhancing.

Throughout the rest of this book, you will be shown different principles that affect your decision-making and how to make the changes consciously and subconsciously to arrive at better informed and life-enhancing decisions. The principles and tools you learn will help you to take full responsibility for the decisions you make and positively improve your life experience.

Principles That Influence Our Decisions

Let us now touch on some other areas that can and will affect your decision-making. One of the biggest influences on our decision-making process is pain and pleasure. Every decision you make is either from your desire to experience pleasure or your need to avoid pain. These two twin powers have caused many to suffer from their decisions and many to grow from them.

Your perceptions of people and events around you have an impact on decision-making. Most people judge a person within the first 10 seconds of meeting. This is a perception based only on the subconscious data your mind has available. Yet, we tend to base our decisions about that person on these perceptions.

Our beliefs, whether conscious or subconscious, have a direct influence on all our decisions and choices. These beliefs are formed by the experiences and interactions we have throughout our lives. When it comes time to make a decision, our mind immediately accesses our belief system for guidance. These conscious or subconscious beliefs will determine our decision.

Just as our beliefs affect our decisions, so do our values. If you do not have a strict set of life values, then your subconscious mind will assign a value when it comes time to make a decision. Next are our needs and wants. When it comes time to make a decision, we tend to answer to our wants rather than our needs. This causes us to make many poor decisions.

Our habits also become involved in our decision-making process. Again, many of our habits are subconscious and can cause a decision we cannot explain. What we focus on at the time of a decision has a great impact on how the decision will turn out.

Our focus is closely tied to our state of mind. If our state of mind is positive, then we are likely to make a good decision. But if we are in a negative state, it can surely change the decision result. Finally, our environment has a large part in determining our decisions. Who you are with, where you live and the culture are a few of the environmental factors that will affect your decisions.

I have briefly mentioned several principles that can influence your decision-making process. In the following section, we will discuss in detail each of the principles. We will learn how they guide all our thoughts, decisions and actions as we travel down the path of life. As we discuss each area, you will discover many principles and tools to help improve your decision-making and thus enhance your life experience.

Summary

In this chapter, I have presented one of the most crucial steps to taking your life back—a method to take control of your destiny. No matter where you have been and what you have done in the past, you have the power in you to make empowering decisions and change your life. The future is in your hands.

If you understand how to gain control of your decisions by guiding your thoughts and actions, you will forge the direction of your life toward the vision you created and remain in alignment with your life purpose. With the proper decisions, you have the ability to live life on your terms and achieve your dreams and desires.

Remember, your decisions and not your life conditions determine your future and happiness. Making a truly committed decision will give you the power to radically change the direction of your life. When you ultimately decide that your life is not determined by the conditions around you but by the decisions you make, you are on your way to a life of happiness and fulfillment.

CHAPTER SIX

Your Perceptions

How you interpret things

"To change ourselves effectively, we first
had to change our perceptions."
— **Stephen R. Covey**

In This Chapter
- ➤ How Perceptions Are Formed
- ➤ The Effects of Perception
- ➤ Changing Perception into Informed Discernment
- ➤ Improved Decision-Making
- ➤ Summary

The decisions we make in life are not random. As discussed in the previous chapter, many principles affect our decision-making process. Our perceptions are one of these principles, and we will now look into how this happens.

Perception means the way we try to understand the world around us. Perception is the ability to capture, process and actively make sense of the information that our senses receive. It is the cognitive process that makes it possible to interpret our surroundings with the information that we receive through our senses. This important perceptive ability is essential to our daily lives because it makes it possible to understand our surroundings.

How many times have you met someone for the first time and formed an opinion of them only to find you were way off? They turned out to be the complete opposite of the person you imagined them to be. This is perception, and we all do it both consciously and unconsciously all the time. Our perceptions are usually formed within seconds of our interaction. We not only perceive the people we meet but also create perceptions of places we come upon and situations we face. We are also constantly developing perceptions about comments and stories we hear from others and through the media during our life journey.

Perceptions have a great effect on the decisions we make. If we have a negative perception about a person, place or situation, it can cause us to miss out on an opportunity that could have enhanced and brought joy to our lives.

In this chapter, you will discover what a perception is, how it is formed, how it can affect your decisions and life path, and how to take control and change your perceptions into informed discernments. This study will help lead to better decision-making and reduce the chance of a poor decisions and missed opportunities along our life journey.

How Perceptions Are Formed

Understanding how our perceptions are formed gives us the power to reform them. If we can control our perceptions, we can change our life.

Each day, we are meeting new people, arriving at or looking into different locations in the world, or hearing comments and stories about people, places and events from others and through the media. We are also encountering many different situations as our day progresses. In each case, we make a first impression or a snap perception about the person, place or situation. This perception is formed unconsciously in seconds by the data we have programmed in our mind through past experiences, examples and teaching.

In all our perceptions—from vision and hearing to the images we form of people's character, our unconscious mind starts from whatever objective data are available to us, usually spotty, and helps to shape and construct the more complete picture we consciously perceive. In order to offer us this more complete picture, our unconscious employs clever tricks and educated guesses to fill in some blanks. In our perception of people (and their perceptions of us), the hidden, subliminal mind takes limited data and creates a picture that seems clear and real but is actually built largely on unconscious inferences that are made employing factors such as a person's body language, voice, clothing, appearance and social category.

Our perceptions are influenced by a complex array of factors. For instance, they can include labels we assign to others based on age, sex, ethnic background, sexual orientation, social status and religion. These stereotypes may have been learned in childhood and can be difficult to overcome. They lead to inaccurate and unfounded assumptions without a thorough review of evidence.

Selective perception or tunnel vision occurs when only a few facts become your main focus while you simultaneously ignore or minimize all others. This often occurs when a person is trying to solve a problem. They see only one solution and in doing so may minimize or ignore other solutions. However, the chosen solution may have negative consequences or even disastrous results.

Factors Influencing Perception

A number of factors operate to shape and sometimes distort perception. These factors are:

- In the perceiver
- In the object or target being perceived
- In the context of the situation in which the perception is made.

Several characteristics of the perceiver can affect perception. When an individual looks at a target and attempts to interpret what he or she sees, that interpretation is heavily influenced by personal characteristics of the individual perceiver. The following major characteristics of the perceiver influence perception:

Attitudes: The perceiver's attitudes affect perception. For example, suppose Mr. X is interviewing candidates for a very important position in his organization, a position that requires negotiating contracts with suppliers, most of whom are male. Mr. X may feel that women are not capable of holding their own in tough negotiations. This attitude will doubtless affect his perceptions of the female candidates he interviews.

Moods: Moods can have a strong influence on the way we perceive someone. We think differently when we are happy than we do when we are depressed. In addition, we remember information that is consistent with our mood state better than information that is inconsistent with our mood state. When in a positive mood, we form more positive impression of others. When in a negative mood, we tend to evaluate others unfavourably.

Motives: Unsatisfied needs or motives stimulate individuals and may exert a strong influence on their perceptions. For example, a person who is insecure perceives another person's efforts to do an outstanding job as a threat to their own position. Personal insecurity can be transferred into the perception that others are out to "get me," regardless of the intention of the other person.

Self-Concept: Another factor that can affect perception is the perceiver's self-concept. An individual with a positive self-concept tends to notice positive attributes in another person. In contrast, a negative self-concept can lead a perceiver to pick out negative traits in another person. Greater understanding of self allows us to have more accurate perceptions of others.

Interest: The focus of our attention is influenced by our interests. Because our individual interests differ considerably, what one person notices in a situation can differ from what others perceive. For example, the person who has just been reprimanded by their boss for coming late is more likely to notice his colleagues coming late tomorrow than he did last week. If you are preoccupied with a personal problem, you may find it hard to be attentive in class.

Cognitive Structure: Cognitive structure, an individual's pattern of thinking, also affects perception. Some people have a tendency to perceive physical traits, such as height, weight and appearance, more readily. Others tend to focus more on central traits or personality dispositions. Cognitive complexity allows a person to perceive multiple characteristics of another person rather than attending to only a few traits.

Expectations: Finally, expectations can distort your perceptions in that you will see what you expect to see.

Frequently Used Shortcuts in Judging Others

Perceiving and interpreting what others do are burdensome tasks. As a result, individuals develop techniques for making the task more manageable. These techniques are not foolproof. Several factors or barriers lead us to form inaccurate impressions of others. These barriers to perception include the following:

Selective Perception: We receive a vast amount of information. Therefore, it is impossible for us to comprehend everything we see. That is why a boss may reprimand some employees for doing something that when done by another employee goes unnoticed. Because we can't observe everything going on around us, we engage in selective perception. Selective perception is also our tendency to choose information that supports our viewpoints; individuals often ignore information that makes them feel uncomfortable or threatens their viewpoints. Selective perception allows us to "speed-read" others but not without the risk of drawing an inaccurate picture. Because we see what we want to see, we can draw unwarranted conclusions from an ambiguous situation. Perception tends to be influenced more by an individual's attitudes, interests and background than by the stimulus itself.

Stereotype: A stereotype is a generalization about a group of people. When we judge someone on the basis of our perception of the group to which they belong, we are using the shortcut called stereotyping. Stereotypes reduce information about other people to a workable level, and they are efficient for compiling and using information. It is a means of simplifying a complex world and it permits us to maintain consistency. By using stereotypes, we can deal with an unmanageable amount of information. When stereotypes are accurate, they can be useful perceptual guidelines. However, most of the time stereotypes are inaccurate. Attractiveness is a powerful stereotype. We assume that attractive individuals are also warm, kind, sensitive, poised, sociable, outgoing, independent and strong. Are attractive people truly like this? Certainly all of them are not. In organizations, we frequently hear comments that represent stereotypes based on gender, age, nationality, etc. From a perceptual standpoint, if people expect to see this stereotype, that is what they will perceive, whether it's accurate or not.

First-Impression Error: Individuals place a good deal of importance on first impressions. First impressions are lasting impressions. We tend to remember what we perceive first about a person, and sometimes we are quite reluctant to change our initial impressions. A first-impression error means the tendency to form lasting opinions about an individual based on initial perceptions. Primacy effects can be particularly dangerous in interviews, given that we form first impressions quickly and that these impressions may be the basis for long-term employment relationships.

Contrast Effect: Sights and sounds that contrast with the surrounding environment are more likely to be selected for attention than are the sights and sounds that blend in. A contrasting effect can be caused by colour, size or any other factor that is unusual or that distinguishes one thing from others. For example, a man walking down the street with a pair of crutches gets more attention than a common man. A contrast effect is the evaluation of a person's characteristics that are affected by comparisons with other people recently encountered that rank higher or lower on the same characteristics. The contrast principle essentially states that external sights and sounds that stand out against the background or are not expected will receive our attention. The contrast effect also explains why a male student stands out in a crowd of female students. There is nothing unusual about the male students, but when surrounded by females, he stands out.

Here's an example of how contrast effects operate in an interview situation in which the hirer sees a pool of job applicants. Distortions in any given candidate's evaluation can occur as a result of his or her place in the interview schedule. The candidate is likely to receive a more favourable evaluation if preceded by mediocre applicants and a less favourable evaluation if preceded by strong applicants.

Projection: It is easy to judge others if we assume they are similar to us. This tendency to attribute one's own characteristics to other people is called projection. Projection can distort perceptions made about others. People who engage in projection tend to perceive others according to what they are like rather than according to what the person being observed is actually like. When people engage in projection, they compromise their ability to respond to individual differences. They tend to see people as more homogeneous than they really are.

Implicit Personality Theories: We tend to have our own mini-theories about how people look and behave. These theories help us organize our perceptions and take shortcuts instead of integrating new information all the time. Implicit personality theory is forming opinions about other people that are based on our own mini-theories about how people behave. For example, we believe that girls dressed in fashionable clothes will like modern music and girls dressed in traditional dress like a sari will like Indian classical music. These implicit personality theories are barriers because they limit our ability to take in new information when it is available.

Self-Fulfilling Prophecies: Self-fulfilling prophecies occur when our expectations about people affect our interaction with them in such a way that our expectations are fulfilled. Self-fulfilling prophecy is also known as the Pygmalion effect, named after a sculptor in Greek mythology who carved a statue of a girl that came to life when he prayed for this wish and it was granted. The Pygmalion effect has been observed in work situations as well. A manager's expectations of an individual affect both the manager's behaviour toward the individual and the individual's response. For example, suppose a manager has an initial impression of an employee as having the potential to move up within the organization. Chances are that the manager will spend a great deal of time coaching and counselling the employee, providing challenging assignments and grooming the individual for success.

Much of what we have experienced in life is programmed into our minds, is subconscious and is drawn upon to form our perceptions, for example: white, black, Mexican, Muslim, Christian, Liberal, Conservative, rich, poor, homeless, salesperson, politician, preacher, hooker, men, women, elderly, teenager, baby.

Chances are you have a perception regarding at least a couple of those labels. How did that happen? The answer to how our perceptions are formed lies within the coming together of two elements.

The first element in understanding how our perceptions are formed is an experience. Our parents get a divorce. We go to our first school dance. We go to college. We don't go to college. We start a business. We fail at a business. We get promoted. We get married. Life's significant experiences are filled with emotions, events and thoughts that play a big role in how our perceptions are formed, but it's only half of the equation.

The second element in the union of perceptions is our information. We are told that marriage is good, or we are told that it is bad. We are informed how to look at rich people, homeless people, preachers and hookers. Information surrounds us. In fact, we live in the information age. Unfortunately, a lot of that information came from wrong and unreliable sources. Bad experiences and bad information result in faulty perceptions. These faulty perceptions generally lead to bad decisions. Regardless of whether it is good or bad though, our information is what we use to process our experiences and form our perceptions.

Here's the bottom line regarding how our perceptions are formed. Bad experience and bad information result in faulty perceptions. Faulty perceptions will then lead to bad decisions. We take wrong paths in live and avoid the relationships that would be healthy and beneficial.

On the other hand, better experiences and better information result in proper perceptions. Proper perceptions will then lead to better decisions. We'll put things in the proper perspective, make the right choices and create healthy connections with the people in our lives.

It is within our power and ability to become aware of how we are forming our perceptions and then implementing the steps necessary to take control and turn our perceptions into informed discernment.

The Effects of Perception

Perceptions can make a lasting impact that is hard to shake. This is related to a phenomenon called the halo effect, in which a person's initial positive perception carries through to similarly positive perceptions in the future, whether warranted or not. The reverse is also true. If a negative first impression is made, it becomes difficult to replace with a positive one. Unfortunately, the halo effect distorts reality. These false impressions are the reasons why con artists can fool so many victims and why innocent people are sometimes wrongly accused of crimes they did not commit.

Perceptions can cause confirmation bias, which is the tendency to interpret and search for evidence to confirm your own beliefs even in the face of contradictory information. It involves a discriminatory reasoning whose effect is strengthened in emotionally charged situations. People will interpret information in a biased manner to support their own conclusions. On occasion, tunnel vision will occur due to a person's own biased search, interpretation and memory of evidence in the face of extreme disagreements between people. Another manner in which people confirm their own bias is by perceiving a false association between two events.

Perceptions can also cause the anchoring effect, which is our tendency to contrast and compare only a few limited characteristics. We then fixate on a single situation, which we then use as the benchmark to compare with everything else. For example, if we see a police car behind us, we often think they are focused on and watching our every move, looking for a chance to stop us. We become nervous and start to wonder if we have done something wrong. We tend to focus on the perception not reality; they are coincidentally driving behind us en route to their next call.

How you perceive your world influences your attitude, which in turn affects what you attract. If you perceive a world of abundance, your actions and attitude attract abundance. Conversely, if you perceive your life as lacking what you need, you worry more about conserving what you have rather than attaining those things you want and need.

The way in which you perceive your world also impacts your general emotional state. People who perceive abundance are likely to be happy. Those who perceive their life as lacking tend to be sad. Two people who are facing the exact same circumstances can have opposite perceptions. The one with positive perceptions has a tendency to thrive while the one with negative perceptions tends to struggle.

As you encounter various circumstances, do you perceive solutions and success or do you envision problems and failure? Successful people are adept at finding solutions for any problem.

Those who continuously perceive life as a struggle have a tendency to find problems in every situation. There is a solution for every problem, but it's your perception that enables you discover it.

What about life in general? Do you perceive it as good or bad? When you perceive life as good, you have a much greater degree of happiness than someone who perceives it as bad. The person who perceives life as bad can provide a long list of reasons justifying their perception. However, the person with a good perception will provide just as many reasons for their position.

The bottom line is that you control your perception. If you're not happy with the direction of your life or your circumstances, the first place to look is your perception. If you see the proverbial glass as half empty, start considering it half full. Start looking at your life as one of happiness and abundance. Especially when you encounter adversity, it will be your positive perception that gets you through.

Also, don't allow others to taint your perception with theirs. You may be accused of being unrealistic or viewing the world through rose-coloured glasses. But remember, someone else's perception of you is irrelevant. The most important thing is your own perception of your life.

Changing Perception into Informed Discernment

The way you view the world around you reveals the filter through which you see the world. You have created this filter through your reactions to the various life events that you have lived through. The major events—significant emotional events—create the structure of your perception of reality, while the small events fill in the gaps. The problems that come from this arise when you fail to be aware of the power of the filter you have created.

When you look beyond the reality, you see and accept that it is not the "truth" of what is happening but an "interpretation" that you have created. Then you are on the way to changing the filter you see the world through. You only see the world through your perceptions and when you change your perception (your filter), the world changes.

Have you ever wondered why people see the world in so many different ways? Do you think about why people have such strong arguments about matters of politics in relation to the world they live in? The answer is simply the variety of filters people see the world through.

It took me many years to see that my perception of the world as an unfriendly place, full of people who wanted to put me down, was the perception I created for myself. I did this because of how I felt I was treated by others and because of the negative experiences I encountered along the way. Once I saw this, I was able to change my understanding of these influences, change my view of the world and change the world I lived in. Not only am I now a different person, but the world is a different place.

Find voices of wisdom. We spend most of our time with people who are the same age and have the same information that we do. In many cases, these people have similar negative perceptions about life as we do. It is time to expand your education. Spend time with people who are happy and positive and have been around longer than you have. Listen to what they have to say and learn from their example. Find leaders, books and organizations that have or are doing what you want and listen to them.

Understanding how our perceptions are formed gives us power to reform our perceptions. If we can change our perceptions, we can change our world. The following four characteristics greatly influence how a person perceives others in the environmental situation:

- Knowing oneself makes it easier to see others accurately.
- One's own characteristics affect the characteristics one is likely to see in others.

- People who accept themselves are more likely to be able to see favourable aspects of other people.
- Accuracy in perceiving others is not a single skill.

Taking responsibility and controlling our perceptions of ourselves, others and the world around us will give us the power to make informed life-enhancing decisions to help us achieve and live our dreams.

Improved Decision-Making

Think about some of the major decisions you've made in your life: whom to marry or not, whether to have children or not, where to attend university or not, which congregation to attend or not, which profession to pursue and where to retire. From the day we can think independently until the day we stop doing so, we constantly make choices and decisions. "Life is the sum of all your choices," said the French philosopher Albert Camus.

Now, think about how you made those major decisions. Did you gather information before deciding? Did you consult with certain trusted individuals? Did you pray about it? Was your perception an informed discernment or was it your uncontrolled subconscious mind at work?

How we go about making decisions will largely determine the quality of our life. The process matters as much as outcome primarily because the process that we use will to shape the outcome. We need to have control of how we perceive others, places and events. We need to consider multiple viewpoints. We need to analyze the many voices we are hearing and what God's voice is telling us to do. These are matters of discernment, which can be defined as "keen perception or judgment." Once our perception is based on sufficient discerned information, we can move on to make an informed and empowering decision.

Summary

We have in ourselves the power and ability to live a happy and fulfilling life if we decide to. We have the power to control our future and not leave it to old and misleading subconscious programming. I pray that you will start to take control of your life decisions starting with recognizing and discerning your perceptions. This will allow you to make the empowering decisions required to live a life full of happiness and joy and to achieve the dreams you have always desired and deserve.

CHAPTER SEVEN

The Power of Pain and Pleasure

The controlling force

"The secret of success is learning how to use pain and pleasure instead of having pain and pleasure use you. If you do that, you are in control of your life. If you don't, life controls you."
— **Anthony Robbins**

- -

In This Chapter
➤ What Is the Pain and Pleasure Principle?
➤ Examples of the Effect of Pain and Pleasure
➤ How Pain and Pleasure Are Affecting Our Lives Today
➤ Using Pain and Pleasure To Make Empowering Decisions
➤ Pain and Pleasure Exercise
➤ Summary

- -

Have you ever wondered why an addict who has been clean for a long period of time suddenly, without warning or reason, uses again, or why someone walking down the street and spotting a house on fire would go and risk their life to save a complete stranger? Why does someone like Kim Jong-un abuse his own people as leader in North Korea and yet someone like Mahatma Gandhi risks his life to help the people of India gain their independence?

Why do people with a strong and positive upbringing go on to become criminals and people who were neglected and abused as children go one to become successful and happy? Some people who have it all—fame, money, relationships—end up taking or destroying their own lives while an immigrant arriving with nothing and unable to speak the language becomes a great success in the business world or as a leader in the community.

What is the cause that creates such different results in people's lives or the force that drives all human behaviour? The answer is pain and pleasure. These two influencing powers are the force that is controlling everyone. Everything we do is either our need to avoid pain or our desire to gain pleasure.

The pain-pleasure principle lies at the core of everything you and I do and of everything we are. Your beliefs, values and psychological rules are all built upon this principle. The decisions you make, the actions you take and the habits you indulge in are all based on this principle. In fact, every part of your psyche is influenced in some way by the pain-pleasure principle. Therefore, you are who you are today because of how you have interpreted and acted upon the experience of pain and pleasure in your life. And as we all know, action always begins with a decision.

Before every decision you make, you unconsciously ask yourself the following set of questions:

- What does this mean?
- Will it lead to pain or pleasure?
- What should I do about it?

Your decision will depend on how you interpret pain and pleasure in your life. And how you interpret pain and pleasure depends on your past experience of pain and pleasure. Thus, learning to use pain and pleasure is the key to taking control of your decisions and your life.

What Is the Pain and Pleasure Principle?

Of the several factors that influence our decisions and actions in life, the most powerful influence is pain and pleasure. Everything we do, we do out of our need to avoid pain and our desire to gain pleasure. Whether consciously or subconsciously, our mind places a reference of pain or pleasure on all our thoughts.

The pain or pleasure that our subconscious creates is developed from past events or experiences in our lives. It is what Anthony Robbins terms neuro-associative conditioning, which are experiences while we were in an intense emotional state and experiencing a strong sensation of pain or pleasure. This pain or pleasure becomes neurologically linked into our subconscious.

These neuro-associations now come to the surface to influence and form our decisions. Let's say you are on a strict diet trying to lose weight. A friend unknowingly brings you some chocolate cake for your birthday. Now a decision is required. Without realizing it, your subconscious mind associates more pleasure to eating the cake than pain to breaking your diet. The decision is made. You eat the cake, satisfying your desire for pleasure and then feel depressed (pain) that you broke your diet.

You cannot understand why after all these weeks you broke down and ignored your diet. It was simply a subconscious decision. Your mind chose the dominate choice of pleasure over pain. Even though the act caused you pain, the overpowering desire for pleasure won out. Your short-term pleasure came with long-term pain, in this case guilt.

What drove your behaviour was an instinctive reaction to pain and pleasure and not an intellectual calculation. Intellectually, you may know that eating the cake was bad for you but you still ate it because you were driven not by your intellectual thinking but by what you have learned to link pain and pleasure to. Without knowing the pain and pleasure principle, you would be unable to ever change this result.

In many situations, the dominance of pain and pleasure can reverse itself, thus bringing about a completely opposite decision and result. Have you ever found yourself procrastinating about something you know you need to do? You know it needs to be done, but you still don't do it and cannot understand why. The answer is simple: you believe that taking action at this moment would be more painful than putting it off. You continue to put it off until suddenly you start to associate more pain to not doing it than doing it so you simply do it.

An example of this is when you are out with friends after work and you know your spouse has plans for both of you that evening. You call and say you will be home in time and truly mean it. You are enjoying yourself and time slips away. Your spouse calls, asking where you are. You respond that you are just leaving but continue to enjoy yourself with your friends. Suddenly you get a demanding call and you immediately get up and head home. You have changed what you link pain and pleasure to. You have now linked more pain to not taking action than to putting it off.

Here's another example, which I went through. One day at a party I was introduced to crack cocaine by my friends. Having not experimented with drugs much in my life, I was shocked at the instant shot of pleasure I received when I ingested it. It was a pleasure like I had never experienced before. Because this was my first time, I had no pain to associate with using crack and plenty of pleasure associated with it. Over several months the increased use of crack started to overtake my life, and there was plenty of pain being realized by my family and me. The problem was the pain I was experiencing was less than the pleasure that I associated with what I was doing, and crack became an addiction that took over my life and threatened everything I held dear to me.

I knew what I was doing was wrong and I hated myself for doing it, but I continued to use. My conscious mind associated pain to what I was doing but my subconscious mind was just the opposite. It was acting on the original programming of that first use.

I attended several addiction programs designed to help me overcome this addiction and all failed. I had short-term successes but in the long run my subconscious desire to gain pleasure kept on overpowering my desire to avoid pain. It was only after I came to understand the pain and pleasure principle that I was able to use it to associate more pain to using and eventually overcome my addiction completely without any struggle or suffering.

The principle of pain and pleasure is very real and responsible for controlling many of the decisions we make on a daily basis without our understanding. It is only after a person understands this power and how to control it that they can regain control of their decisions.

Why is it that we experience all this pain but cannot change? The reason is we have not experienced enough pain yet. You have not yet hit what Anthony Robbins refers to as the emotional threshold. We all know people who have remained in a destructive relationship; they are very unhappy but not willing to change. This is because they have not yet reached their emotional threshold. Then one day they say "I have had enough," and they make a decision they are no longer going to live this way. They have hit their emotional threshold and now associate more pain to the relationship than pleasure. This is when change starts.

The transformational moment is when we start to use pain as our ally. Our pain causes us to take action and produce new results. What you link pain to and what you link pleasure to will dramatically change your life. Understanding this one principle will help you radically improve your life and lead you to the life you have always desired. Without knowing the pain and pleasure principle, you would be unable to ever change this result.

Examples of the Effect of Pain and Pleasure

Donald Trump not only became a successful and well-known businessman but, against all the odds, became the President of the United States. Let's look at what has driven him to achieve all the success he has experienced.

Trump is a man who received a lot of pleasure from amassing property and buildings that stand out and bear his name. From large hotels, casinos and office towers, his name has also been trumpeted from his planes, yachts and other possessions. He has even trademarked his name. He enjoys being in the spotlight and addressing large crowds. But pleasure is not the only thing that drives Donald Trump. He receives pain from bad business decisions, criticism, negative publicity and losing. Thus, pain and pleasure have moulded him to become the person he is today.

Another real-life example of the effect of pain and pleasure is Mother Theresa. She was a woman who not only witnessed the pain of the poor and suffering in India but felt the pain too. To help overcome her pain, she was guided to a life of reducing the suffering of the poor wherever she could. As she acted to help reduce the pain and suffering of the poor around her, she found her mental pain disappeared as well. By answering her spiritual calling and witnessing the ease and comfort of the people that she helped, she brought pleasure into her own life. Her journey was a difficult one in which she not only witnessed the pain and suffering of the poor but suffered greatly herself both emotionally and physically. It was the power of pain and pleasure that led her to become a saint and example to all.

During my life, I have also experienced the effects of the power of pain and pleasure. As a prison chaplain, I have witnessed the effect and power of pain and pleasure on the prisoners and staff of the prison as well as on the innocent victims affected by crime. I was also proud to see how lives were completely changed when many of these people and victims, who had struggled and suffered for years, were able to completely change their lives by learning to use pain and pleasure rather than let it continue to control them. Many prisoners completely changed the direction of their lives and become happy and contributing members of the community. Many victims learned to forgive and positively move on with their lives.

How Pain and Pleasure Are Affecting Our Lives Today

Today, our personal life decisions are being controlled by the neuro-associations of pain and pleasure. That is not the only way pain and pleasure are affecting our lives. Others have learned how to use pain and pleasure to influence how they think and act, including who to vote for and how to live their lives. They also use pain and pleasure to get all the rest of us to purchase the products they are selling. If we do not learn how to use and control pain and pleasure, then not only will we continue to make self-harming decisions but we will allow others to continually control us.

We will now explore how pain and pleasure experiences from our past become associated neurologically with our subconscious. I will use Christmas as an example. For many of us, Christmas is a deeply spiritual time of the year while for others it is not. Why is it that most people, whether spiritual or not, seem different during the Christmas season?

At this time, people seem more patient and loving towards each other or just the opposite. People who are regularly pleasant and inviting suddenly become cold and reclusive. During the days leading up to Christmas, people who gave and thought little of the poor and marginalized in their community suddenly start to donate and help. Christmas dinners for the homeless and poor pop up everywhere and family food hampers are provided in greater quantities than usual. Are these people only in need of food and supplies at Christmas time?

Many talk pleasantly to people they turn away from or avoid the rest of the year. Families come together and strangers are more welcoming to each other. Is there a special spirit that comes from above, like a potion that affects people's thoughts and behaviours? I think not. What accounts for the drastic change by so many and for such a short period of time?

The answer is pain and pleasure. For many, while they were growing up Christmas was a pleasant and encouraging time. There are memories of fighting parents suddenly being respectful and loving towards each other. The pleasure of giving is experienced in the home and in the community. Family members who regularly have little time for each other come together lovingly for a while. The love and concern people show for each other bring pleasant and welcome feelings into their hearts.

Yes, Christmas is so full of pleasant memories that we all want to experience them again, and during Christmas we are given permission to do just that. Yet for many, Christmas is a time of pain and suffering. Relationships were strained, tragedies were experienced, and people lost loved ones or felt alone. These feelings of pain and suffering affect how many people act today during Christmas and explain their different behaviour.

As you can see, the heightened past experiences of pain and pleasure are neurologically associated into our subconscious, ready to come out and express themselves in our thoughts and actions. Most of the time, this happens without our realizing why. Some of the experiences are so traumatic that they are well hidden from our memory. This is one example of how pain and pleasure affect our decisions and behaviour.

I am sure if you think about it, you can come up with many more examples of times when heightened experiences of pain and pleasure could have been neurologically associated into our minds. Some examples may include birthdays, weddings, school, early relationships and times we tried something for the first time or stepped out of our comfort zone. There are many events and experiences of pain and pleasure from our past that we would prefer to forget or do forget that affect us subconsciously when called upon. These references are what control our decisions and the path our life takes.

Pain and pleasure can also be used by others to control our lives and get us to act the way they desire us to. It is usually for their benefit, not necessarily ours. We will begin with the power of advertising and how it uses pain and pleasure to influence our subconscious and thus our decisions and actions.

Just like Pavlov's dogs were trained to salivate every time he rang a bell, so too can we be trained to believe something or act a certain way by outside forces with the use of the pain and pleasure principle.

The mission of all advertising companies is to influence what we link pain and pleasure to. They fully understand that what drives us is not our intellect as much as the perceptions we link to their product. They have become experts in using images, music, colour and other elements to place us in a high emotional state so they can use repetition to neuro-associate pleasure messages linked to their product into our subconscious.

Images like beautiful men and women, beaches and water, success, romance and love, and freedom and independence are only a few of the images they link to their product with the idea if you have the product you will feel pleasure and be happy. Political campaigns use the same principle but they often use pain to move us in the direction they desire. They show us the pain and suffering we will feel if their opponent is elected. Some organizations use a combination of pain and pleasure. Special interest groups such as animal rights groups will show the pleasure a pet can provide and the pain they suffer if their message is not adhered to. Child sponsorship groups are famous for this. They start out showing you children who are hungry and suffering all kinds of physical and mental atrocities. Then they show how a small donation from you will fix everything and bring pleasure to the child and your heart.

Companies also link taglines to pleasure and their product, for example, Nike: "Just Do It"; Coke: "The Real Thing"; McDonald's: "I'm Loving It"; KFC: "Finger Licking Good"; Kellogg's Frosties: "They're GR-R-R-reat"; and of course De Beers: "A Diamond is Forever." I am sure you have your favourites. But consider when you desire something, what first comes to mind? Could it be the product of one of the slogans? What first comes to your mind has been subconsciously neuro-associated into your mind and you have probably acted on it in the past without realizing it.

Another way our subconscious is programmed is through religious, cultural and community groups. Each has its own agenda and system they want you to believe and follow. They are all masters at using pain and pleasure to program you to their way of thinking and living. They can even manipulate your intellectual thinking if given the chance. Some are honestly looking out for your welfare and believe what they tell you, not always fully understanding their own beliefs. This is not to say they are all wrong. But if you are not prepared, the tool of pain and pleasure can make you a dependent follower rather than a rational thinker and member.

If you truly look at what I and others have presented in the area of pain and pleasure, you will recognize that if someone is not aware of the pain and pleasure principle, their decisions can negativity affect their life. But if you do comprehend the principle, you will see that it is possible to use it to help you make empowering decisions and build the life you have always desired.

Using Pain and Pleasure To Make
Empowering Decisions

As mentioned above, the first step to taking control of the power of pain and pleasure and its influence on your decisions is to fully understand the principle. Only then will you be able to progress and improve your life by using pain and pleasure to make empowering decisions and adjustments towards how you approach your short- and long-term activities.

You will come to understand that in most cases it is not actual pain that drives us but the fear that something will lead to pain that influences our decisions and actions. The same is true for pleasure. It is not actual pleasure but the sense that somehow thinking or acting a certain way will bring about pleasure.

The great news is that this new revelation makes it possible for you to easily use the power of pain and pleasure to implement positive and healing change in your life, take back control and live the life you have always desired. You have the power within you and no one else can stop you, not people, world events or even bad luck or misfortune. Now, it is time to take responsibility for your future and learn how to use the power of pain and pleasure rather than continue to be a victim of the power of pain and pleasure.

Learning how to use pain and pleasure for improving your life is not difficult at all. It begins by becoming aware of how the power of pain and pleasure is currently influencing your decisions. For example, let's say that you have a problem saying "no" to people. You need to review a few of the times this happened and the circumstances around your decision. Start by asking yourself "why did I not state my real feelings and say 'no'? What perceived pain was I avoiding or what perceived pleasure did I think I would experience?"

This process will help make you more aware so you can reverse the process when you move on to the next step. Just as pain and pleasure influenced the decisions and actions that led to results you did not desire, you can use it to achieve what you truly want.

If you want to take control of your decisions and resulting actions, you need to reprogram your pain and pleasure references. It starts by linking massive pain to the decisions and behaviours you do not want. This can be done through a technique developed by Anthony Robbins out of years of research. He calls it the science of neuro-associative conditioning. It is a tool to help you reprogram your subconscious mind and use pain and pleasure to produce positive and empowering decisions in your life.

A perfect example is if you want to quit smoking, then you need to list all the negative and painful experiences and results that smoking causes. If you find it difficult, then think back to the pain you have experienced as a result of smoking. You can also research the negative impacts of smoking through the internet or medical and historical sources. If you are truly committed, you will find many situations and results to help in your new programming.

Once you have determined the actions that bring about these results, you need to picture them affecting you personally. Close your eyes and create a live moving scene of the painful results you are experiencing. Make the pain real by linking so much pain to the action that you cannot bear it. Continue this until any time the action comes to mind, you start to immediately experience the great pain the action causes.

Next, call to mind all the perceived pleasure you have received in the past associated with when you avoided taking that action. Now once again focus on the pain you receive from taking that action. Continue this over and over until every time you think of the action, you feel the massive pain it would give you as well as the pleasure you get from avoiding that pain.

You have now reprogrammed your subconscious to make you aware that by taking that action you will receive massive pain and not the pleasure you previously were programmed to believe. This process will help guide you to make a more empowering decision and experience a more pleasurable outcome.

The formula provided above, showing you how to take control of pain and pleasure rather than letting pain and pleasure control you, may look simple. The truth is it is simple. We as humans have a tendency to think that implementing positive change into our life will be difficult and requires a lot of work and time. This is not always true. Some areas do require a lot of attention, but there are also processes we can do in an instant that will bring about the change we seek. The pleasure and plan process is one of these instances as all it requires is understanding how the process works, believing it will work and implementing it.

The pain and pleasure reprogramming process is solely responsible for my success overcoming a serious and destructive crack addiction. Once I understood the principle and how to use pain and pleasure to my advantage, I began to implement the strategy.

I recalled all the negative effects I experienced as a result of my addiction. I investigated each negative situation one at a time and focused on it. I formed a picture in my mind as if I were experiencing it at the moment. I felt the pain of it and made it real. I focused deeply on the pain and negative effects it gave me.

First, I pictured the police catching me while I was using. I felt the pain of being arrested and going to jail. I pictured my wife and children struggling without my support. I focused on the pain and disappointment that they felt because of my actions. I felt the guilt and pain for the suffering I was causing them. I pictured and felt the pain that dying from an overdose would cause.

I focused on the pain I felt from allowing people to use me just so they had someone to use with. I focused on how degraded and bad I felt searching through the carpet on my knees looking for a piece of crack. I focused on the money I was wasting on the drug and what I could have done with it. I focused on how weak I was not being able to control my own actions. I focused and felt the pain of all this and brought it together as one flash video in my head. The pain was real and massive, the disgust was real, and the guilt was real. I had envisioned and felt enough pain to reach my emotional threshold.

I decided then and there I would never use again. I then started to picture and focus on the pleasure I would receive by not being a slave to the drug and how happy my life would become. I had completely shifted my pain and pleasure references. Every time a craving or desire arose, the massive pain I have associated with using kicked in. I was then able to quickly decide that I did not want to use. My pain references were quickly replaced by the pleasure I received from being able to make a positive decision.

I became stronger each time the situation arose until over time the cravings and desire disappeared. This tool broke my desire to use instantly and I was able to focus on the pleasure of the successful empowering accomplishment I had just experienced. As the weeks and months went by, I was able to quickly change my thought pattern when something would trigger a using desire, and this ability grew until it became automatic. Implementing this life-saving process started me on the path to purpose, success, happiness and fulfillment.

I now use the pain and pleasure process in many other areas of my life. I have been able to reverse the destructive direction my life was headed. No matter what your past experiences and actions are, by using the power and taking control of the pain and pleasure process in your life and then implementing the resulting empowering decisions, anything is possible. Many people have done it and many more will experience its enlightening and healing power.

The reason the process of pain and pleasure works is because it changes the neuro-associations we program into our mind. Our subconscious is reprogrammed by what we truly desire not by random input. By changing our neuro-associations, we are not only fixing the problem but are eliminating the problem for good.

We can successfully reprogram our mind to associate what is good for us and what will hurt us. This new understanding will become a powerful influence on our decisions and how we live our lives.

Pain and Pleasure Exercise

Here is a chance to use this powerful tool to make a positive change in your life.

First, write down something that you want to change in your life. It can be something that you have been putting off, such as stopping smoking. Do you want to repair a relationship? Is there a behaviour that you want to change?

_____

_____

_____

_____

_____

Second, write down why you haven't made this change. This may help you discover some hidden pain. You should describe what pain you link to making the change will cause you.

_____

_____

_____

_____

_____

Third, write down all the pain caused by not changing. The pain can be emotional or it can be something like not enough time. List as many pain statements as you can. The more you discover, the sooner you will reach your emotional threshold.

_____

_____

_____

———————————————————
———————————————————

Fourth, write down all the pleasure you have received by not making this change. What are you doing now that is providing you pleasure? It may be instant gratification or something more.

———————————————————
———————————————————
———————————————————
———————————————————
———————————————————

Fifth, write down what it will cost you if you do not change. What are you losing or hurting by not changing?

———————————————————
———————————————————
———————————————————
———————————————————
———————————————————

Sixth, write down all the pleasure you would get by making the change. How would you feel emotionally? Would you be healthier either mentally or physically? Would it benefit a relationship?

———————————————————
———————————————————
———————————————————
———————————————————
———————————————————

Once you have completed the questions, take some quiet time to reflect. First, look at your reason for not making the change. How does it make you feel? Hold that feeling and make it real.

Now, focus on what it will cost you and how it makes you feel. Feel each consequence. Ask yourself "do I really want this pain?" As you do, focus again on the pain. Become able to close your eyes and feel the pain.

Tell yourself that you do not have to feel this way. You have the power to stop it. Make a decision not to allow this to happen again.

Now, picture and feel yourself overcoming all the obstacles in your path and having made the change or reached your goal. Again, feel the pleasure that will give you.

Next, imagine again that you are achieving your task. When the negative thoughts start to appear, immediately focus and feel the pain you have practised. Let it take control. As soon as the old negative thoughts subside, then feel the pleasure of success. You will now be inspired to make the right decision on how to proceed.

I urge you to complete this exercise and learn to use the pain and pleasure principle to help you overcome the negative habits and areas of your life that have been causing you to run off course. You can also use the process on other concerns and start to build strength and motion towards changing your life and living your dreams.

Summary

If understood and used properly, the twin powers of pain and pleasure have the ability to change a life of suffering and despair into one of hope, vision, achievement and happiness. No matter who you are or what you have done in the past, you have the ability and power within you to accomplish great things.

This chapter has provided you with a life-changing principle and process that can help you to reprogram your subconscious and assist you in making empowering and life-enhancing decisions as you venture ahead in your journey through life.

By using neuro-associative conditioning, you are able to take control of your decision-making and life. No matter how you have lived in the past and what you have experienced along the journey, be assured that you have within you the power to change. Only you can implement the tools required to change the scope and direction of your life to achieve your dreams and live the life you have always desired and deserve.

CHAPTER EIGHT

Your Beliefs and Values

The guiding force

"People who live a life of purpose have core beliefs and values
that influence their decisions, shape their day-to-day actions,
and determine their short- and long-term priorities."
— **Frank Sonnenberg**

In This Chapter
- ➤ Understanding Belief Systems
- ➤ What Is a Belief?
- ➤ How To Change Your Beliefs
- ➤ Belief Exercise
- ➤ What Are Your Values?
- ➤ Value Exercise
- ➤ Summary

The beliefs and values we have etched into our minds over the years
have a strong controlling influence on the decisions and actions we
take in life. Before we make any decision, we reference our beliefs

and values for guidance. Our subconscious forms beliefs from life experiences over time. These beliefs help form our values, which in turn help decide what our resulting attitude and actions will be.

Two separate people who have identical past experiences can have different beliefs and values. When they are facing the same situation, these different beliefs are responsible for the completely opposite outcomes. For example, two brothers of an abusive alcoholic father had different outcomes, whereby one grows to become a self-destructive drug addict and criminal and the other becomes a loving husband, father and leading member of the community.

Beginning to form at an early age, our beliefs and values are unique to our individual perspectives, become the driving catalyst of all our decisions, actions and life outcomes. In this chapter, you will discover how your beliefs and values are formed, how they affect your decisions and actions, and how you have the power to eliminate limiting and harmful beliefs and values and replace them with positive and empowering ones.

Understanding Belief Systems

Most of us have been misled into believing that outside forces control our lives and these forces are the cause of who we are today. There is nothing further from the truth. This myth was created so we are able to place the blame of our failings elsewhere instead of taking responsibility for our own outcomes in life. The circumstances around us do not shape our lives; we are shaped by the beliefs we create about what those circumstances mean.

How we interpret the circumstances that we experience is what forms our beliefs. These beliefs help shape who we are today and who we will become tomorrow. Beliefs are what distinguish a lifetime of joy and happiness from a life of suffering and misery. Beliefs can provide us purpose and direction or lead us to a life of aimless desperation. They are the guiding force that tells us what will lead to pain and what will lead to pleasure. Whenever we are required to make a decision, our subconscious asks two questions: "will this lead to pain or pleasure, and what do I need to do to avoid the pain or experience the pleasure?" These beliefs were formed subconsciously by generalizations of what we have experienced and learned and they define for us what will lead to pain and pleasure. These beliefs will then influence our decisions and the direction and quality of our lives.

The generalizations we have made about our experiences and what we have learned can be misleading and create limiting beliefs. An example of this is when someone says that if you fail the test you are about to take, it means you are stupid and can't learn anything. You in turn fail the test and it causes you embarrassment and guilt, which leads to pain. You then create a belief that this pain was caused because you are stupid and unable to learn. Once you believe this is true, it anchors into your subconscious and becomes a self-fulfilling prophecy. This limiting belief was formed by one small incident in your life and causes you to give up and quit school. This example shows how the generalization about one event can create a limiting belief that negativity affects the rest of your life.

The problem with limiting beliefs like the one above is that they become roadblocks to advancement in future decisions and negatively affect who you are and what you are capable of. As demonstrated in this case, most of the beliefs we form throughout our lives are not done consciously. They are based on a limited amount of information without any scrutiny to confirm if they are valid or not. Once the belief is formed, we do not think about how it was formed and we treat it as a reality. Over time, our experiences will strengthen it so that we will no longer question it and will even begin to defend it.

Beliefs have the power to create and the power to destroy. Beliefs are the driving force behind such destructive actions as terrorist attacks, war, prejudice, bullying and many other hurtful actions. These actions harm not only innocent people but the one who has created and is acting on their belief. Negative and misunderstood beliefs have been the cause of so much needless death and suffering in the world.

Adolph Hitler believed that a natural order existed that placed the so-called Aryan race at the top. This belief influenced his decision that anyone who did not meet his idea of the perfect race should be eliminated. It was this belief and the actions triggered by it that led to the Jewish Holocaust and millions of innocent lives lost.

Yet, just as beliefs are behind so much of the evil and tragedy in the world, so too do they have the power for so much good in the world. On September 11, 2001, the passengers of United Airlines Flight 93 were faced with the ultimate decision after it was overtaken by terrorists. They had heard about the events that had taken place at the World Trade Centre in New York City. Based on the information available, they formed a belief that if they did not act, they would all die and so would many other innocent people. This belief led to their decision to try and overtake the hijackers. They believed they either had to take control of the plane or cause it to crash into a secluded location to spare the lives of many other people. This belief was formed by their associating more pain to the possible overall outcome than to their own imminent deaths.

The two examples above are only two examples of the many events throughout history in which the power of beliefs brought out goodness in people or caused them to inflict pain and suffering on others. We all have the power to investigate our beliefs, ensure they are sound and empowering and in turn make life-enhancing decisions from them. Let us not become implicit victims of our groundless, unintentional and limiting beliefs.

Another area in our lives in which beliefs have a major effect is in our health and welfare. Our beliefs have the power to cripple us not only emotionally but physically. They have the power to bring about sickness or the power to heal. There are many examples of people who were diagnosed with cancer who went on to live many healthy years while others died quickly after discovering the news. Much of this was the result of the belief they attached to the diagnosis.

Many people questioned the diagnosis and took the time to get second opinions, surround themselves with positive people and become informed. Armed with this information and support, they were able to form a belief that they could overcome this setback and enjoy a healthy and happy life. Some of these people may not have lived a long time but they lived the rest of their life with hope, fight and happiness. The power of their belief was even at times responsible for the physical improvement they experienced.

Just the opposite resulted for the people who accepted the news and created a limiting belief that this was their destiny. The result was a path to self-destruction and misery. Even the people who went on to live for years longer than diagnosed lived their lives in self-pity and suffering. Their limiting belief told them their life was over and that influenced their decisions and the resulting actions or lack of actions they produced. In some cases, this limiting belief helped the affliction to advance.

A great deal of evidence from the scientific community shows that people's minds have the capability to heal their bodies if they have a strong enough belief. There are documented cases of people with multiple personalities who have physical diseases like diabetes in one of their personalities. When their personality changed, the disease associated with that personality completely disappeared. There were no physical effects of the disease present in their bodies. Yet when they changed back to the first personality, the disease was again present.

Here is another way that beliefs can affect your health and body. I am sure you have heard of the placebo effect. The mind can have a powerful influence on the body, and in some cases can even help the body heal. The mind can even sometimes trick your body into believing that a fake treatment has real therapeutic results, a phenomenon known as the placebo effect. In some cases, these placebos (often sugar pills) can exert an influence powerful enough to mimic the effects of real medications.

But the placebo effect is much more than merely positive thinking. This is where belief comes into play. In order to understand why the placebo effect is important, it is essential to understand a bit more about how and why it works. The placebo effect is defined as a phenomenon in which some people experience a benefit after the administration of an inactive substance or sham treatment. They believe they have received a medication that produces a certain result and may even have side effects associated with it. What exactly is a placebo? A placebo is a substance with no known medical effects, such as sterile water, saline solution or a sugar pill. When this response to a fake treatment occurs, many patients have no idea that they are responding to what is essentially a sugar pill. The results have shown that a portion of the people who received the placebo experienced the same effects as the ones who received the real medication. In some cases, they even experienced the believed side effects.

There are numerous studies of people divided into two groups where one group received the real medication and one received the placebo. They are both informed they are receiving the medication. The positive results are very similar in both groups. These studies have proven the power that the mind has on the body. Thus, you can see that our beliefs, whether conscious or subconscious, have a great impact on our decisions and the resulting actions we take. Our beliefs are responsible for whether we are living a life of purpose, joy and happiness or a life of quiet desperation and misery.

The only way we can create effective, empowering and lasting change in our lives is look into our beliefs and change the limiting beliefs that are holding us back. It is important to understand that just as we have the power to create limiting beliefs in our life, we also have the power to destroy those beliefs and replace them with new empowering beliefs, ones that will improve our decisions and empower us to strive for and realize success, joy and happiness throughout our lives.

What Is a Belief?

If you want to improve your life by taking control of your decisions, you must first become aware of and manage both your conscious and subconscious personal beliefs. Before this can be done, you need to understand what your beliefs are and how your beliefs were formed. When you become aware of a belief and are able to determine how it came to be formed, then you will be in a position to evaluate whether it is enhancing or limiting your life. Only then will you be in a position to make informed and life-enhancing decisions.

What exactly is a belief? Most people live their lives simply accepting that their beliefs are there. They never question them, what they really are or where they came from. Beliefs are not something that appeared from nowhere. A belief is created from a thought or idea that you have a feeling of certainty about.

A belief is formed by a conscious or subconscious feeling that comes in three levels of certainty and intensity. First is an opinion. An opinion is something you feel relatively certain about but is only temporary and can be changed easily. An opinion's foundation is constructed of weak and uneven reference blocks that are usually hearsay and unverified. These reference blocks can easily be chipped at and bring the whole foundation tumbling down.

Next is a belief that is formed when you develop much more even and stronger reference blocks. A belief has a strong foundation of certainty and emotion. A belief is rarely shaken. People with a belief have a strong level of certainty and are usually closed to new input about the topic.

Third is a conviction. A conviction is a belief with an emotional intensity so high that a person is so convinced that they will get angry when it is questioned. A person with a conviction is never willing to even question their references. The certainty and the strength of all three of these components in your life were formed through your past life experiences both consciously and subconsciously.

If you believe that you are likable, this simply means you are thinking and feeling certain that you are likable. The question or idea "am I likable" allowed you to tap into your past experiences and use those experiences as references on how certain you feel about whether you are likable or not. It is that feeling of certainty that is call your belief.

Let's say you believe you can change a flat tire. What you are really saying is that because you either have done it in the past or have enough references on how it is done, you feel certain you can do it. The strength of your belief is determined by those references. If you have successfully changed a tire in the past, your certainty that you feel you can do it will be stronger than if you had only watched a YouTube video on how it is done. Your decision on whether you attempt to change the tire yourself is influenced by the strength of your belief or the certainty you feel that you can successfully do it.

Then how is a question or idea turned into a belief? To change anything into a belief, you must develop a feeling of certainty and this requires references. The more references you have, the stronger the feeling of certainty. You need to build a foundation of references around the idea, and the stronger the foundation the stronger the belief. A strong foundation is built out of several building blocks of personal experiences or references. These experiences or references can be real, imaginary or influenced by others. The more references you have that support the idea, the stronger the feeling of certainty and belief.

Think about a belief you have. Ask yourself "what is it that I am certain about and why do I believe it to be so? How certain am I about it?" Then ask "is this belief enhancing my life or is it limiting it and causing me to suffer?" You will then start to tap into your belief foundation and recall the references and foundational blocks that created and determined your belief as well as the feeling of certainty about the idea. In some cases, the references you find may not be events or feelings that you have personally experienced but ones that your imagination has created or others have influenced.

A great example is you are asked to jump off the high diving board for the first time. You imagine landing flat on your stomach and being in a lot of pain. This is a reference that in turn causes you to believe and feel certain that you cannot do it. Another example is a religious belief. Many people follow certain religious traditions because of the influence of their parents or the faith group around them. They have not personally researched the doctrine but follow it faithfully because of these outside influences. This is why cults have existed in the world. In the examples above, you can see how we can use references, whether real or not, to form our beliefs.

Another important influence on our references and the strength of feeling they produce is the emotional state felt during the reference experience. If you are in a high state of emotion, whether positive or negative, it will affect the feeling differently than if it is not emotional at all. Let's say you are receiving an award for something you did. The emotion felt around you while you are receiving the award will affect the feeling it produces.

Say that you are presented the award on stage in front of hundreds of co-workers. They are all standing, clapping and shouting congratulations. You become captivated by their attention and the number of people who approach you to shake your hand and congratulate you personally. Now in contrast, you receive the same award at home in the mail in an envelope with a letter of congratulations. You open it, review it, smile and place it on the counter. How do you think these two references would support the belief or the feeling of certainty that you are a winner? It is clear that if this were the only reference to draw upon, then the feeling of joy experienced at the award night would provide a much stronger belief and feeling of certainty that you are a winner than receiving it in the mail.

One factor that can affect your beliefs and the actions you take is your subconscious ability to form negative beliefs and use events to support them. Emotion is usually involved when this happens. I will use an example I experienced, which caused me a lot of pain. I played a lot of craps (gambling with dice) over the years. This game fed my addictive behaviour and would usually take control of me. Because money was involved, my emotions were extremely high. I discovered that I had created an unsupported negative belief that affected my emotions and my game play, which produced negative results.

In the game, I had my money spread on several numbers and I would get paid if those numbers appeared when the dice were thrown. If a seven was thrown, I would lose all the bets on the table. Somehow my mind created the idea that if during play the dice were accidently thrown off the table, the next throw would be a seven and I would lose everything. Thus, every time the dice left the table, I would expect a seven to be thrown next. When it did happen, I stored the experience as another reference block until I had a strong foundation and came to believe and feel certain this would happen every time.

This belief began to affect me so much that if the dice went off the table, I knew a seven was coming next. You would think with this belief that I would remove my bets so as not to lose. Wrong! I had another belief that hurt even more and that was it took a lot of rolls to build up my bet and I would lose the potential winnings by taking them down. Then, when a seven did come out, I would be mad at myself for not taking the bets down, which would eventually lead me to change how I played the game. It was this emotionally caused change in gameplay that influenced me to get away from my regular structure and eventually lose. The loss and pain I experienced from it was all brought about by a negative limiting belief.

When I learned about beliefs and how they work, I explored this belief. I started by questioning how it came to be. I realized that my reference was formed by the dice leaving the table a few times and a seven coming up next. I then decided to explore this reference and recorded how often a seven was thrown after the dice left the table. I was surprised to find it happened less than 20 per cent of the time, a far cry from my belief that it would happen every time. With this new proven reference, I was able to change my old negative belief and improve not only my game but also my emotions and enjoyment.

There are many areas in our lives in which we have taken an idea and unknowingly turned it into a negative belief. Once created, our belief would cause us to focus and look for experiences and references that supported it. How many of these limiting beliefs do you think you have right now that are negatively affecting your life? Understanding the importance that emotional feelings have on the creation of our beliefs will help when it comes time to take control of your beliefs rather than let them control you.

The beliefs that each person forms can lead them to either an optimistic or pessimistic outlook in all they do. Beliefs are what brought about the realization of many objects or processes once thought impossible. The horseless carriage, flight, space travel, harnessing nuclear energy and the four-minute mile are all examples of ideas many believed impossible but made possible by the beliefs of others. Again, it was the different references that formed these beliefs and people who believed that the impossible could be made possible.

Every person is limited only by what their beliefs allow them to do. You have heard of examples where the impossible became possible, where health and physical features were changed, and where great technical breakthroughs were achieved. These all transpired because people believed enough to overcome any obstacle that crossed their path. They believed enough to never give up.

Yet, so many people allow adversity to form their beliefs. They become pessimistic and do not push themselves enough to overcome their negative beliefs and move on to conquer their adversity. This was evident in the Jewish Holocaust we discussed earlier. Many believed they were going to die and gave up. I would encourage you to read *Man's Search for Meaning* by Victor Frankl. You will see firsthand how beliefs were formed and how they influenced many people's lives.

By discerning and understanding the beliefs you have formed over the years, you have the ability and power within you to take control of them. You can then eliminate your limiting beliefs and form new empowering beliefs to help you create the passion and ability required to overcome any adversity or pessimistic attitude you will experience. You also can achieve the impossible.

I pray that you now understand that beliefs are feelings that we grow to be certain about. When understanding the makeup of beliefs, the effect emotions play in their creation and the reference foundation principle, you are on your way to positive change. Now you can start to research what beliefs you have both consciously and subconsciously. Once you start the process, you can determine if they are real, imagined or influenced by others. Are they enriching or limiting? This information will allow you to eliminate your limiting beliefs and implement positive and inspiring beliefs that will lead you to live a life of joy and happiness.

How To Change Your Beliefs

You may now be asking yourself "if I believe something, how can I change my belief? There must be references defining the belief or I would not have it in the first place." You are right.

Without the proper tools and know-how, a belief or conviction cannot be changed. If you are not consciously in control of your beliefs, then your subconscious is. As I mentioned earlier, all our beliefs were built on a foundation of references. Most of these references were created subconsciously. If you want to change a belief, you must consciously change your references that your subconscious has created, and this is done in three steps.

First, you must start to question your limiting beliefs. Questions cause doubt, and it is this doubt that will bring down the foundation of the belief that you created. By asking questions like "why do I believe this?" you will discover and introduce doubt into the references you have created. If you continue questioning the references that have formed the foundation of your belief, the doubt you create will then begin to chip away at each of them and weaken the overall foundation.

An example is if you have a belief that you cannot stop smoking, you would start by asking yourself "why do I believe this? Why is it that I am so convinced that I can't stop smoking?" When you start to ask yourself questions like these, you will find that the references you have created in the past will start to appear and defend your belief.

Examples of these references might include the following: you tried to quit many times in the past but ended up giving in to your cravings and started again; it is an addiction that you have no power over; you don't really want to quit; it helps keep you calm. These are a few of the references that may start to appear in your consciousness. These are references that your subconscious has created over time to build your belief foundation.

By questioning each of these references individually, you will then start to introduce doubt into them. When you question anything enough, eventually you will start to doubt it. This includes even our strongest convictions.

I am sure that you can recall a time when you had a belief about something and you were certain it was true. Maybe you thought someone did not like you. You believed this from what you heard from others and from what you thought were signs from them. One day, you had a conversation with them. As you talked, you found them to be friendly and you began to question your references that led you to believe they did not like you. After a few questions, you realized your belief was totally wrong and they never disliked you. It is the doubt that you formed by asking yourself questions that weakened the foundation of the belief you had created.

Using the above example, if you have tried unsuccessfully to quit smoking in the past, you could ask questions like "what was happening when I started again? What led to me giving in?" As you continue to question your reference, the answers that start to appear will begin to weaken the certainty of the reference.

If you realize that it was stress that caused you to start again, you would go on to ask "is smoking the only way I could reduce stress? What else could I have done besides smoking that could have helped?" When you keep digging deeper with more questions, you will discover choices that were available that you missed and did not chose. It is the discovery of these choices that will help weaken the reference. Once you have built enough doubt to weaken your references and overall belief, you are ready to implement the second step.

The second step to changing a belief is to introduce massive pain to your old limiting belief, a pain so real and strong that you decide you will no longer accept what the belief causes in your life. As mentioned in Chapter Seven on pain and pleasure, you can also use this powerful principle to help you eliminate those beliefs that negatively affect your life. Pain is the most powerful way to change a belief.

When you start questioning a belief, you need to ask yourself "this belief is causing me what pain today? If this belief continues, what future pain will I experience?" If you associate enough pain to the belief and allow yourself to feel the pain deep within yourself, change will not only be possible but become essential. Next, ask yourself "do I want to feel this way the rest of my life?" If you answer these questions honestly and if you truly experience the pain this belief causes, you will have the power to break down any belief foundation you have created.

Once you have weakened your limiting belief with doubt and pain, you are ready to move to the third step. It is time to replace your old limiting belief with a new empowering one, a belief so compelling that you can turn it into a conviction. It will be a belief that is built with a strong foundation constructed from new, reliable and empowering references.

Creating a new empowering belief to replace your old limiting belief will not only empower you but inspire you to reach for and achieve the things you have always desired to have and experience. By replacing the old belief with a new one that brings joy to your life, you are ensuring that the old belief will not work its way back into your life.

If your belief was "I cannot stop smoking," you could replace it with one like "I will not smoke under any circumstances." You will then support your new empowering belief with a strong foundation of references built on informed and lasting information.

Let's investigate now a real example of how this life-changing process can be used. During my tenure as a prison chaplain, I was blessed to meet Ryan. Ryan was a career criminal and drug addict who was in and out of prison on a regular basis. He was what we used to refer to as someone doing life on the installment plan. Ryan came to a program that I had been facilitating in the prison. I had recognized him from one of his previous stays in the institution.

One day I asked him to come and see me after the program. During our discussion, Ryan made it clear that he believed he was destined to be a criminal and drug addict, spending the rest of his life in and out of jail. I began to question him as to why he believed this. As we continued to talk, many of the references that were the foundation of this belief began to appear. His references included that his mother was an addict and his father was always in and out of jail. Ryan had been sexually abused when he was young. He quit school because he was told he would never graduate or become anybody. He had no skills so he only knew how to sell drugs and use crime to survive. No one liked him or cared about him. There were many more references.

Over a couple of months, I worked with Ryan, getting him to start questioning where each of his references came from. I asked questions like "why do you believe that because your father spent most of his life in jail it means you have to do the same? Does your father make your decisions or control what you do? Do you know anyone with a similar upbringing as yours who has gone on to be successful? Is there a possibility that you could be better than your father?"

With questions like this, Ryan began to see the flaws in his references and started to doubt their reality. As we questioned each reference that surfaced, Ryan began to doubt his belief that crime, drugs and prison were his only future. Now that he had doubt about his belief, I moved him to the second step. I had him start to associate massive pain to the belief that he was destined to spend most of his life in jail. I again used the tool of questions like "how does it make you feel knowing that you will spent the rest of your life in jail? Is that something you really want? What will you be missing out on while you are in jail?" The more I questioned, the more pain surfaced until Ryan broke down sobbing, saying he couldn't take it anymore as the pain was too much.

I then asked, "Do you still believe with certainty that this life of pain is your only choice? Could there be another course for your life?" This was the moment when the doubt and the pain Ryan experienced destroyed his limiting belief. He said, "No, I believe there must be more. There has to be something different." I then asked, "What would something different look like?" At this point, Ryan visualized a different future than he previously believed was in store for him. It was a life of purpose and joy. Using questions, Ryan was able to design a better, more empowering future and start to build references towards this future that created a strong foundation to a new empowering belief and life.

Empowered by his new belief, Ryan began to implement positive changes in his attitude and actions that strengthened his belief. After his release, Ryan went on to learn how to repair motorcycles and moved on to start his own successful motorcycle shop. He also met a girl, got married and has two wonderful children. Ryan is an excellent example of how strongly embedded limiting beliefs can be erased and replaced with empowering beliefs that inspire you to passion and happiness.

A person does not need someone else to help them grow through this process. If you use the three steps I have described, then you can change any limiting belief you have. It starts with the desire to change. I truly believe if you are still reading this book that you have this desire. You have within you the power to overcome any limiting belief in your life and replace it with a new set of life-enhancing beliefs that will lead you not only to enjoy your life but to achieve the dreams you have always desired.

Is this the time to start implementing this life-changing process in your life? Complete the exercise below that uses the three-step process of change. You will eliminate the limiting beliefs that have been causing you pain, and you will also create new empowering beliefs to replace them, new beliefs that will help you achieve the future you desire and deserve.

Belief Exercise

I have given you a lot of information about beliefs and how they can affect your life. It is now time to explore how your beliefs are controlling your life. In this exercise, you will need to take some time to identify what your beliefs are and how they are influencing your life.

To better help you understand this principle a little better, I would like you to take a moment to brainstorm some of your empowering and your limiting beliefs. In the spaces below, I want you to spend the next 10 minutes and list all the beliefs—both empowering and limiting—that are affecting your life today.

Think about where you are, what you have, who is in your life and what you do to earn a living and for enjoyment. List all the beliefs that come to you. Some thoughts that arise may seem simple or not all that important at the time. If they came to mind, then they are important. Don't try to rationalize them; just write them down. You will want to list all of the following beliefs: if/then beliefs, I am/am not beliefs, I can/cannot beliefs, and global beliefs.

We will start with your if/then beliefs. These are beliefs that if you do something, you are certain a specific result will transpire. For example, "if I allow myself to fall in love, I will surely get hurt" or "if I don't do it myself, then it will never get done."

List your "if/then" beliefs here:

Empowering Beliefs   Limiting Beliefs

_____   _____

_____   _____

_____   _____

Now you will list your "I am/am not" or "I can/cannot" beliefs. These are the beliefs about who you believe you are or are not and what you believe you can and cannot do. For example, "I am a great cook, I am not a salesman, I can dance, I cannot sing."

List your "I am/am not" and "I can/cannot" beliefs here:

Empowering Beliefs   Limiting Beliefs

_____   _____

_____   _____

_____   _____

Finally, list your global beliefs. These are your beliefs about the world around you. They include: how you view the world and all that is in it; beliefs about people, religion and politics; whether you believe everything is destined or you live in a random world; people are selfish, the government is corrupt, or there is no justice in the world. These are examples of global beliefs.

Now list the "global" beliefs that you feel empower or limit you here:

Empowering Beliefs   Limiting Beliefs

_____   _____

_____   _____

_____   _____

I hope you took enough time to list at least 10 of each of your empowering and limiting beliefs. I know it can be a difficult thing to delve into our conscious and subconscious. Change doesn't just happen. It takes effort and commitment. If you do not have at least 10 empowering and 10 limiting beliefs listed, I want you to go back and complete your list. As we continue this exercise, you will be happy you did.

Now that you completed your list, I want to ask you "what did you learn from doing this and how did it make you feel? Did any 'ah-ha' moments arise?" I would now like to show you how you can use this exercise to enhance and strengthen the empowering beliefs you already have.

Look over your list and circle your top three empowering beliefs, the ones you are certain are enhancing and bringing joy into your life. Look them over, explore them and ask yourself "how are these beliefs empowering and strengthening my life? How have they positively affected the path my life has taken?" Feel the satisfaction you experience from the results these beliefs have provided. Notice how the power of your belief enhances your life and how you feel about yourself.

I remember how surprised I was when I first completed this exercise and acknowledged that I had empowering beliefs. My life was not transpiring as I had hoped. Until then, I believed I had no empowering qualities at all. When I discovered I like to help other people and see them happy, my life changed. This one belief, when exposed, led to many more life-enhancing beliefs and qualities that were waiting to be explored and implemented. By taking the time to explore and discover our life-enhancing beliefs, we are able to recognize the positive affect they have in our life. It is the feeling we experience from this discovery that strengthens and enhances our belief.

This too is available and will work for you if you take the time for self-discovery and embrace your empowering beliefs. I want you to not only review your list of life-enhancing beliefs regularly but also add to it. Use the positive outcomes and feelings these beliefs produce in your life to increase the certainty of your beliefs until they become convictions.

Now it's time to review your limiting beliefs. I want you to look over the list you made and ask yourself "what is each of these beliefs costing me both emotionally and personally? What are the consequences they are producing in my life?"

Now write down the two most disempowering beliefs you have:

1. _____

2. _____

How does the negative effects these beliefs are producing in your life make you feel? Now decide that you are no longer willing to allow this belief to cause you any more pain. It is over. Tell yourself "I am in control and will decide for myself what I will believe or not."

You are now ready to chip away at the foundation references that have built the belief. Start by asking the following questions and allow doubt to weaken and break down your disempowering belief foundation:

1. Why do I believe this?

   _____

2. What proof is there that this belief is real?

   _____

3. How did I come to believe this?

   _____

4. Is the source of my belief credible?

   _____

5. What will it cost me emotionally if I do not change this belief?

   _____

6. Is this belief negatively affecting my family or relationships?

   _____

7. What is this belief costing me physically or financially?

   _____

8. Can there be another option?

   _____

9. What will this belief cost my future if it is not changed?

   _____

As you ask yourself these questions and others like it, you will probably notice your belief start to weaken. You have used doubt to chip away at the foundation.

It is now time to implement the second step of the process. You must link massive pain to your old belief. As you focus, feel the loss and pain this belief is going to give you. Picture in your mind that your spouse is leaving you. Feel the disappointment and pain your child is experiencing as you enter the prison and leave all you cherish behind. See your health failing and the people shaking their heads at your funeral. As you do this, you will break apart the remaining foundation of your disempowering belief and it will come tumbling down.

Finally, you cannot break down a limiting belief without replacing it with a new empowering one. What is the opposite result of the belief you just eliminated? If your old belief was that you were a loser, you would replace it with a belief that you are a winner and no one else can change that.

Now choose a new empowering belief to replace your old one and write it down. Make it real and powerful. You do not have to be convinced of your new belief at this point. This will be done later. You are simply writing a belief you would desire.

New belief 1: _____

New belief 2: _____

Now imagine your new beliefs in action. How are they impacting your life? What are the results and feelings you experience because of these new beliefs?

This process will help you discover and develop many positive references. These references will begin to construct solid foundations for your new beliefs. Your subconscious will continually look for examples and sources that will strengthen your new beliefs. If you are having problems finding positive references, you can look to someone who is already succeeding with a similar belief and someone who is achieving the results in their life that you would like to experience. Role models and mentors are the best source of positive and proven references through their example.

By completing the exercise above, you have now eliminated some old destructive limiting beliefs and replaced them with new and empowering beliefs that will produce positive influences on all your future decisions and the results they provide in your life. If you are not getting the results you want in life, it is because of poor decisions you have made that were influenced by your limiting beliefs. If you want to change any part of your life, all you have to do is use the above process and you will achieve your dreams and desires.

What Are Your Values?

The values we hold within our heart and mind guide our every decision and therefore the overall direction our life progresses. Our values are the leading factor that influences our decisions and directs our behaviour. Values are the beliefs we have at the highest level of our being. Because a value in reality is simply a belief, they are created and influenced in the same way all our regular beliefs are. As a result, we are not always the true author of our values. Similarly, we are not always consciously aware of all our values.

There are two categories of values that we adhere to in our lives. The two categories are our cultural values and our personal values. A culture is a social system that shares a set of common values. These common values help a person to understand the social expectations and understandings for the common good. Cultural values are the values that society broadly influences, shares and places upon us. Cultural values are how the community defines good and evil, what is right and wrong, what is acceptable and not. They have geographical, religious and political influences in their creation. Our cultural values are the values we need to uphold so we don't come in conflict with our community. When we breach cultural values, we are usually held accountable by the community that created them.

The other set of values has the greatest impact on how our lives are lived and evolve, and they are our personal values. Our personal values exist within the cultural values of the time and are either in agreement or at odds with one or more of them. These values are the most important to us and reflect what we truly stand for. They guide every decision we make. Our personal values provide an internal reference for what we believe is good, beneficial, important, useful, beautiful, desirable and constructive.

Our personal values are divided into two types: our ends and our means values. If I were to ask you "what do you value most?" Your reply might be love, family or money. If your reply was love, that is the ends value that you are pursuing. In other words, it is the emotional state you are seeking. If you were to answer money, then that is a means value. Money is a means that will provide an emotional state.

If you are not fully aware of what your values are or of what you truly believe deep down, then you may be living a life of chasing the emotional state you desire. You are also vulnerable to others determining what you value. If you want to live the most fulfilling and joyful life possible, there is only one way you can accomplish it: you need to decide what you most value in life and why. Then you need to live those values each and every day. People who know their values, why they have them and live them daily are happy even when things do not go their way. Why? Because they stuck to their value system, knew what they desired and then did everything possible to accomplish it.

Unfortunately, most people today do not do this. They have no idea what is truly important to them. They are not firmly knowledgeable about any issue around them and are easily led in their decision-making. They find it hard to commit to a relationship, job, hobby or idea because they do not understand what they want and why.

There is no better evidence of this than in today's politics. People vote because of a news article that is not reliable to base their decision upon or they do not vote at all. They act as though they value their choice but in reality they have no idea. Then they complain when government policies affect them negatively.

If you are not clear on what is truly important to you, what you stand for and why, then how do you expect to make decisions that will empower you and increase your self-esteem? Have you ever found yourself in a situation where you found it difficult or impossible to make a decision? It was because you did not know what your true values were. Remember, all decision-making comes down to values and beliefs clarification.

It is also important to realize that our values can conflict in many situations. If you are not certain about the clarity and importance of your values, then you are left in a stressful and sometimes hopeless situation. A good example is a recruit who joined the army in hopes of gaining a career. The recruit has grown to value that a solider must serve their country and defend it at all costs. They also have a deep value that they should never take a life. When asked to go into combat and face the possibility that they may have to take a life to survive, they become distressed and do not know what to do and cannot understand why. They have two conflicting values and have never taken time to understand and rate their importance to them.

Values exist whether you acknowledge them or not. Life is so much easier when you determine and live by a set of defined values. When you know what is most important to you and why it is important to you, then decision-making and life itself become simple. If you strongly value family and then work a 70-hour week and miss quality time with your family, you will feel internal conflict and stress. If you value competition and work as a highly competitive sales professional, then you will be happy and satisfied with your job. These are two examples of how understanding your values can help you make empowering decisions in your life. When you know your values, you can use them to make empowering life decisions. You will be able to answer questions like:

- What job should I pursue?
- Do I want a career or family?
- What do I enjoy doing?
- Should I get married?
- Do I want to travel?
- If I could do anything I wanted, what would it be?

Now it is time to discover and get to know what your present values are. As you go through the exercise below, keep in mind that important values from the past may no longer be relevant. Do not dwell on old limiting values. They can be discarded by using the same process you learned to change a limiting belief into an empowering one.

Values Exercise

It is time to define your values. When you define your personal values, you discover what is truly important to you. A good way to do this is to look back on your life. You will investigate times in your life when you felt happy and confident and made good decisions. You will also contemplate the times when things did not go so well, times when you made poor decisions, struggled and failed. You will look at what the values were that affected how you felt and how you made your decisions.

Complete the following steps for both the personal and employment areas of your life.

Step 1: Identify the times you were happiest. What were you doing?

_____

_____

Who were you doing it with?

_____

_____

Why did it make you feel good?

_____

_____

What other factors contributed to your happiness?

_____

_____

Step 2: Identify times when you were most proud. Why were you proud?

_____

_____

Did others help or share the moment with you? Who?

_____

_____

What other factors contributed to your pride?

_____

_____

Step 3: Identify the times when you felt most fulfilled and satisfied. What need or desire was being fulfilled?

_____

_____

How and why did the experience give your life meaning?

_____

_____

What other factors contributed to your feeling of fulfillment?

_____

_____

Step 4: Identify times when things went opposite to how you wanted. What was the event or situation?

_____

_____

Who else or what other entity was involved?

_____

_____

Who did you blame and why?

_____

_____

How did you feel about the outcome?

_____

_____

Step 5: Identify times when you felt helpless and did not know what to do. What was happening?

_____

_____

Who else was involved?

_____

_____

How did you feel and why did you feel that way?

_____

_____

Step 6: Go through the list of values below and assign one or more value that you can associate to each of the situations in Steps 1 to 5. If you come up with values not on the list, write them down.

Step 1 values: _____

Step 2 values: _____

Step 3 values: _____

Step 4 values: _____

Step 5 values: _____

List of Values

Accountability	Excellence	Perfection
Accuracy	Excitement	Piety
Achievement	Expertise	Positivity
Adventurousness	Exploration	Practicality
Altruism	Expressiveness	Preparedness
Ambition	Fairness	Professionalism
Assertiveness	Faith	Prudence
Balance	Family-focused	Quality-oriented
Being the best	Fidelity	Reliability
Belonging	Fitness	Resourcefulness
Boldness	Fluency	Restraint
Calmness	Focus	Results-oriented
Carefulness	Freedom	Rigour
Challenge	Fun	Security
Cheerfulness	Generosity	Self-actualization
Clear-mindedness	Goodness	Self-control
Commitment	Grace	Selflessness
Community	Growth	Self-reliance
Compassion	Happiness	Sensitivity
Competitiveness	Hard work	Serenity
Consistency	Health	Service
Contentment	Helping society	Shrewdness
Continuous improvement	Holiness	Simplicity
Contribution	Honesty	Soundness
Control	Honour	Speed
Cooperation	Humility	Spontaneity

Correctness	Independence	Stability
Courtesy	Ingenuity	Strategic
Creativity	Inner harmony	Strength
Curiosity	Inquisitiveness	Structure
Decisiveness	Insightfulness	Success
Democracy	Intellectual status	Support
Dependability	Intelligence	Teamwork
Determination	Intuition	Temperance
Devoutness	Joy	Thankfulness
Diligence	Justice	Thoroughness
Discipline	Leadership	Thoughtfulness
Discretion	Legacy	Timeliness
Diversity	Love	Tolerance
Dynamism	Loyalty	Traditionalism
Economy	Making a difference	Trustworthiness
Effectiveness	Mastery	Truth-seeking
Efficiency	Merit	Understanding
Elegance	Obedience	Uniqueness
Empathy	Openness	Unity
Enjoyment	Order	Usefulness
Enthusiasm	Originality	Vision
Equality	Patriotism	Vitality

Step 7: Edit and prioritize your values.

This will probably be the most difficult step for you because you will need to look deep within yourself to complete it. It is also the most important step because, when you are required to make a decision in the future, it is vital that you have the proper understanding of your values and their importance to you. In many cases, you will have to choose between two conflicting values.

Start by asking yourself the following questions for each of the values you listed above. How important is this value to me? Where did this value come from? Do I need it at all? Does it benefit me in any way? Is there a better value I could replace it with that would enhance my life more?

You should now have a refined value list, one in which you decided to eliminate certain values and add new ones.

Now go over the value list provided and see if there are any values you do not have listed that inspire you. Ask yourself "if I lived this value, what would it bring me?"

After you have added any new values that you have chosen to your list, I would like you to start at the top and compare the first value on the list with the second. Determine which one is more beneficial in your life. It might help to visualize a situation where you could see the values in use. For example, the first value listed may be contribution and the second security. If you were faced with a choice of helping someone financially but not having enough to help them and maintain a certain savings level, then how would you resolve the conflict and still feel positive about your decision? Choose the one you believe would enhance your life more and move down to the next one and complete the same process again. Follow this process until you have a complete list of your values in order of importance to you.

Step 8: Reaffirm your values.

Now it is time to check your top life value list and make sure they fit with your life and your vision of yourself. Ask yourself these questions:

- Do these values make you feel good about yourself?
- Are you proud of your top five values?
- Would you feel comfortable and proud to tell these values to people you respect and admire?

- Do these values represent things or ideas that you would support, even if your decision isn't popular and puts you in the minority?
- Are you willing to do whatever is required on a daily basis to try and live up to these values?

When you consider your values in decision-making, you will maintain your sense of integrity and what you know is right as well as approach decisions with confidence and clarity. You will also know that what you are doing is best for your current and future happiness and satisfaction.

Making value-based decisions may not always be easy. However, making a decision that you know is right is a lot less difficult in the long run.

Identifying and understanding your values is a challenging and important exercise. Your personal values are a central part of who you are and who you want to be. By becoming more aware of these important factors in your life, you can use them as a guide to make the best decision in any situation.

Most of life's decisions are about determining what you value most. When many options seem reasonable, it's helpful and comforting to rely on your values and use them as a strong guiding force to point you in the right direction.

Summary

If you ever want to regain control of your life and move it in the direction you desire, your beliefs and values must be involved. Identifying and understanding our beliefs and values are crucial steps in making life-enhancing decisions. If you are able to grasp this one vital process, you are well on your way to a life of happiness, achievement and fulfillment. I ask you to complete the exercises in this chapter. I know they are difficult, but the information you discover and work through and the processes taught will enhance your life tremendously.

I know in my heart that you have the desire and ability to take this information and use it to introduce many changes to your attitude and decisions. You will open your own eyes to how successful and happy you can be, and others will take notice and start to give you their trust and support. Now go and develop an arsenal of strong, positive life-enhancing beliefs and values that will lead you to achieve the dreams and desires you deserve.

CHAPTER NINE

Your Needs and Desires

The driving force

"Evaluate your needs. What are they? Are they being met? If not, how can you meet your needs? Look after yourself and your needs before you try and look after others and their needs. You'll be a lot more effective in whatever you do."

— Akiroq Brost

- -

In This Chapter
- ➢ How Personal Needs Work in Our Life
- ➢ Six Personal Needs to Happiness and Fulfillment
- ➢ Meeting Your Personal Needs in a Healthy Way
- ➢ Personal Needs Exercise
- ➢ Summary

- -

Over and over throughout my life, I have experienced the feeling of frustration after achieving something I thought I wanted. After successfully completing a goal, I wondered, "Is that all there is?" I had completed my goal, overcame all the obstacles, achieved what

I desired and you would think I would feel elated. I should have felt fulfilled and happy. But that joy was missing. There was an emptiness. The reward of happiness I desired and expected was not there.

There were even times while I was striving to achieve my goal and everything was going right, yet I found myself in a funk. Even though I had a plan and was on course, I was not able to understand why I felt so disconnected when everything was going according to plan and I should be riding high. I would start to disengage and self-destruct. I would turn a positive and healthy situation into one of destructive actions and total failure.

Only after I began to search for the reasons why people act and feel as we do, I was able to discover the answer to this mystery. It all comes down to whether our personal needs are being fulfilled. Only by becoming aware of and understanding what our needs are is it possible to align our goals and life to achieve the happiness and fulfillment we all desire.

In this chapter, I will introduce you to the concept of personal needs. You will discover the control and impact they impose on our feelings and motivation in life. I will introduce you to a concept I learned from Tony Robbins called our six human needs. This information should help you to understand that if a person knows the makeup of their personal needs and designs their goals and life around meeting these needs, they can and will achieve the happiness and fulfillment they desire. We will start by learning about our personal needs.

How Personal Needs Work in Our Life

What motivates people, what causes their desire to do their work well and how can they be encouraged to perform even better? To get a better understanding of this process, the psychologist Abraham Maslow developed a Hierarchy of Needs model in 1934, in which he described five different levels of gratification of needs that every person has. The hierarchy of needs is known as the Maslow Pyramid or the theory of human behavior and is still used in other sectors as well.

According to Maslow, people are always motivated to satisfy their needs both at home and at work. He does not make distinctions based on age. He categorized human needs into five hierarchical levels (Hierarchy of Needs). He made the assumption that an advanced level can only be reached when the previous level of needs has been fulfilled.

Maslow states that it is not possible to skip a level of the Hierarchy of Needs. That is why it is important to fulfil the need that has been skipped or lost at a later date. The lowest level of Maslow's Hierarchy of Needs is the foundation of the pyramid. This is where the needs pattern begins. These basic needs apply to everyone. The higher the level in Maslow's Hierarchy of Need, the more difficult it becomes to satisfy the needs. Here are the five levels of needs:

1. Physiological Needs

These include the most basic needs that are vital to survival, such as the need for food, water and sleep (primary needs). Without fulfillment of these primary needs, people cannot function properly and they can fall ill. In terms of our work, a salary pays for most of these basic needs (such as food and drink).

2. Safety Needs

Every person wants security, safety and stability (secondary needs). This can also be translated into peace, order and health. This needs category also includes the security of a roof over one's head. If you make the transition to work, steady work, such as a long-term contract, provides stability and security for the long term. This ensures security with respect to housing and providing for the family.

3. Belonging

People are social beings and need social contacts. They wish to belong to a group. Friendship, acceptance, caring for other people and intimacy are important needs. In regards to work, an employee will only invest time in social contacts on the work floor and be loyal to colleagues when they have been given the security of a long-term contract. The employee now feels that they are a part of the group.

4. Esteem

After investing in social contacts, people need esteem and recognition for what they do (recognition needs). Self-respect is crucial in this. Only when these needs are met, they will feel esteem, recognition and respect from other people. In the transition to the work place, the employer holds a motivator with this needs category. Apart from the size of the salary, there are other factors that can motivate an employee. Thus, compliments, trust and autonomy become important motivators for an employee.

5. Self-actualization

Because of the full development of certain qualities, this needs category will grow (development needs). This can take place in different ways, from taking a course or night classes to taking on hobbies. In terms of the workplace, employees might be allowed to take certain courses or studies. The incentive and appreciation for doing voluntary work, by offering a subsidy or leisure time, are part of this category.

Even when all the needs in the pyramid have been met, people will not be satisfied. According to Maslow, people will always have the urge to develop themselves, to chase after new needs and to be better at what they are good at. A top sportsman wants to perform even better, an artist wants to pour more soul into their work and a manager wants to have an even bigger company. This need is also called self-actualization.

Each person has a unique set of personal needs (above basic survival needs) that must be met in order to be at their best; they are critical in order to thrive. As important as personal needs are, few people are aware of them. As a result, they generally go about meeting their needs unconsciously, often in ways that are at odds with living a fulfilling life. Once you spend time discovering your personal needs and how to meet them in successful ways, your life tends to work much better.

There are several characteristics of personal needs. Meeting your personal needs is critical for you to thrive and live a life you love. Your needs are neither good nor bad and they can be met in positive or negative ways relative to your desired results. Think of your personal needs as the underlying experience or feeling you are attempting to create through your actions.

Some examples of personal needs include:

Acceptance	Control	Influence
Accomplishment	Creativity	Intellectual stimulation
Acknowledgment	Discovery	Intensity
Adventure	Drama	Intimacy
Attention	Excitement	Power
Autonomy	Freedom	Recognition
Challenge	Harmony	Simplicity
Connection	Importance	Safety
Contribution	Independence	

This list is by no means exhaustive; it is intended to provide examples, which will be a starting point for you and will be helpful to you in identifying similar (or different) words that accurately describe your personal needs.

In order to thrive, it is important to meet your personal needs in positive ways that enhance your enjoyment of life and the quality of your relationships. Examples of positive ways to meet your needs and some of their possible associated personal needs are included below. Any of these activities/outcomes may have one or several personal needs associated with them (including others not listed as examples).

Activity/Outcome	Possible Personal Needs
Learning a new skill	Accomplishment, control, power, acceptance, discovery, autonomy
Taking more "me" time	Independence, connection, control, discovery, strong relationships, acceptance, acknowledgment, creativity, harmony, intimacy
Work smarter, not harder	Challenge, excitement, control, freedom
Bungee jumping	Connection, challenge, excitement, freedom
Financial security	Safety, independence, control
Expressing your feelings	Attention, control, freedom, intimacy
Writing a book	Recognition, accomplishment, creativity
Volunteer work	Contribution, connection, discovery, power
Playing team sports	Challenge, excitement, connection, recognition
Hiking	Adventure, freedom, challenge, connection

Identifying the patterns, behaviours and outcomes that you repeat that detract from your enjoyment of life or the quality of your relationships can help you determine what your personal needs are. Examples of negative patterns and associated personal needs are outlined below. Any of these patterns may have one or several personal needs associated with them (including others not listed as examples).

Ineffective Pattern	Possible Personal Needs
Whining	Security, control, power, acceptance, attention, procrastination, safety, independence, excitement
Being late	Challenge, power, control, attention, excitement over-committing, connection, challenge, excitement, acceptance
Under-achieving	Safety, independence, control
Yelling	Attention, control, independence, power
Watching TV	Autonomy, discovery, recognition, safety

Whether we are conscious of it or not, we spend much of our life attempting to meet our personal needs. We do everything in our lives in the quest for experiences, the experiences that are most important to us to fulfil our personal needs. The more you know about yourself and what is important to you, the more likely you will be to choose positive ways to meet your needs so that you get what you truly want. Awareness of your personal needs is the first step toward meeting them in ways that are positive, which contributes greatly to the likelihood that you will thrive and live a life you love.

Six Personal Needs to Happiness and Fulfillment

Have you ever asked "what causes a person to feel fulfilled or unfulfilled? How do you ensure that you are happy, even when things are not going your way?" To answer these questions, you need to understand the path to happiness. You require a road map with signs showing that you are on the right path. This path should be your goal in life. The problem is most people do not know this path yet expect to achieve happiness. This is why they struggle. They are trying to achieve a goal that they do not understand or know the path to. As a result, they try random paths, hoping that it will eventually lead them to their ultimate goal of happiness and fulfillment.

I remember when I had a goal to become the winner of the sales and marketing person of the year for the city's home building industry. This was a prestigious and coveted award. I believed winning this award would not only provide me the validation I so dearly desired but make me feel extremely happy and fulfilled.

As I worked to achieve this goal, the anticipation of how I would feel grew as I got closer. When the day finally came and my name was called as the winner, I made my way to the stage for my acceptance speech. I was elated and had a big smile as I walked up. Unfortunately, that elation was short lived. After proudly accepting congratulations from people and the festivities ended, I made my way with my wife to the awaiting winner's limo. As we drove to the hotel, the adrenalin started to wear off and I found myself thinking, "Is that it? There has to be more."

I did not feel fulfilled at all and started to wonder "was this worth all the work I put into it?" I had achieved the goal that I thought would lead to happiness and fulfillment only to feel disappointed with how I felt, which was not at all like I imagined.

This life event stood out like a flashing light when I heard Tony Robbins introduce his topic and lessons on what he determined were our six human needs. It became clear that the reason I felt that way was because I was trying to obtain long-term happiness and fulfillment without understanding or meeting my own personal needs. I did not know the real path to happiness so I tried to forge one.

Most of us have disappointment and pain in our lives because we do not know or meet our six needs. In most cases we are meeting more than one need through what we seek or do.

These needs are:

1. Certainty
2. Uncertainty/Variety
3. Significance
4. Love and Connection
5. Growth
6. Contribution

Needs of the Personality

The first four needs are the needs of the personality. We all find ways to meet these needs in some way.

1. Certainty

The need for certainty could be viewed as a need for security. You want to be certain that the water you drink is safe. In other words, you looking for security from the sickness you could get with polluted water. You want to be certain that your partner loves you. In other words, you are looking for security in your relationship. We are looking for certainty about anything that could affect us. If we are not certain about something, then the doubt that arises can cause fear and that fear equates to pain. That fear of pain influences our decisions and the outcomes we experience in life.

2. Uncertainty/Variety

Just as important as certainty is to us, so too is uncertainty or variety high on our needs list. It may seem conflicting to want to be certain about something and at the same time want to be uncertain about it. It is but it isn't. You may want to be certain that your spouse will greet you each day when you get home, but you would like variety or uncertainty about how or whether it will happen. Using the greeting example, let's say your spouse met you at the door each day with a kiss. If it was the same every day, it would lose its magic and become routine. Would you not prefer to be surprised each time not quite knowing what to expect?

Another good example is my enjoyment of gambling. I learned a certain way to bet, which makes me certain I have the best chance to win and feel the pleasure that winning emits. There is an excitement not knowing for sure if you will win, but you are counting on it because you are certain your method of play will allow it. But how much would you enjoy it if you won every bet? It would soon lose its appeal and become boring. You need an amount of uncertainty to enjoy it.

The above two examples are a couple of ways to show how you need both certainty and uncertainty in your life. I am sure if you think about your past, you can find similar examples of this concept once you understand it.

3. Significance

One deep desire that drives every human heart is the need to be significant. We need to know we matter. We want to be recognized and accepted. We want to feel unique and that our life matters. It is this need for significance that influences our actions in positive manners but in many cases it leads to actions that are destructive in the long run. How many stories have you heard in which someone has done something dangerous to be noticed? It is their need for significance that drives them to overpower their own safety and risk themselves. Many people use illness to get attention and meet their need for significance. This need can also be a great positive motivator. It can give you the energy and drive to accomplish great things. Many athletes use their need for significance to motivate them to win. They want to be at the top and be recognized as the best.

By understanding this powerful need, you can use it to achieve many positive outcomes. Ask yourself "am I doing this for me or am I doing it to please or be noticed by someone else? What could the consequences of my actions be? Is it worth the risk?" Your answers will help you decide if you should continue. You will also be able to use other people's desire for significance to assist you when dealing with them. Whether to change your actions and results or improve your interactions with others, the need for significance can be a great tool to assist you.

4. Love and Connection

We all have a need to connect with others in our lives. We were all created to be in community. Our need for love and relationship can motivate us to move mountains and it can cause us a great deal of pain and suffering. We each have our own personal type and amount of relationships we need. For some people, a close partner to share their life with is all they need. For others, a large family or being a member of an organization is required.

I have met people who want to be alone, and many of them have been miserable. This is because they are trying to avoid their basic need for love and connection. Our need for companionship is so great many have imagined a relationship. An example of how far someone would go to meet their need was evident in the movie *Cast Away*. In the movie, Tom Hanks plays a Federal Express employee whose plane crashed and left him stranded on a remote island. To meet his need for companionship, he drew a face on a soccer ball and attached hair. He named his new friend Wilson. Wilson was his companion for years until the ball was lost at sea just before his rescue.

If our need for love and relationship is achieved in a positive and healthy way, it will be a leading factor in helping a person achieve happiness and fulfillment in their life.

Needs of the Spirit

The next two needs we will discuss are the needs of the spirit. These needs are more difficult to satisfy and are rarely met by most people. When these needs are met, we are truly fulfilled.

5. Growth

The need to become a better person is a need we all have but many people overlook. They are so consumed with meeting their needs of the personality that they have little time to think about their personal growth let alone address it. People often believe that obtaining a university degree or specialized knowledge in a certain field will produce personal growth. These advancements are actually meeting their other needs like certainty, significance and connection. They are certain that a degree is the best way to ensure employment and income in the future. They achieve significance by graduating. They have companionship during the process.

The growth referred to in this need is personal growth, or becoming a better person. This is accomplished by learning who you are and what you need to do to become a better person to yourself, your relationships and the world around you. Personal growth is not doing something to meet another need. Another example of this is when a person takes a workshop and helps others around the office to get a promotion so they can rise up in the company and earn more money. In this case, there are two other needs being met, certainty and significance.

True growth is looking deep within yourself to see what kind of person you are and determining what kind of person you want to be. This is a difficult process as it is usually painful to do this properly and that is why most people do not do it. The fear of facing yourself can bring pain. It takes a strong commitment and desire to meet this important need.

There are many ways we can grow personally if we are doing it for the right reason. Studying to improve your knowledge and understanding of life is a valuable tool for personal growth. Learning and practising your faith is another excellent tool. Addressing your health, attitude and talents are all ways to grow personally. As you grow and become a better person, you start to feel better about yourself. You begin to like who you are and eventually become proud of who you are. Now you start to experience true happiness and fulfillment.

6. Contribution

It is when a person unselfishly gives of themselves to others that they start achieving their need to contribute. We all have a deep need to go beyond ourselves because we were created to contribute to the betterment and happiness of ourselves, those around us and the world in general. Contribution is when our motives are focused on the needs of others.

There are times in our lives when we help others under the guise of contribution. This is when our actions help someone else but we have an ulterior motive for our actions. We are using our kindness to meet one of our own personal needs. An example of this is providing a donation to a charity and receiving a lot of fanfare with it. The question you need to ask yourself is "am I doing this to help others or am I satisfying my need for significance?" The answer to this question is important for your own happiness and fulfillment. In most cases, there will be a split in your answer: some feeling of truly wanting to help and some satisfaction towards your need for significance. It is alright to satisfy some of your personal needs if they are not the main reason for the action.

In my work with prisoners, I used the following example to illustrate the difference. I would ask "how many of you do things for others because you know they will owe you and that may be handy in the future?" Most of them acknowledged that is the case most of the time. In their minds, they would only contribute when it would meet one or more of their own needs. I asked them how they felt about themselves in regards to this, and the majority responded they did not feel great but that it was necessary to survive.

I then asked them to think of a time when they helped someone just because they needed the help, such as a situation in which the person would not be in a position to repay the gift. I told them to dig deeply because we have all done it on occasion. After a moment, I asked them to think about how they felt while they were carrying it out. You would immediately see smiles come to their faces. They were experiencing the feelings of joy and pride for their unselfishness. That is the difference. True contribution brings about happy and healthy feelings whereas selfish giving results in guilt and unhealthy feelings. Saint Francis said, "It is in giving that we receive."

Contribution is not reserved only for others but we must also contribute to ourselves. Giving to others at the detriment to yourself is not healthy and is counterproductive. To help others, you must first help yourself and place yourself in a position to be able to contribute. A balance of contribution to one's own self as well as to others around you is the best way to realize the joy, happiness and fulfillment that people desire. By having a healthy amount of self-respect and vision, you will be in a position to feed your need of contribution and receive all the benefits that meeting this need provides you.

Meeting Your Personal Needs in a Healthy Way

Meeting your six personal needs in a healthy way is the key to achieving joy, happiness and fulfillment in your life. I have given you a brief explanation about these needs and how they interact in your daily life. Acknowledging their existence will help you to realize positive change in your life. What I ask you to do is to research and learn more about your personal needs, how they affect your life and how to satisfy them in your daily living.

In every decision you make, take the time to ask yourself "what needs am I meeting through this decision and is it healthy?" This one tool will help you make better decisions and help you to start feeling better about yourself as a person.

In any decision or action we commit to, we are doing it to meet one or more of our needs. As we get used to asking ourselves the question above, we will realize that we are addressing more than one need and in many cases these needs are conflicting with each other. This is good. By recognizing the fact we have more than one need involved and that there is conflict between them, we are in a position to prioritize our needs, which will help us make an empowering decision. To achieve happiness and fulfillment, you will want to meet as many of the six needs as possible.

To illustrate this, let's say you want to go out with your friends after work for a few drinks. Several of them had approached you and said you are the life of the party and they need you. Your spouse had asked you to come immediately home after work because she had dinner plans for both of you. You want to go out because you have not spent any time with your friends in a while. You call your spouse and ask her if you can go out with your friends, but she says she has prepared for the dinner party and says you can go out another night. You have to make a decision whether to go out or go home. What would you do?

Ask yourself "what needs will I be meeting by each decision and what conflict in needs will arise because of the decision?" If you go home, you will meet your need for love, significance, certainty, contribution and growth. Love will be met by showing your spouse that she is more important than your friends. Significance will be met because you are important to your spouse. Certainty will be met because you know your spouse will be happy with you and not upset that you chose to be with your friends. Contribution will be met by going home because you are unselfishly giving of yourself because you would have liked going out with friends.

Growth would be met because you were able to think of others first rather than yourself.

Going out with your friends would meet your needs of significance, certainty, companionship and uncertainty as follows: significance because your friends called you the life of the party; certainty because you know you will have a good time; uncertainty because you are not sure how your reception will be when you get home later; and companionship with you friends.

Can you see the conflicting needs in this decision? By breaking down the situation, you are able to review how each need will be met and the satisfaction you will receive towards each need. You are now in a position to prioritize each need and make an informed decision that will better meet your needs.

In the example above, either decision will leave some unmet needs. However, by examining the situation, you were able to justify your needs and meet the ones that were most important to you. At first, it will take effort and commitment to implement and use this needs tool. As you use it more and experience the results, it will become second nature. You will start to feel joy, happiness and fulfillment enter your life.

Personal Needs Exercise

Can you think of activities in your life that you love to do, that empower you and that you find effortless to do? It is probably because these activities are meeting all six of your needs in a tremendous way. If you want to experience joy happiness and fulfillment in your life, you need to start with awareness. This exercise is designed to help you become more aware of what needs are and how they can be met at the highest level. It is time to open your heart and mind. Thoughtfully complete the exercises below and get to know what your needs are and how fulfilling them will improve your daily life.

A. Find your needs that empower you.

1. Think of some activity that you love to do, something that you feel the need to do and seems effortless to you.

_____

_____

On a scale of 1 – 10, how much does this activity meet your need for:

Certainty	_____	Uncertainty	_____
Significance	_____	Love and Connection	_____
Growth	_____	Contribution	_____

How does this activity make you feel about yourself when you are doing it, when you are not doing it and in general?

_____

_____

2. Think of some activity that you hate to do, something that you try to avoid.

_____

_____

On a scale of 1 – 10, how much does this activity meet your need for:

Certainty	_____	Uncertainty	_____
Significance	_____	Love and Connection	_____
Growth	_____	Contribution	_____

How does this activity make you feel about yourself when you are doing it, when you are not doing it and in general?

How does this activity make you feel about yourself when you are doing it, when you are not doing it and in general?

_____

_____

Notice that you are meeting your needs when you do things you like to do as well as when you do the things you do not like to do. The lesson is to see what needs you are meeting when you are avoiding doing something because you don't like doing it and when you are doing something that has a negative impact on you. In the exercise below, you will learn how to use your needs to change a limiting behaviour or a decision into an enhancing one.

B. Change limiting behaviours and decisions into enhancing ones.

Write down some activity that you avoid and do not like doing, something that doesn't feel good but is good for you, good for others and serves the greater good.

_____

_____

Turn this limiting behaviour into an enhancing one by finding ways to meet all six needs at a higher level.

- **Certainty:** What could I do or believe to make thinking about this activity feel not only comfortable but pleasurable?

_____

_____

- **Uncertainty:** How could I bring more variety to this task?

_____

- **Significance:** How can I appreciate how important this is?

_____

_____

- **Love and Connection:** How can I feel more connected while doing this?

_____

_____

- **Growth and Contribution:** How can I use this to grow personally and contribute to others?

_____

_____

By using the above exercise, you have a tool to help you change a limiting behaviour into an enhancing one. You will have the ability to effect positive change into all areas of your life by taking control of your decisions and actions. If you truly want to have joy, happiness and fulfillment in your life, then start to use this tool on a daily basics. Use it for every serious decision you are making. It will be difficult at start, but as you grow and feel the results, it will become a natural part of your daily life.

Summary

We have explored the important role our needs play in deciding what we do and avoid doing in our lives. We are created to have all our needs met and will do whatever we can do to accomplish this. This explains why we sometimes do things that bring about negative consequences into our lives. The power to have our needs met when we are not aware of them or do not understand them fully has caused us to make many poor decisions in the past.

In this lesson, we have learned that if we become aware of our needs and how they are being met in each situation we face, we will be able to evaluate them and make the adjustments needed to make better and empowering decisions and life experiences. Start to use the tools I have presented to you today, and in a short time they will enhance your life and help you on the road to achieve your life dreams and desires.

CHAPTER TEN

Your Habits and Rituals

The repetitive force

"Repetition of the same thought or physical action
develops into a habit which, repeated frequently
enough, becomes an automatic reflex."
— **Norman Vincent Peale**

In This Chapter
  ➤ What Are Habits?
  ➤ How Habits Work
  ➤ Taking Control of Your Habits
  ➤ Habit Exercise
  ➤ Summary

Habits, whether good or bad, are an unavoidable part of life.
The habits we have formed over the years either empower us to
achieve positive outcomes in our lives or bring about negative
consequences to our health, progress and happiness. Our lives are
largely determined by factors we never fully notice: our habits,

those unthinking, automatic choices that surround us each day. They guide how we get dressed in the morning and fall asleep at night. They affect what we eat, how we do business and whether we exercise or have a beer after work.

Each of our habits has a different goal and offers a unique payoff. Some are simple and others are complex, drawing upon emotional triggers and offering subtle neurochemical prizes. But every habit, no matter its complexity, is flexible. The most addicted alcoholic can become sober. The most dysfunctional families can transform themselves. A high school dropout can become a successful executive.

Changing habits is not merely a matter of willpower, despite what you've probably learned. Sure, we all have habits we've tried to break and failed, and we've had good habits we've tried to acquire and dropped. But the real obstacle to change for most people is not a lack of determination—it's a lack of understanding how habit works.

As it happens, habits all get modified in somewhat the same way. When an individual successfully quits smoking or an organization changes collective behaviour to improve its safety standards, there are certain universal patterns at work. It is important that each of us discover what our habits are and the patterns that form them. We can then work toward eliminating our limiting habits and developing a strong set of empowering habits.

The first step is to learn what a habit is, how they are formed and what can be done to take control of the habits that are affecting our life. If you have a problem behaviour that you are ready to part with (and who doesn't), this chapter will help you discover how to use habits to improve your life and achieve the joy, happiness and fulfillment you desire and deserve.

What Are Habits?

Habits are routine behaviours done on a regular basis. They are recurrent and often unconscious patterns of behaviour and are acquired through frequent repetition. Many of these are unconscious, as we don't even realize we are doing them.

Merriam-Webster's online dictionary defines habits as:

1. An acquired mode of behaviour that has become nearly or completely involuntary
2. The prevailing disposition or character of a person's thoughts and feelings
3. A settled tendency or usual manner of behaviour
4. A behaviour pattern acquired by frequent repetition or physiologic exposure that shows itself in regularity or increased facility of performance

Habits define your character, your thoughts and feelings, and your "usual" behaviours. You can also see that habits are behaviours that are nearly or completely involuntary and because they are repeated frequently, they become stronger and more controlling.

A habit can also be an addiction. Some believe the term addiction should be reserved for describing a physical dependency on chemical substances such as alcohol and drugs. Other addictions include a range of compulsive behaviours such as gambling, eating, shopping, playing videogames, working and using the internet. This type of addiction is typically described as psychological addiction, a form of habit with a stronger reward influence.

How Habits Work

Habit formation is the process by which new behaviours become automatic. If you instinctively reach for a cigarette the moment you wake up in the morning, you have a habit. By the same token, if you feel inclined to lace up your running shoes and hit the streets as soon as you get home, you've acquired a habit.

Habits form when you engage in a behaviour repeatedly in the presence of consistent stimuli. They are "automatic" responses to familiar environmental cues. Countless studies have shown that habits are comprised of three main parts: an environmental stimulus, a behavioural response and a reward.

Stimulus → Routine → Reward

You develop habitual responses to familiar stimuli that you encounter on a regular basis. This stimulus can be a location, the time of day, your emotional state, a thought, people, a pattern of behaviour or anything that can trigger an emotional response. This stimulus triggers a habitual routine that has developed over time and whose intensity is determined by the amount of times it has been triggered in the past. This routine is composed of one or more actions or responses that your mind has associated to creating some kind of reward.

For example, if you're a smoker, your cravings are typically triggered by a stimulus that you associate with smoking, for instance, stress, driving, eating a big meal, drinking a beer or seeing another person smoking. In this example, the stimulus was seeing a friend smoking. The stimulus triggered them to pull out a cigarette, light it and take a long drag to inhale the smoke. This was to achieve the mental reward that the mind had conceived and the related physical reward that would be achieved by smoking a cigarette. The physical pleasure supports the mental reward. Some of the habits we have created over the years are clearly evident to us while others are hidden in our subconscious. All of our habits were created by information we gathered from many different sources, such as family, experiences, events or our imagination. Our habits are real in our mind, and we rarely question them, no matter how silly or unrealistic they may seem.

We've all heard the story of a mother who was visiting her daughter at a family reunion. In the evening while preparing dinner for the family, the mother cut the back quarter off the ham before placing it in the roasting pan. When the daughter questioned her mother about why she cut the piece off, the mother replied that was how her mother used to prepare the ham. Still baffled, the daughter ask why her mother did it to which the reply was "I am not sure." To find the answer, she called her grandmother and asked her. She replied, "I had to cut some of the ham off so it would fit into the pan. Back in those days, the ovens were not as large as they are today and we had smaller roasting pans."

The moral of the story is that the mother had learned a habit from her mother when she was young and continued to implement the habit without questioning it even though it no longer made sense. That is the power of habit.

Old habits can be difficult to break, and healthy habits are often harder to develop than one would like. That's because the behavioural patterns we repeat most often are etched into our neural pathways. The good news is that, through repetition, it's possible to form—and maintain—new habits. And even long-time habits that are detrimental to one's health, behaviour and well-being can be shaken with enough determination and a smart approach. Maybe it is time to start to question your own habits. Ask yourself "do they make sense and is the outcome desirable?"

Taking Control of Your Habits

Some habits form out of repetition and routine. Other habits form as a way of avoiding unwanted (but often necessary) activities. Whether you've decided to make personal change, to make a New Year's resolution or to change up your day-to-day routine, changing a habit can be the start of a meaningful personal transformation. As discussed earlier, a habit is a learned and repeated behaviour aimed at receiving a specific reward. Because a habit is the result of repeated behaviour, it is only reasonable to assume that to change a habit it will take newly learned repeated behaviour.

I have worked with many people over the years at successfully eliminating old detrimental habits and forming new enhancing ones. Many of these people had tried in vain over the years to eliminate the negative habits and corresponding results in their life. It's all too easy to fall short in the pursuit of behaviour change, whether the ultimate aim is to nix a disruptive habit or to establish a new one. Excuses, fatigue and the vagueness of our goals can spell doom for such endeavours.

One of the largest errors promoted and attempted by people is that you can make change merely by using your willpower to change your behaviour. The concept promoted is that if you want it bad enough and you focus on changing the behaviour with the use of willpower on a continual basis, you can overcome anything. This is very misleading. Some people have been able to use willpower to overcome minor habits but the more complex ones require more than just willpower. Using willpower alone to overcome complex negative habits or form lasting empowering ones is a path to failure. Willpower alone will not get the job done.

We all have a limited amount of willpower and will deplete it quickly. In 1998, psychologist Roy Baumeister made a startling discovery. People who were forced to exert willpower (in this case, resisting eating cookies placed in front of them) did worse on puzzles and problem-solving tasks than people who indulged themselves. Thinking that perhaps it was a fluke of five particularly hungry people, he and other psychologists ended up testing this over and over again across multiple scenarios and found the same thing: people who are forced to exert willpower and focus on one task are worse at exerting willpower and focus on subsequent tasks. Thus, our willpower is finite and can be drained. We each have a "fuel tank" of willpower that can be spent, and once we use it all up, we are far more prone to give up and indulge our whims, impulses and habits.

It is important to understand that willpower is still a major component in habit change. The good news is willpower is like a muscle. It can be exercised, practised and built up. Just like going to the gym and building up strength and endurance, you can build up your discipline and willpower over a long period of time by setting and accomplishing a series of tasks on a consistent basis. You can make your fuel tank bigger and bigger by draining it on a consistent basis. For there to be successful change, your willpower must be combined with other components to have a real possibility of success. What are these other components of change?

The first component is to change the component we are focusing on, the behaviour. Habit researchers have found that in order to create new habits (or break old habits), we should not focus on the behaviour but rather focus on the stimulus that triggers the behaviour. We spend so much time and effort on creating or eliminating the behaviour itself, when instead we should be dedicating our willpower to consciously creating or reorganizing the stimuli in our environment that trigger those habits.

For example, let's say you want to start working out on a regular basis. Instead of focusing on developing the habit of working out, focus on developing a routine around initiating a workout. This may seem like a subtle difference, but it's actually huge.

An easy way to do this is to choose a stimulus that already occurs regularly in your daily life, such as getting home from work. Then, during the early stages of developing your workout habit, focus your effort on going straight to your room after you get home and changing into your workout clothes. Then go fill up your water bottle and head straight to the gym or hit the running trail or whatever. You want to develop the habit of putting yourself in the position to work out regularly, which makes it more likely that you will work out regularly. After a while, you'll start to notice that when you get home from work (your environmental trigger), it takes little to no effort to go to your room, throw on your workout clothes and head to the gym (habitual response). You'll even start to look forward to it, and maybe even feel like something in your life is off when you don't work out. And that's the power of habit.

The "reward" component of the habit equation above is used to reinforce your target behaviour after you've successfully completed it. With our exercise example, you might get done working out and treat yourself to a healthy snack or maybe schedule a post-workout rest session by watching an episode of your favourite television show. Some people derive enough reward from the exercise itself (e.g., "runner's high"), which acts as powerful reinforcement for their habit. Whatever you do, be sure to incorporate a healthy reward into your habit routine.

In the above example, you saw how to initiate a new empowering habit. Let us now see how to use this process to eliminate or change an existing negative habit.

The first step to eliminating or changing an existing habit is that you need to understand the habit. Start by noting which specific stimuli are triggering your habits routine. Think of instances when your habit was in action and try to determine what was happening moments before it engaged. Where were you, what did you see or hear, what were you doing, how did you feel? Try to recall all the influences that could have triggered the habit. Just by recognizing and becoming aware of the stimuli that trigger your habit, you are beginning the process of change. By being aware that this stimulus triggers a habit, you will be able to recollect that it is a habit trigger each time you encounter it. This awareness will help you to stop the triggering process before the habit routine begins. This one step alone may provide all you require to eliminate your habit.

Another component to eliminating or changing a habit is to review the habits routine. Once you know how the routine is structured, you will be able to change it up by creating a new, more empowering routine or eliminate it altogether. The result is that your limiting habit has been converted to an enhancing habit or eliminated completely.

Finally, you can discover what the reward is that the habit provides you. Similar to the last step, the awareness you achieve will allow you to determine if the reward is real, perceived or even desired. Understanding the reward realized from anything we do allows us to change it or the routine required to achieve it.

In summary, we have discovered that to change or eliminate a habit you need to discover what stimulus triggers your habits and the meaning you associate to that stimulus. You can then associate a trigger that either avoids the old routine or one that runs a newly created empowering routine for it to follow. You have the ability to review a habit routine and its sequence. This will allow you to implement structural change to it and achieve a more positive result. By knowing the reward you receive from your habit, you have the ability to redefine what the reward means to you and an empowering way to achieve it.

Habit Exercise

The best way to understand how a concept works is by trying it. In this exercise, I would like you to work through recognizing, eliminating, changing and creating a habit. Follow the exercise and you will discover how simple it is to create change. I say simple but it is not necessarily easy or done in a short period of time. The effort and time needed are dependent on your willingness to change and the strength of the habit you desire to change.

1. Identify your negative or limiting habit.

List a habit you have that has been negatively affecting your life:

_____

_____

Describe the rewards you receive as a result of this habit:

_____

_____

What are the outcomes you are experiencing because of this belief?

_____

_____

How does this make you feel?

_____

_____

How would changing or eliminating this habit enhance your life?

_____

_____

2. Identify the stimulus that triggers your negative habit.

List any stimuli that you believe trigger this habit:

_____

_____

How obvious are they to you?

_____

_____

How often do they appear?

_____

_____

What do they trigger?

_____

_____

How could you stop these stimuli from triggering your habit routine?

_____

_____

3. Identify the routine that supports your habit.

Describe the routine in sequence that transpires when your habit is triggered:

_____

_____

How could you stop this routine from transpiring?

_____

_____

List changes you could make to the routine to change it from limiting to enhancing:

_____

_____

How would stopping or changing the routine make you feel?

_____

_____

4. Identify a new empowering habit.

Describe a new empowering habit you would like to have:

_____

_____

How would this new habit enhance your life?

_____

_____

Create a routine that this habit would require to be successful:

_____

_____

List the rewards having this habit would provide you:

_____

_____

Which stimuli could you incorporate to trigger this new habit?

_____

_____

If you thoroughly completed the exercises above you will have provided the awareness required to acknowledge your negative and limiting habits, the stimuli that trigger them, the routine they follow and the rewards or pain they provide. You will also have acknowledged new empowering habits that, if implemented, will enhance your life. I would like you to take this information and, using the tools described in this chapter, do the following:

- Identify and eliminate one negative habit.
- Change one limiting habit into an empowering one.
- Create and implement one new life-enhancing habit.

You now have the knowledge to take control of your personal life habits and commit yourself to following only empowering habits created by you on your own terms. No longer will you tolerate your subconscious or the outside world deciding which habits you will follow.

Summary

As we have learned above, our habits have a large impact on the way we live and experience our lives. If we take the time and effort required to identify our habits, both those that are evident and those that operate from our subconscious, we can develop the awareness required to implement positive change.

By learning the stimuli that trigger our habits, we can learn to control them or eliminate them altogether. In understanding the routine and sequence our habits follow as well as the perceived rewards we receive, we are in a position to implement corrective change and turn negative habits into ones that will enhance our lives. We now also have the ability to create new empowering habits that will help us to move towards achieving our dreams and desires.

CHAPTER ELEVEN

Your State and Focus

How you feel and what you see

"To me, true prosperity begins with feeling good about
yourself. It is also the freedom to do what you want
to do, when you want to do it. It is never an amount
of money; it is a state of mind. Prosperity or lack of it
is an outer expression of the ideas in your head."

— Louise Hay

- -

In This Chapter
 ➢ Your State of Mind
 ➢ Focus Is Power
 ➢ Changing Your Focus and State of Mind
 ➢ Cancel, Cancel, Cancel
 ➢ Summary

- -

Have you ever experienced an event when you were in a state of
pain and sorrow and out of nowhere you are suddenly laughing
and happy? Maybe you are at the funeral of a long-time friend

who had unexpectantly passed away. At the reception, you are with a group of close friends and wiping tears from your eyes when someone suddenly brings up a funny, memorable story about the departed friend. Suddenly, you are all laughing and high-fiving each other. You went from a place of pain and sorrow to laughter and happiness in a split second. What just happened?

You have changed the state you were in by changing your focus. The state you are in is how you are feeling and perceiving things at that moment. The decisions you make and how you act is influenced by that state. In the case above, you were in a state of loss and sadness because of the death of your friend. Your focus was on the perception that you lost a good friend and need to feel and act sad and sorrowful. Out of nowhere, you hear something that instantly redirected your focus and this caused a state change from one of loss and sadness to a state of joyful memories and happiness.

During each and every moment of our lives, we are in a state that is manipulated by our current perceptions, emotional feelings and focus. How we feel is directly proportional to how we perceive things and what we focus on. What we focus on and how we perceive things is influenced by how we are feeling. Our focus, perceptions and feelings all feed off each other, influencing our decisions and actions.

Understanding how to control the state you are in and what you focus on at any given moment is vital to our being able to make empowering decisions and achieve the joy, happiness and fulfillment we desire.

In this chapter, you will learn how this important dynamic in your life affects your overall decision-making and resulting life experiences. You will then be able to understand how they function and how you can better use them to enhance your life.

Your State of Mind

George, a sales manager at a car dealership, wakes up late, scrambles to get showered and dressed, has an argument with his teenage daughter over breakfast, then gets stuck in traffic on the way to work and realizes he will be late for his first meeting.

Sally, a marketing executive, wakes up at 6 a.m. and completes her daily spin on the exercise bike, takes a moment to stretch and relax, takes a relaxing shower, dresses, feeds her two kids before walking them to the bus, then catches the train to the office.

Which executive will have a more productive day at work? That depends on whether George—who's had the more difficult morning—is able to manage his state of mind.

Of all the things that impact human performance, your state of mind or mindset is one of the most important. We all have the power and ability to choose how we feel at any given moment. It is up to us to decide if we want to be happy or sad, in control or helpless. The state you are in will affect your behaviour and it influences what you say, the decisions you make, how you behave and even your heart beat, biochemistry and skin colour. The problem is most people allow their state of mind to function randomly.

Everyone tends to move in and out of various states of mind throughout the day. At times, you might experience a sad state and at other times happy states. States are sometimes referred to as moods, as when you are in the mood for some task or not in the mood. If you are a writer, you may notice that in some states writing is effortless and the words come with no work on your part. However, you may experience other states in which writing is a painful chore and nothing seems to flow.

Many of the things you want in life are states or are attained through the appropriate state. For example, self-confidence is a state. So too is creativity a state. Sometimes you want actual physical things, such as wealth along with the feelings and the benefits that wealth provides you.

We are all choosers and everyone can choose to be the master of their states or be the servant of them. Actually, you are always the master of your states, but some people create the belief in themselves that they can do nothing about their states.

States of mind are the product of mental events like what you see in your mind, what you say and hear in your mind, or what you feel in your mind. They are also the product of physical actions like posture, facial expressions or breathing. Outside influences have a large impact on the state you place yourself in.

Your state of mind or mindset is powerful and can lead you to great victories or down the path of failure and despair. Henry Ford once said, "Whether you think you can or think you can't—you're right." Your mindset, coupled with consistent action, is the key to achieving and sustaining success. The mind steers almost everything. Mahatma Gandhi once observed, "Your beliefs become your thoughts, your thoughts become your words, your words become your actions, your actions become your habits, your habits become your values, your values become your destiny."

Your mindset (thoughts, beliefs and expectations) are the lenses through which you perceive the world. And these lenses affect how you live and the choices you make every day. Your mindset is formed by a combined interaction of thoughts and corresponding emotions and images. The mindsets people adopt have everything to do with their judgment of anything. When you are constantly hearing and repeating stories about "the way things are," the narrative gets daily reinforcement.

Your state of mind or mindset is not any beliefs. It is composed of beliefs that position our reactions and tendencies. They serve a number of cognitive functions. They let us frame situations; they direct our attention to the most important cues, so that we're not overwhelmed with information. They suggest sensible goals so that we know what we should be trying to achieve. They prime us with reasonable courses of action so that we don't have to figure out what to do. When our mindsets become habitual, they define who we are and who we can become. William James said, "Believe that life is worth living and your belief will help create the fact." Your state of mind influences your body, and you cannot easily separate the interdependence of mind and body.

Think about it: when you get up in the morning and you're in a bad mood, worried about something going on in your life or feeling overwhelmed by work, that mood translates to your behaviour and overall performance. When you approach the day with positivity and purpose, everything changes. Your lenses or perceptions determine your response in any given situation.

When your emotions and thoughts are repeated regularly, a neural network is formed that regulates your mindset. That mindset develops a habit that becomes effortless over time. This explains how you can master a habit such as reading, writing, eating healthy, meditating or exercising. Your neural network has the habit in place after much practice and repetition. The more the same action is performed, the stronger your mindset becomes about that action.

Therefore, when you feel as if you are resistant to change, it is not that you are a weak individual; the strength of your neural network makes you feel as if you cannot change. However, you can change. If you are willing to change, then you are going to be able to change your mindset. What you believe affects what you achieve; once your mindset changes, everything on the outside will change along with it.

Your attitude and your perspectives are part conscious and part unconscious and can be learned, unlearned, programmed and reprogrammed in a variety of ways. A simple change of mind can help you become your best self. Mindsets affect your life expectancy. People with negative mindsets are less likely to proactively engage in healthy behaviours such as eating healthy, exercising or living in the moment. The mindsets you have developed over time have serious implications on how you live your life. If you are constantly thinking about everything wrong with your life, you are more likely to be stressed than people who choose to focus on the bright side of life. One mindset can flood your system with stress hormones and make you anxious all the time. Another can make you feel confident, happy and cheerful.

It's not what happens to you, but how you react to it that matters. As we go through life, we pick up beliefs that help us navigate the world. These beliefs have very real consequences for our psychology, physiology, behaviour and performance. It's up to you to choose your responses in life carefully. You have much more power than ever believed to influence your physical and mental realities.

Your mindset is not fixed. The idea that change is difficult is simply a mindset. Your mindset is recognized by your body—right down to the genetic level, and the more you improve your mental habits, the more beneficial response you'll get from your body.

You can't control what has happened in the past, which shaped the brain you have today, programmed your cells and caused certain genes to switch on. However, you do have the power today—right now and going forward—to choose your mindset, perspective and behaviour, which will change your brain, cells and genes.

Be bold and willing, and you can change your mindset and your life. By using your personal power of responsibility and choice, you can change your state in an instant allowing, you to improve how you respond to every situation in life and work.

Focus Is Power

Your focus determines your reality. Remember the story I told in Chapter Eight about my experience playing craps? What happened when the dice went off the table during a roll? As soon as it happened, I shifted my focus from everything else that was happening to my belief that the next throw was going to be a seven. When a seven did come up, it supported my belief that it happened all the time. My focus now shifted to the frustration and distress it caused and that would negativity affect my game until something changed my focus. When an event happened such as a sudden long profitable roll, my focus would be shifted to the sudden winning streak and the positive feelings that went with it. This all happened in a moment and I would change my whole demeanour without a single conscious thought.

Our focus is something we don't think about much of the time, but let us now give it some consideration. Have you ever woken up in the morning and started to think about the miserable items you need to do later in the day that you do not want to do? How did your day go? I can predict that you probably had a miserable day. Now imagine if you woke up and focused instead on what a wonderful gift your life is. You said to yourself, "What a beautiful day! I am ready to conquer anything that comes my way." How would your day go now? I bet you'll have a great day and accomplish many things.

If we let our attention jump from one thing to another, we will have a busy, fractured and probably unproductive day. If we focus entirely on one job at a time, we may lose ourselves in that job, and it will not only be the most productive thing we do all day but be enjoyable. If we focus on being tired and wanting to relax in front of the television, we will get a lot of television watching done. However, if we focus on being healthy and fit, we will become healthy and fit through exercise and good eating.

This may seem simplistic, but it's completely true. This is the magical power of focus. Let's look at some of the ways you can use focus to improve different aspects of your life. Let's start by focusing on a goal. In my experience, focus is the most important determination of whether you'll achieve a goal or stick to creating a new habit. Not self-discipline, not rewards, not sheer willpower, not even motivation (also an important ingredient, however) will work as well as focus. If you can maintain your focus on a goal or habit, you will more often than not achieve that goal or create that habit.

If you can't maintain your focus, you won't achieve the goal, unless it's such an easy goal that it would have happened anyway. It's that simple. Why does focus matter so much? Let's say you decide you want to declutter your house — that's your goal for this month. On the first day, you're completely focused on this goal, and you fill up boxes and trash bags with junk. The second day, you're still focused, and you fill up a bunch more boxes and you've cleared most of two rooms with progress on another. This goes on for a few more days, with your focus being on this goal, and you make lots of progress.

However, let's say that a week into your decluttering, you decide you want to become a runner. You are now focused on running, and not only do you go out to jog for a few days, but you buy running clothes and a Fitbit and start to read running blogs and magazines. However, you've lost your focus on decluttering, and soon you aren't doing much of it. This is because your focus has now shifted to running. In fact, you've even added more clutter because you've bought all the running equipment, magazines and books.

If you had maintained your focus on decluttering the entire month, by the end of the month you would have achieved a nice, simplified house all through focus. This is why I am constantly advocating focusing on only one goal at a time. Having multiple goals spreads out your focus and makes it less likely that you'll complete any of the goals. It's possible, but with a diffused focus, it's much more difficult.

Even with only one goal, maintaining focus can be difficult. You need to find ways to keep your focus on that goal. Some examples to help you are to read about your goal as much as possible or create a vision board, like I mentioned in Chapter Three. You could post your goal and photos on your wall, refrigerator and computer desktop. Send yourself reminders using an online calendar or reminder service. Tell as many people as possible about your goal and post your progress on social media. Set a time each day to work on your goal, with a reminder in your schedule. Maintain your focus on your goal, and you've won half the battle in achieving it.

You must always focus on the now because focusing on the present helps reduce stress, increases enjoyment of life and increases your effectiveness. Focusing on now, rather than the past ("I can't believe they said that to me!") or the future ("what am I going to say in the meeting today?"), isn't easy and takes a lot of practice. I suggest you read *The Power of Focus* by Jack Canfield, Mark Victor Hansen and Les Hewitt. This book can change your life, if you follow the suggestions in it. It helped me better understand the power of focus and improve my life.

By focusing on the task at hand, you will develop a hidden strength that will not only motivate you but produce insights that you were unaware of. Have you ever completely lost yourself in a task, so that the world around you disappears? You lose track of time and are completely caught up in what you're doing. Ideas are coming from everywhere. That's the popular concept of flow, and it's an important ingredient to finding happiness. Having work and leisure that gets you in this state of flow will almost undoubtedly lead to happiness. People find greatest enjoyment not when they're passively mindless but when they're absorbed in a mindful challenge.

How do you get into flow? It takes a bit of practice, but the first step is to find things to focus on that you're passionate about. Seriously, this is an extremely important step. Find hobbies that you're passionate about. Turn off the television—this is the opposite of flow—and get outside and do something that truly engages you. Next, you need to clear away distractions and focus completely on the task you set before yourself. This is the part that takes a lot of practice.

Always focus on the positive. One of the key skills I've learned is how to be aware of my negative thoughts and to replace them with positive thoughts. I learned this through quitting smoking and goal setting. There are many times when you feel like giving up, and if you don't catch these negative thoughts in time, they'll fester and grow until you actually do give up.

This is how you can change your state and mindset in a moment. Instead of allowing a negative state to manipulate you, learn to focus on changing your thoughts to something that is positive. Think about how great you feel. Think about examples of how other people have done it and start telling yourself that you can too. Think about how good it will feel when you accomplish what you're trying to do. This change in focus will change your life. Also learn to see the positive in just about any situation as this results in happiness. In my experience, if you don't focus on the bad parts of your life, you will not feel them as much. But if you focus on the good things, you will attract more goodness into your life. Always be thankful for what you've received.

Changing Your Focus and State of Mind

How To Change Your Focus

Changing your focus is a skill you can use to improve your results in any situation. When you're up against a wall, life has got you down or you're facing the unexpected, you need a way to change your focus. Asking yourself the right questions is the solution. It works because thinking is just asking and answering questions. If you ask yourself better questions, you get better answers. If you want to change your focus, change the questions you ask yourself.

By changing the questions, you change your focus, which improves your results. If you tell yourself to focus on something else, that doesn't work. In fact, the more you tell yourself not to focus on something, the more you end up focusing on it. Instead, you can put your brain into a fully resourceful state simply by asking the right questions. Your brain is great at solving problems, but you need to ask the right way. You'll also find that as you improve the questions you ask yourself, you'll improve your energy.

Here are some techniques that will help guide you to use questions as a tool to control your focus:

- First, you can ask questions instead of make statements. Don't tell yourself what to focus on. Instead, ask questions. For example, instead of telling yourself, "don't focus on the layoffs" ask "am I prepared if there are layoffs and if not what's the best thing I can do today to prepare myself?"

- You should always ask "how" questions over "why" questions. For example, don't ask yourself "why am I always late?" Ask yourself "what can I do to make sure I am on time from now on?"

- Always focus on what you want, not what you don't want. When you are driving and sliding on the ice, don't look at the tree and think "I don't want to hit the tree." Instead, look at where you want to go and say to yourself "stay on the road." Most people focus directly on the tree they do not want to hit and drive right into it because it was what their mind was focusing on.

- Focus on the future not the past. The past is about blame or justification. You cannot change the past but only learn from it. The present is about values. The future is about opportunity. For example, ask yourself "how can I make the most of this situation?" or "what's my next best move?"

- If it's not working, change the questions. Little tweaks to your questions produce amazing results. For example, "what do I want to do?" is an entirely different question than "what do I want to accomplish?" One can get you stuck, the other can get you out.

- Use questions to change your emotions. Which feels better: asking yourself about the worst part of your day or asking yourself about the favourite part of your day?

Here is a starter set of questions to help you change your focus and make the most of what you've got:

- What do I want to accomplish?
- What's my next best move?
- How can I make the most of this situation?
- How can I solve this? If I knew how to solve this, what might I do?
- Who can I learn from?
- Who can I team up with?
- What's unique that I can bring to the table?
- What's the ideal solution? What's the minimum solution?
- What would good look like?
- What can I learn from this?

As you can see, asking questions can help switch your focus to a more positive and empowering idea. You can use this same process to change your state or the mindset you are in.

How To Change Your State of Mind

You can instantly shift your state of mind by taking the following these four actions:

1. Shift your mental focus. As introduced above, this is where it starts. You have the ability to choose what you think about. For example, you can think, "Argh, I have to write again today." Or you can think, "Wow, by writing today I am one step closer to completing my new book." This tool is so important that I have literally created a mental script that I recite before I begin to write. Here's what I say to myself to prime the pump:

* "I am not here by accident. God sent me. To these people. At exactly this time.
* That's because He has a purpose; therefore, I have a purpose in being here.
* Through Christ, I can do all things. He has given me every resource I need to succeed.
* I have the energy, the passion and the message to make a huge impact—now and for eternity.
* What I have to share today is vitally important. It matters. To them and to their loved ones.
* Those that read it will be changed forever. Years from now, they will look back on today and say, 'It started here.'
* By God's grace, I am prepared. I am strong. I am energetic. I am outstanding. My heart is wide open. I will connect and make a difference!"

2. Change your posture. Do you know that every emotion has physical attributes? For example, if I say to you "act like you are depressed," you would likely slump your shoulders, tilt your head down and rub your face. You would frown and your breathing might slow down.

If I say to you "act like you won the lottery," you would likely jump up and down, thrust your arms up into the air and scream with joy. You would smile and your breathing might speed up.

Does the emotion cause the action or does the action cause the emotion? The truth is, it doesn't matter. For example, if you smile and hold it for several seconds, it will change your biochemistry. In an article published in the *Journal of Personality and Social Psychology*, a team of psychologists at Clark University in Worcester, Massachusetts, showed that simply having people put their facial muscles in a configuration typical of a given emotion produced the feeling that the expressions represent. (See this article in the *New York Times* and this one in *Scientific American*.)

3. Watch your language. Our words are more important than we think. They reflect our thinking, but they sometimes influence our thinking as well. Words have tremendous power. But rarely do we apply these words to the language we use in talking to ourselves. For example, you ask someone, "How are you doing?" They respond, "Well, I'm surviving." Strangely, those words shape their reality—or at least their perception of it. They end up barely getting by.

Conversely, I always reply, "Fantastic!" This shapes my reality. I always seem to be doing well. I know I have challenges, but these words empower me and give me the hope and resources I need to overcome them. When I hear myself say "fantastic," I start to believe it and feel energized.

4. Change your environment. Your location and what is going on around you at the moment can affect your state. From busy city streets to pockets of nature, quiet residential living to crowded multifamily complexes, or addict and criminal gatherings to church picnics, the environment around us shapes our feelings but also the decisions we make and the actions we take.

If you are in a negative environment, it is likely to influence your state. If you are a recovering addict and you attend a party where people are openly using drugs, you will be tempted. No matter how strong you think your willpower and determination are, your environment is steering you into a state of desire to join the others. Change your environment and leave, and your state will also change.

Honestly, this formula works for me every time—almost like a recipe. If I am deliberate about taking these four actions, my emotional state shifts. The good news is that this puts me—and you—in control. And often this spells the difference between success and failure. Have your doubts? Take the seven-day challenge. Try this for seven days and see if it doesn't make a difference.

Cancel, Cancel, Cancel

Many times throughout the day, we find ourselves entering a negative state because of outside stimuli that influence our decisions and actions. You may be driving along and out of nowhere a car cuts you off. This unprovoked event is the stimulus that triggers a frustrated and upset state or mindset. "How dare they do that to me? What a jerk they are." These are a few of the ideas entering your mind. They grow until you work yourself into a revengeful state and take off after them to express your frustration. Most of this is done unconsciously and in an instant. Suddenly, you are in a negative revengeful state that could lead to serious consequences for yourself or someone else.

What if you had the power to stop this process at the beginning before your subconscious takes control of you? I am happy to inform you that you do have this power if you choose to use it. It is called interrupting your state, changing your focus and creating an empowering solution in a moment. The technique is to use a tool to interrupt the state-changing process before it begins to manifest and take control. It is a tool I call Cancel, Cancel, Cancel.

The first step in this powerful tool is to become aware of an area in your life that you fall prey to negative state change. In the above example, the negative state change was triggered by the stimulus of another driver doing something that was considered wrong or offensive by the person. Most of our past negative state changes have stimuli that we can define and recall if we put our mind to it.

Once you become aware of the stimulus that triggers your negative state change, you must admit to yourself that this has happened in the past and that you are susceptible to it happening again in the future. Once you have acknowledged the stimulus and how your state change functions, you will be able to identify it in the future when it appears. As soon as you consciously realize that a negative state change has been triggered, you can interrupt it and stop it dead in its tracks.

To accomplish this, you need to say or do something that will interrupt the process and change your focus. By changing your focus to awareness and away from unconsciously forming a negative state, you are now able to consciously focus on creating an empowering state.

This is when the words "Cancel, Cancel, Cancel" come in. These three words are a tool I have learned to use and have found effective in changing my focus and breaking my state changes. By blurting out "Cancel, Cancel, Cancel," I quickly stop what I am thinking about in its tracks and become fully aware of what is transpiring. I am then able to refocus and stop the negative questions and begin asking new empowering ones. My focus is now changed, and I can begin to resolve my feelings of frustration in a satisfying manner.

It is the sudden change of focus that allows me to change the information my mind is considering and positively resolve, the feelings that were triggered. This may sound too simple of an idea to work. We have been taught that change is not easy and is complicated. Let me assure you, this is not the case.

The tool I have just given you to change your focus is as simple as I described it. I have been using it for years and continue to use it today. I ask you to give it a try on a negative state change in your life that you are aware happens quite often, one that leads you to produce negative decisions or actions. As soon as you notice you are falling victim to a negative state change, yell out "Cancel, Cancel, Cancel" until it interrupts the pattern and changes your focus enough to formulate an empowering solution to the situation. You will immediately start to experience the feeling of accomplishment and relief as you undergo this process.

Summary

One of the best ways to have a good day is to open your eyes in the morning and say aloud, "Thank you, Lord, for another glorious day. Show me how I can share my blessings and happiness with the world today." Then clap your hands together, get up, look at yourself in the mirror and say to yourself "today is going to be a great day" three times aloud. This all may feel a little silly at first, but when you begin to experience the positive results it will produce in your life, you will become convinced.

What we focus on and the state we place ourselves in when we get up are critical to give us the confidence and desire we require to overcome any obstacle we encounter and to provoke in us an optimistic and energetic presence throughout the day.

Only you have the power to choose what to focus on and what state you will approach the day from. There may be many outside forces trying to take control of your focus and state but only you have the power to choose whether to let them or not. Even when bad things happen to us through no fault of our own, we have the power and ability to decide what it means to us, how we will feel about it and what we will do. How we approach and attend to our focus and state will determine whether we have a successful and happy day, merely survive the day or experience a day of failure and sorrow. It is up to you—choose well, my friend.

CHAPTER TWELVE

Your Environment

The influencing force

"You are a product of your environment. So choose the environment that will best develop you toward your objective. Analyze your life in terms of its environment. Are the things around you helping you toward success - or are they holding you back?"
— **W. Clement Stone**

- -

In This Chapter
- ➤ What Is Your Environment?
- ➤ How Your Environment Impacts Your Life
- ➤ Managing Your Personal Environment
- ➤ Change Starts with You
- ➤ Environment Exercise
- ➤ Summary

- -

One of the biggest influences we have in our lives is the environment we surround ourselves in. The relationships we have, the community we live in, our daily employment, the faith we celebrate, the hobbies we choose and the culture we identify with all influence our decisions and behaviours.

Every day, we face several options. They bombard us from when to get out of bed to what we should do next. A great deal of this happens subconsciously. We are unaware of the decisions and choices we are making that will directly affect our day and life journey. Some of these choices are tough. Others require patience and dedication. And then, there are the tempting choices that we try to resist. They can creep up on us when we don't realize it. By the time we do, it's too late. Like any other cautionary tale, we end up falling prey to certain choices because of the environmental cues around us.

Environmental cues are the people, objects, beliefs, practices and events in our surroundings that trigger certain thoughts and desires, causing us to behave in certain ways. Your decisions are largely influenced by what's around you. Here are some examples:

- The people around the office like to gossip, and you get caught up with them by saying things you know are not true and will hurt them if they get out.
- The plates you use for dinner are large, so you tend to fill them up with more food than you need.
- A community you are in promotes destructive ideas you do not agree with, but you go along with them by justifying to yourself it's not all that bad.
- Your friends like to party, overindulging in drugs and alcohol, and you follow suit.

Even when you set out with the best of intentions, it's no use if your environment dictates otherwise. We look around ourselves at other people, objects and the way our environment is set up to determine how we should act. They serve as reference guides for us on how we should act and respond.

Making changes to your environment makes it easier to do what's right without having to think about staying motivated. If you set up your surroundings so that making the best decisions comes easily, then you can set yourself up to make better decisions and to practise better habits.

In this chapter, I will discuss what our environment is, how it affects us and how we can make empowering changes to our personal environment that will guide and support us towards achieving our dreams and desires.

What Is Your Environment?

How would you describe your environment? When we hear the word "environment," most of us immediately think in terms of the Earth or nature, but what we're going to focus on now is your personal environment. Your personal environment consists of everything and everyone you come in contact with each day, your physical as well as social surroundings, the relationships, sights, sounds, smells and even the words you use on a consistent basis.

To a large extent, it is true that you are a product of your environment because different types of surroundings affect your behaviour and overall life satisfaction in a very real way. Our quality of life depends on our surroundings. The people we encounter throughout the day and the environment around us have a great deal of impact on our feelings and perspective. It can positively or negatively influence a person's well-being.

Whether you realize it or not, the company you keep plays a huge role in who you are. Think about any period in your life when you were introduced to a totally new crowd, for example, when you transferred schools, joined a club or moved to a different city. Didn't you adopt the new environment's slang, mannerisms, popular way of dressing, even their perceptions of various issues?

It is much easier to be influenced by your environment as a child, but do not assume that as an adult you are impervious, because I assure you that you are not. Spend enough time in any crowd and you are bound to pick up a trait, a habit, and a point of view or two. Coupled with your own thoughts, habits and mannerisms, what you pick up from the people around you integrates to determine who you become, what character you have, what thoughts you have and what perceptions you have of the world.

You may argue that you are a conscious, intelligent and self-aware individual who is not easily swayed by the crowd, and this may all be true. But if you are constantly in an environment where you are surrounded by pessimistic, fear-based people, it is bound to impact your own confidence in yourself and the possibility of your dreams, thereby slowing your progression.

However, if you surround yourself with confident, optimistic and insanely ambitious people, you are bound to pick up on their confidence, which will influence you to fiercely believe in the possibility of your own visions and follow them to the end.

It is quite simple: if you are spending time with people who are holding you back, you will lag behind. If you are spending time with people who are fuelling the fire in your soul, you will thrive. It's simple mathematics, so to speak.

Think about how your own mood can be impacted by a salesclerk who smiles and is helpful and kind versus one who is rude and unhelpful. In one case, the clerk's happiness creates a positive connection between you, while the other experience may leave you feeling frustrated or even angry. In both cases, a complete stranger's attitudes influenced your own and you may, in turn, pass that attitude along to others either through your good mood or your irritation.

Each day has 24 hours and of the 24, we spend an average of 10 hours with other people, and in most cases (unless you're travelling), you spend time with the same people. In the hours you spend with others, most of it is spent engaging one another in conversation. Through these conversations, you will pick up schools of thought, perceptions, character traits and even simple habits such as hand gestures, voice intonations or body postures.

This may all sound so harmless, and you may be thinking that your own character is strong enough to repel such subtle influences, but observational learning has been defined to be a mode of learning where you learn through observing others. While you may not notice it, you may take a similar posture to your best friend's.

If your best friend is a confident person, you will find yourself being more confident whenever you take up their posture. If your friend is not confident, you will find yourself feeling less confident whenever you take up their posture.

Whether it is apparent to you or not, who you are as a person drifts towards the direction of the people you spend the most time with because all important traits are contagious—your beliefs, values, mood, attitude, mannerisms and habits—and they begin to change. Your desire to be liked and belong help fuel this process. We all have a fear of rejection and will do almost anything to avoid this fear becoming a reality. You become exactly what you surround yourself with. It is a human inevitability that you will be influenced by your surroundings, which is why it is important to choose who you surround yourself with very carefully.

As a prison chaplain, I have witnessed hundreds of prisoners completely change their personality and beliefs to fit into the environment. The gangs and prison culture have transformed addicts, who would have never committed a crime if they did not need to feed their addiction, into career criminals with little regard for others.

Creating a positive and empowering environment around you is fundamental for you to start thriving and being happier, more focused and relaxed. It is a fact that our environment can affect our mood, our productivity and our creativity. Positive surroundings make us happier, more creative and productive. They give you the hope and motivation to engage and follow through with the tasks required to create positive and lasting change.

It is essential that we surround ourselves with positive energy and positive people. Maintain an environment that keeps you upbeat and positive. Everywhere you go, you will meet people who can lift you or drop you. Therefore, every individual must make a conscious effort to protect their personal space from negative energy, as energy is contagious. Don't expect positive changes in your life if your personal environment is filled with complainers, vicious people, constant negativity, highly critical people or anything that disrupts your peace of mind.

How Your Environment Impacts Your Life

The environment we live, socialize and work in has interesting ways of encouraging (or discouraging) and enabling (or dis-enabling) our behaviours. Given that our individual and collective behaviours create the results we achieve, it is critical that we explore the impact our work, social, community and home environments are having on us. If we want to improve the results we're getting and the direction our life is moving, we know we need to change what we're doing (our behaviour), and one powerful source of influence that can help us do that is our environment.

Here's how outside environmental influences can affect your decisions and behaviour:

1. Influence your mood
- » For some people, siting in the dentist's waiting room can cause such anxiety that they develop a headache or nausea.
- » Watching your team either win or lose the championship game can leave you in a state of elation or somber disappointment and loss.

2. Impact your behaviour and motivation to act

» Ad agencies design clever ways to connect the fulfillment of our needs and desires to the consumption of their product. Many manufacturers will promote their product using male and female models portraying themes of enhancing sexual attractiveness and attainment.

» Often the people you are with decide to do something you do not really want to do, but you do it anyway to go along with the crowd.

» When describing a goal you would like to pursue, others say you cannot do it. You question your ability and drop the idea, leaving your desire as a past dream.

3. Facilitate or discourage your interactions with others

» Your family and friends shun someone, thus encouraging you to avoid them.

» You are told that you are not worthy or good enough to meet someone.

» You boycott a business against your will because of peer pressure.

4. Create or reduce stress and self-confidence

» Agreeing to go somewhere or do something that makes you uncomfortable will cause stress.

» A competitive or confrontational atmosphere at work or a group you participate in may make you feel uncomfortable. A co-ordinated team working together can help build your self-confidence.

» Being involved with a group that is focused on and helping others in need can reduce stress and build self-confidence.

» Family turmoil can create personal stress.

You can evaluate and control your environment so that it serves you and becomes a partner in your success. In the previous chapter, I discussed using your mindset to improve your performance.

There is no denying that there is a "head game" that is important in propelling us toward whatever transformation or goal we are pursuing. What goes on in your head absolutely affects how you act and behave as well as your moods. It affects your path in daily life and how you interact with others. It affects your ability to fight off difficulties on your path to success. There is a lot of science behind how your environment can influence changes in your thinking and affect how you act and feel and ultimately the quality of your day-to-day life.

What is often missing in the "change your mindset" conversation is that environment predicts much of our behaviour. By changing our environment, we can support other changes that we are trying to make, allowing those changes to be attained far easier. Often the challenges of a particular change can be greatly improved by making sure that we set up an external environment to support the change in behaviour and change in mindset that we are working on achieving.

I recently worked with a client wanting to make one environmental change by clearing everything out of his office that reminded him of his partner's business failure and the pain it caused his family. The problem was that every time he went in the office and saw her old files, it distracted him from his goal of working on his own business needs. His mind would change focus from his objective to her problems. He would become frustrated that he could not solve her problem and became stressed. This would strip away any motivation he had for doing his job.

My suggestion was to remove anything that reminded him of her or her business from the office and to write out his goals and objectives and place them where he would see them as soon as he entered the office. This was to stop him from losing focus and thinking about her problems when he entered. I instructed him to discuss her concerns and needs anytime except when he was in his office. At first, he didn't think it was possible. It took some encouragement from me and some exploration on his part. But he committed to the change and did it. He was now aware that if there was any reminder of the situation in sight, he'd be distracted by it. It would grab his focus and interrupt his work. Once he set up his environment to support his focus on important work and keep the distractions at bay, he was able to do what he knew he needed to be successful.

There are many areas in our lives in which our environment is negatively influencing our decisions and actions. It is incumbent upon us as individuals to investigate which of our environmental influences are limiting and which ones are enhancing our lives. Only then will we be in a position to implement the changes required to create an environment that focuses on and supports our dreams and desires.

Managing Your Personal Environment

There are four areas of your personal environment that influence your life decisions and actions. They are the people you interact with, the community you live in, the way you earn a living and the community groups you are a part of. We will discuss all four below.

The People You Interact With

What is your personal environment like? Are there people around who make you feel negative, drained, annoyed or depressed? This includes family, friends, co-workers, group members and acquaintances. Does anyone ask you to do things they know you shouldn't and could cause you negative consequences? Then, it is the best to avoid them, ignore them or even better delete them from your personal space, if possible.

Implementing constructive change into your life can and will be challenging. You need to surround yourself with positive and supporting people. There are five types of people that you should have in your life:

People who inspire you: Inspiration gives you great confidence and improves your morale because the person who is inspiring you has successfully achieved something that probably you wish to accomplish. Inspiration works as an example: if that person has achieved a goal, then why can't I? These people can give you the fuel you require when things are not going well. You can use their example to help you overcome any obstacle you encounter.

People who motivate you: There are many people out there who want to see you succeed. They are always willing to support and encourage you. Always positive, they help encourage you to keep going when you may not feel like it. No matter what you have done, they shift your focus towards your goal. They help you create ideas to overcome perceived or real obstacles along the way. They highlight your success along the way. When you are down, feeling dejected, facing fear or unsure of your ability to do it, they are there to help you. Their push will get you over the moment and back on track.

Open-minded people: Having open-minded people around you will give you the ability to say what you think. You won't feel judged every time you see them. They will help you to look at the situation from all angles. They will understand things from your perspective and will not try to force you to accept their own rigid views. Open-minded people will help you find a solution that is best for you.

Passionate people: When you associate with passionate people, their passion can wear off on you. Passion is an important trait to have in your life. It is passion that leads to fulfillment. Learning how to live with passion is a key to success and happiness. When you surround yourself with passionate people, you are sure to become passionate about your life. Their passion is also a great motivator.

Grateful people: Grateful people think about the world in a more positive way. Grateful people will help you to focus on the good in things in your life and eliminate the negative thoughts that affect your decisions and actions. Seeing how grateful others are in time of struggle is a powerful tool to help you survive your time of struggle and disappointment. Their influence in your life will help you keep focused on what you have achieved and are striving for when things go wrong. This will give you the power to keep moving forward and becoming grateful that you overcame the setback.

If you can find and include people with one or more of these five traits in your life, you are on your way to success. It is a tough, negative world out there. If all the people around you are struggling, negative people, then you are sure to struggle and become negative yourself. Give yourself the best opportunity to succeed by replacing the negative people in your life with people who care about you and your happiness and will work at helping you achieving it. The best way to start surrounding yourself with these types of people is to seek out and find mentors who can guide you. We will discuss mentorship in Section Three of this book.

The Community You Live In

Does the community you live in provide the atmosphere and support required to achieve your goals? If not, you may want to make a move. Your surroundings and the people in it can definitely affect your mood, your decisions, your performance and your behaviour. You need to honestly look at your surroundings and the people in it. Learning how your community is currently affecting your life is vital. If it is not enhancing you, it is limiting you.

The realtors have it right: location, location, location. The location of where you live is incredibly important when it comes to personal health and happiness. Though it is entirely possible to craft a happy and healthy lifestyle no matter where you live, it seems that certain communities inspire their members while others limit them.

Some ways your community can influence you include:

Pressures from the community may restrict you to doing jobs you may not like in order to meet societal expectations of success, status, financial stability, gender roles, etc.

People in the community are committing morally wrong, abusive and criminal acts in the streets. We are never born perfect and each of us has stains. However, due to fear of ostracism, punishment or injury, we ignore or do things that we know are wrong and destructive.

Our community limits our behaviours, as we fear being judged. For instance, we don't hug others in public for fear of being accused of something sinister.

Our community can cause us to lie. In order to meet society's expectations and feel dignified or proud in society, some people lie about their achievements.

Community can cause people to fear exposing their character in public. Some homosexuals are afraid to come out for fear of condemnation.

The only people available to form a relationship with are morally corrupt, are lost themselves and will detract you from pursuing happiness and success rather than encourage and support you.

Each person is born into a social and cultural setting—family, community, social class, language, religion—and eventually develops many social connections. The characteristics of a child's social setting affect how they learn to think and behave by means of instruction, rewards and punishment. This setting includes home, school, neighbourhood, and local political, religious and law enforcement policies.

Then, there are also the child's mostly informal interactions with friends, other peers, relatives, and the entertainment and news media. How individuals will respond to all these influences, or even which influence will be the most potent, tends not to be predictable. However, there is substantial similarity in how individuals respond to the same pattern of influences—that is, to being raised in the same culture. Furthermore, culturally induced behaviour patterns, such as speech patterns, body language and forms of humour, become so deeply imbedded in the human mind that they often operate without the individuals themselves being fully aware of them.

Community influences one's behaviour through old and new ideas or external pressure (mob rule) accepted by the majority or by everybody within that community. If your community is influencing and limiting you from positive growth and becoming the best person you can, then change is required.

What you do to make your external environment better support you is a skill you can and must learn. In many cases, people feel trapped where they reside. They feel helpless, believing they have no choice and could not move if they wanted to. This is not true. The only person who has control of you is you. There may be external factors in play and changing surroundings may seem impossible at the time, but if you truly want to, you can devise and implement a plan and the resources required to achieve it.

<u>The Way You Earn a Living</u>

Whether you work for someone else or have your own business, you interact with people, policies and external influences daily. Most people will work an average of 65,000 hours in their lifetime. Being in a positive and supporting environment is the key to living a happy, productive and fulfilling life. If you are unhappy in your job, you will be less likely to perform well and it will negativity affect all areas of your personal life.

All jobs have some level of stress, even on good days. However, if going to work (or just the thought of going to work) makes you tired, depressed or even physically ill, that's more than just general work stress; these are the signs of a toxic work environment. A toxic workplace can be defined as any job where the work, the atmosphere, the people or any combination of those things cause serious disruptions in the rest of your life. Listed below are some solid indicators of a toxic work environment:

- **Employee sickness:** Toxic workplaces lead to employee burnout, fatigue and illness due to high levels of stress that wreak havoc on our bodies. If people are calling in sick or, worse, are working sick, that's a good sign of a toxic work environment.

- **Egotistic leadership:** Your higher-ups demand that you always agree with them, tell them they're right and feel they're above the rules. They expect everyone else to be perfect while they can meet lower standards.

- **Little to no enthusiasm:** Look around the office. Is anyone happy to be working there? Are people smiling? Are conversations positive and upbeat? Is anyone talking at all? A "no" to these questions equals toxicity.

- **Lack of communication or negative communication:** You and others don't get the necessary information to do your job. You work hard with no positive feedback and no recognition, and you might even be told to be glad you have a job at all.

- **High turnover:** When the work environment has nothing good to offer except dysfunction, poor morale and sickness, people will start heading for the door to find a better situation. If you notice a high turnover rate in your company or department, take that as a sign of a toxic workplace.

- **Cliques, gossip and rumours:** Everyone seems to be out for themselves, and there are no genuine friendships among employees. There's much infighting and paranoia as well as gossip and rumours.

- **Duties or tasks you do not enjoy:** Do you enjoy what you do on a daily basis? Of course, there are tasks we do not enjoy from time to time that are required to be done. But if on a daily basis you do not enjoy the work you are doing, it will be hard to motivate yourself. Find a job that inspires you and you want to go to every morning, and your life will become less stressful and enjoyable.

In addition to the list above, trust your gut if it tells you something is wrong. Once you know what you're dealing with, it's time to develop strategies that can help you stay sane day to day.

If you are in a toxic work environment, you need to learn how to handle it. Because it takes time to find a new job and you may not be able to walk away from this difficult situation immediately, it helps to develop ways to handle the dysfunction until you can step into a new job somewhere else. Here are some ways to deal with a toxic work environment:

1. **Find people who feel the same way you do.** Develop friendships with people who feel the same way as you. The hope is that you'll watch each other's back and will share any news with the group.

2. **Do something after work that can help relieve stress.** Go to the gym, do home repairs or learn a new skill. The key is to make sure you're living a fulfilling life outside of work to combat the drama of your 9 to 5 job.

3. **Create lists to keep yourself busy.** A list can help you stay focused on your tasks instead of the toxic atmosphere and gives you a reason to keep going every day.

4. **Document everything you do.** Save emails and write down comments and decisions from meetings, phone calls and every person who interacts with you. If you need to file a complaint, you will need the evidence to back your claim.

5. **Start your exit strategy.** It is possible that things could improve at your job, in which case it might make sense to stay. However, while waiting it out, begin your search for a new job. This will help you stay positive when things get rough. If you need to leave immediately, consider a bridge job that will keep you active while you find something in line with your career.

Knowing the signs of a toxic work environment and how to handle it will allow you to take your next step on your terms and in your time so your next job will be a place you truly enjoy working.

The Community Groups You Are a Part Of

Group identity refers to a person's sense of belonging to a particular group. At its core, the concept describes social influence within a group. This influence may be based on some social category or on interpersonal interaction among group members. In general, people are born into certain groups based on their personal, social and cultural surroundings. People also voluntarily join groups based on shared occupations, beliefs or interests. Membership in these groups influences how people think of themselves and how others think of them.

Social identity theory explains that part of a person's concept of self comes from the groups to which they belong. An individual has a personal selfhood as well as multiple selves and identities associated with their affiliated groups. A person might act differently in varying social contexts according to the groups they belong to, which might include a faith group, sports or athletic group, hobby or activity group, or a gang, among many other possibilities.

There are three types of group mentality:

- **Social categorization.** First, we categorize people in order to understand and identify them. Some examples of social categories include black, white, professor, student, Conservative and Liberal. By knowing which categories we belong to, we can understand things about ourselves, and we can define appropriate behaviour according to the groups that we and others belong to. An individual can belong to several groups at the same time.
- **Social identification.** We adopt the identity of the group that we belong to, and we act in ways that we perceive members of that group act. For example, if you identify as a Christian, you will most likely behave within the norms of the Christian denomination you belong to. As

a consequence of your identification with that group, you will develop emotional significance to that identification, and your self-esteem will be dependent on it.

- **Social comparison.** After we categorize ourselves within a group and identify ourselves as being members of that group, we tend to compare our group against another group. To maintain your self-esteem, you and your group members will compare your group favourably against other ones. This helps explain prejudice and discrimination, because a group will tend to view members of competing groups negatively to increase their own self-esteem.

There is no better place to study how group identification affects behaviour than in a prison. I have witnessed an inmate act in four or more different manners, depending on the identity of whom they were interacting with. If they attending a faith-based chapel program, their actions and demeanours were in accordance with the group's faith identity. This could even change depending on which members of the group were in attendance. If I saw this person out with members of the prison group they regularly associated with, there would be a complete contradiction to the actions and demeanour they had while in the chapel. Now, place them in the gym with others working out and I saw them act and present themselves differently again. Other areas where they acted differently were their workplace or learning classes, one-on-one with staff, self-improvement programs and family visits.

A criminal gang is a perfect example of how the group influences a person's decisions and behaviours. Many people in a criminal gang do not agree with many of the things they are required to do. It is their desire to belong that motivates them to override even their own personal beliefs.

Change Starts with You

How do we protect or change our personal environment? It starts with you. You need to think positively; give your best in everything you do today; eliminate jealousy, gossip and any ill-will towards other people; and focus on the good inside you and around you. As per the Law of Attraction, like attracts like. When you radiate positivity and love to everyone or everything around, it will boomerang to you in the form of positive people and a nourishing environment.

While striving to achieve goals or any type of meaningful life change, most of us focus on self-discipline, willpower, determination and planning. And while these are all important factors, the key to creating sustainable results is an environment designed to not only help you achieve your desired outcome but support the new behaviour or circumstances on a daily basis.

If your environment has little or no structure, conflicts with the change you are attempting to create, or surrounds you with circumstances and people that drain your energy, you will have difficulty sticking to any plans to change or grow, and you're going to be susceptible to increased levels of stress, unhappiness and destructive behaviours.

If you want to foster an environment that nurtures your well-being, brings out the best in you and leads you to greater life satisfaction, then you're going to need to make some choices about your surroundings.

We cannot control the people or our surroundings—there will always be good and bad. Therefore, you need to learn the necessary skills to create your best environment around you and that starts with understanding and acknowledging your current environment.

Once you have implemented personal change, it is time to review your personal environment and decide if each aspect of your environment is enhancing or limiting you. Only when you are aware of your environment can you implement the change required to enhance it and allow it to help you live a joyful and fulfilling life.

Environment Exercise

Your personal environment impacts your life greatly. In this exercise, you will complete an honest review of the four environmental areas in your life.

Summary

As you can see, your personal environment has a large impact on how you live and experience life. It is incumbent upon you to stop your personal environment from controlling your life and take control of it. That begins by sitting down and completing an honest and comprehensive review of the four environmental areas in your life. First, you need to make a list of all the good influences you currently have supporting you, ones that are enhancing your life and supporting the goals you have. These are the environmental areas you want to encourage and strengthen. This will help give you the momentum you require as you move to the next step.

Step two is list all the negative environmental influences in your life. Ask yourself how much damage and pain they are causing in your life. Then start to eliminate or change these limiting factors. At first this may seem overwhelming and it will be difficult. Do it in phases. First, eliminate the areas that do not seem overwhelming. This may be deleting certain friend profiles on Facebook. Then move on the more difficult ones. You may have to end a relationship, change a job or move to a new location. As your environment starts to change and enhance your decisions and actions, your self-esteem will start to grow and your path will become much easier.

I offer one word of caution in regards to changing your location or where you live. Many people I have worked with, including myself, had the belief that if they moved somewhere else and started anew, everything would work out. This is completely wrong and can lead to even worse pain and despair. If you have not changed who you are, you will lead yourself back to the same negative personal environment in your new location.

Many people have moved to a new city to get away from the influence of their addicted and criminal associates. They blame others for their situation and minimized their part. These people always worked themselves back into the same negative and destructive personal environment they escaped. If you don't fix yourself, then your environment will not change even after a move. The move comes after commitment and change, and the move should be well thought out and planned.

Understanding and acknowledging the makeup and impact of your personal environment is the first step to personal improvement and happiness. I pray that you honestly review this important area in your life. Then after implementing the tools you learn in this chapter, wrestle back control of it and live your life in a strong, supporting and life-enhancing personal environment.

SECTION THREE

IMPROVING MYSELF

"No matter who you are, no matter what you did, no matter where you've come from, you can always change, become a better version of yourself."
— *Madonna*

How Do I Do It?

Deep inside you lies an unlimited potential that can only be realized through positive living. Negativity is one of the biggest (if not the biggest) factors limiting individuals from realizing their full potential. We will now put an end to all the negativity.

It all begins with laying a strong foundation of creating yourself first and foremost. No one knows you better than yourself, and as it has been said before, you cannot lie to yourself. You know what ails you, what pulls you back and what stands in your way better than anyone else. Creating yourself first is like laying a blueprint for changing your life for the better, and the faster you can do that, the better.

If you truly want to change your life for the better and to reprogram your mind for success, you have to intentionally bring your mind to accept the fact that your successes or failures are all of your own responsibility and it is your own duty to make it happen for your own self.

There is only one person on this Earth who can help you become all you want to be and that person is you. In the first two sections, you have discovered who you are and why you do what you do. In this third section, you will learn several principles and tools proven to assist you in positively changing who you are and what you do. Whenever you are ready, take a deep breath and let's begin this step-by-step life-changing process.

CHAPTER THIRTEEN

Accept Responsibility

Take ownership of your life

"Success on any major scale requires you to accept responsibility ... in the final analysis, the one quality that all successful people have ... is the ability to take on responsibility."
— **Michael Korda**

In This Chapter
> ➤ You Are Responsible for Your Current Situation
> ➤ What You Are Responsible For
> ➤ Accepting Responsibility
> ➤ Stop Playing the Blame Game
> ➤ Staying Responsible
> ➤ Summary

More than ever in today's culture, people are taking less and less responsibility for their personal lives and relying on society to provide for their needs and happiness. Blame and excuses are the way of the day when things don't go as planned or desired. People's negative actions and life circumstances are the fault of someone or something else. They are victims and were destined to end up as they have.

Individuals find it easier to blame their own actions and circumstances on others. It is the lack of taking personal responsibility for one's own decisions, feelings and actions that is the cause of so much of the distress in people's lives today. The only possibility for achieving success or happiness in your life is to accept and take complete responsibility for your life. It is time to move past the excuses and blame that have keep us from living the life we have always desired.

Accepting complete responsibility is accomplished when we come to understand and accept that everything we have experienced in our lives is the result of decisions we have made in the past. Even when we were the victim of someone else's negative actions, an accident or a natural disaster, it is how we decided to define the event that leads to the outcome we have experienced. You could view the event from the viewpoint of a helpless victim and use the event as an excuse for your negative or self-defeating actions, or you could view it as an event you had no control over and use the event to empower and improve yourself.

Where you are in your life today, how you feel and what you believe are all within your control. The job you have, the place you live, and your health and wellness are all results of your own beliefs and actions. No one else has the power to define your life. You are completely responsible for you.

After reading this you, are probably saying "wait a minute, Gary, I am not responsible for the tornado that destroyed my home. I am not responsible for my partner cheating on me or for having cancer." You are right. There are things outside your control that can and will affect your life. Disasters happen, people do things that hurt or negatively affect your life, and health issues appear. Through no fault of your own, your life is in shambles.

Though you are not responsible for the appearance of these things in your life, you are responsible for how you react to them.

In this chapter, you will learn about how and why you are responsible for every aspect of your life. This information will help you to accept that responsibility and effect the changes you need to take control and live a happy and fulfilled life, no matter what others and the universe throws at you.

You Are Responsible for Your Current Situation

If there is only one thing you take from this book, it should be that you and only you are the one responsible for the quality of your life. In his book *The Success Principles*, Jack Canfield recalls a conversation with his mentor W. Clement Stone. Mr. Stone asked Jack if he believed he took 100 per cent responsibility for his life. Jack's response was "I think so." Mr. Stone said, "This is either a yes or no question, young man. You either do or you don't." Jack replied, "Well, I guess I'm not sure." Mr. Stone then asked him, "Have you ever complained about something?" Jack answered, "Yes, I have." Mr. Stone went on to explain to him that if he has complained or blamed someone else about anything in his life, then he has not taken 100 per cent responsibility. Taking 100 per cent responsibility is understanding and acknowledging that you are the cause of all your experiences.

You are the only one who controls your decisions and actions. You determine what things mean to you and what you do about things. If you complain about issues in your life, you are acknowledging that something is wrong. If you were being responsible, you would seek out and implement a solution to the problem. By complaining, you are passing the responsibility to someone else and hoping or expecting that they will rectify things for you.

The same issue happens when you are making excuses or blaming someone else for your problems. If you were being responsible, you would be proactive and do whatever was required to achieve the result you desire.

For example, let's say you were trying to rent an apartment and had to move in by a certain date because you had to be out of the one you lived in by that date. You had signed the lease but were unable to pay the first month's rent right then because you were waiting for some money owed to you by a friend. The new landlord made it clear that you could not move in until you paid him the rent. On move-in day, your friend was nowhere to be found and you are not able to move in. You become frustrated and start blaming the landlord for not being flexible and your friend for not paying you as promised. You are now homeless and in a state of distress. You complain to others how you were put in the situation by the two of them, and it is their fault that you are homeless.

Though other people were influential in what transpired, you are the only one responsible for the outcome. You knew the consequences of not paying the rent that day. You passed the responsibility on to others rather than being in control of the situation. Even though a promise was made to you, everyone is aware that people break promises all the time. Taking personal responsibility means that you would have a backup plan, if needed. You would not leave all your eggs in one basket. As this example illustrates, even though outside factors can negatively affect us, the outcome is our responsibility and not others' responsibility.

Thus, the first step to accepting 100 per cent responsibility for your own life is to stop making excuses and blaming others for your current situation. Look at where you are and take control by creating and implementing a plan that will take you from where you are to where you desire to be. Stop complaining about what other people do that negatively affects you and find ways to overcome their influence and effect on you.

What You Are Responsible For

The quality of life we live comprises many factors and we are responsible for all of them. When you discover and understand the contributing roles that affect the quality of your life, you will then be able to take 100 per cent responsibility of each of them and control your life outcomes. We will now explore these contributing factors and come to understand the effect each one has in your life.

You Are Responsible for Change

To become the best version of yourself, change will be required in most areas of your life. There is only one person who can implement and solidify that change and that person is you. No one else can change you no matter how much they want to. Change can only come from within and through the desire to change.

Here are five fundamental tools that have been proven time and again to be essential in creating successful change in one's life:

Curiosity: Curiosity simply means a strong desire to know or learn something. If you are not being curious, then you are not able to explore yourself properly. People have many different levels of curiosity. For some, being curious means digging into things they are afraid of. They fear the unknown or even the known. A lack of curiosity is often a tool for protecting oneself from possible pain associated with the truth. Another reason some people are not curious is that they want to avoid something that they know deep down is true.

It is vital that you embrace curiosity as a tenant in your life if you ever desire to create change. You need to become curious about who you are and why you do what you do. Curiosity will allow you to investigate what is stopping you from becoming who it is you truly desire to become.

Walt Disney once said, "We keep moving forward, opening new doors, and doing new things, because we're curious and curiosity keeps leading us down new paths." Start to become curious and you will discover many things that will assist you in your journey through life.

Honesty: To become the best version of yourself, you need to be honest, both honest with others and most importantly honest with yourself. Honesty is integrity and it is all about doing the right thing. If you can't be honest, then how can you expect to become the best you can be? By being honest, you are able to face and accept the truth. Only then are you in a position to implement positive and constructive change.

Openness: The only way to see and acknowledge problems is to be open to them. It is often easier to turn a blind eye to something rather than face it or the impact it is having in your life. You also need to be open to change itself. If you find you are constantly making excuses for not changing something in your life, then you are not open to the change required. You need to investigate what it is that is keeping you from implementing the steps required to bring about the desired change. Only by being open will you have a chance at actually realizing the required change that is needed.

Willingness: Similar to openness, you need to be willing to change in the first place. If you do not have the willingness, then all else will fail. You will find a reason not to do what is required or even ignore it all together. You must create within yourself the desire to change. Find and highlight the reason the change is needed and the personal cost you will pay if you don't change. Then list all the benefits you will get from the changes. Willingness is a decision, and if you use the tools provided earlier in this book, then you will know how to take control of your decision on whether you are willing or not willing. When you are willing, the how will always appear.

Focus: Ask any successful person "what was the most significant tool you used in reaching your success?" and they will answer "focus." Jack Canfield said, "Successful people maintain a positive focus in life no matter what is going on around them.

They stay focused on their past successes rather than their past failures, and on the next action steps they need to take to get them closer to the fulfillment of their goals rather than all the other distractions that life presents to them."

Change requires focus. If you do not focus directly on what is required in executing your change process and the reason you are doing it, you are bound for failure. Without focus, your old habits, a lack of constant action and a weakening desire will set in and divert you off course. That is part of why change can be so difficult. People desire change but do not have the commitment and effort of focus required to successfully carry out the change. If you want real change in your life, then you need to control your focus.

Make sure you involve all five of these attitudes when you are trying to implement any kind of change into your life. Change is hard, but you now have tools that you can use to help reduce the fear and stress of change. Give yourself the best opportunity at successful change and make it with confidence and help.

<u>You Are Responsible for What You Focus On</u>

We will examine the one aspect that has the most effect on our life experiences: what you focus on at any given moment of the day. As mentioned above, your focus has a direct influence on the rest of what you will learn below. As you discovered in Chapter Eleven, what you are focusing on influences how you interpret people, events, your feelings and actions. Focus will determine whether you are enjoying life or on a journey of despair. When you drive a car, the responsible thing to do is focus on the road and what is happening around you. If you lose focus, you will most likely end up hurt in an accident. The same is true as you manoeuvre through your day. You need to keep your focus on the road to personal growth and your goals. If you want to be 100 per cent responsible, then you need to continually direct your focus towards empowering feelings, thoughts and actions. By directing

your focus, you are controlling how you feel and the actions you
need to take to achieve your goals.

You Are Responsible for Your Decisions, Actions and Reactions

Next, you need to become 100 per cent responsible for your
decisions and the resulting actions and reactions they cause.
You cannot allow random dynamics to influence your decisions
and resulting actions. As we discussed earlier, we are in total
control of the decisions and choices we make throughout each
day of our lives. These decisions and choices result in the actions
and reactions you generate. When you control your decisions
and choices, you control your life. That is taking 100 per cent
responsibility. When you are not in full control of your decisions
and choices, you usually experience negative consequences and a
lower quality of life.

If you go out, get drunk and drive home because you let
the alcohol tell you that you are OK to drive or allow others
to influence your decision, you are not being responsible. Being
100 per cent responsible means that you have considered all the
circumstances, options and consequences of what you were about
to do. You would use sound reasoning to help you make the most
empowering and productive decision possible. You would have
been proactive, knowing that you would be drinking and you
are easily influenced while drinking. Being responsible means
that sometimes you must make a decision that is not the most
convenient or personally rewarding at the time. Being responsible
is taking control and doing something like using the tool E + M
+ R = O which we discussed in Chapter Five. By doing this, you
can use reason to arrive at a decision that will be in support of your
life purpose and goals.

Let's say someone you do not like very much said something
insulting to you. If you quickly respond with a return insult or even
worse strike out at the person, then the situation could escalate
with devastating consequences. You might end up in prison for

throwing a punch in frustration or anger and accidentally injuring or killing the person. This may sound extreme, but I have met many inmates in prison who were there because of a similar situation. Being responsible is when you take time to reflect and respond accordingly. You use the tools you are learning in this book and walk away even though it seems the other person is getting away with something or your pride is injured.

A bad habit many people acquire over the years is to comment about something someone else has said or done. In many cases, this comment ends up causing harm to the intended person or the person making the comment. Being responsible is deciding whether a comment is required at all, even though what they said or did is against your strongest belief. I remember in the Disney movie *Bambi* when Bambi's friend Thumper the rabbit said, "My mama always said, 'If you can't say nuffin' nice, you shouldn't say nuffin' at all.' " Sometimes saying nothing at all is the most responsible thing you can do, no matter how difficult it may be.

As a strong-willed and opinionated person I had a bad habit of always letting people know what I thought when, in my eyes, they were wrong, bothering me, allowing others to control them or just stupid. I could not understand why people did not like me, avoided me or plain attacked me. It was only when I discovered this hidden flaw that I was able to take responsibility and implement the needed change. Here is a tool I learned and used that helped me take control of my comments and criticisms of others. This one process has had a strong positive impact on my life and resulted in quality relationships and less conflict and stress in my life.

Try this tool the next time someone says or does something that rubs you the wrong way. Before you blurt out a comment, criticize them, talk behind their back or call them out, take a moment to ask yourself these three questions:

Does this really need to be said? Sure, you want to say or do something, but if you take time to think about what saying or doing something will accomplish, you start the reasoning process.

What are some of the consequences that may result? Is it really that important and worth wasting time on? Is there a better way to deal with it? These questions will help you to overcome the emotion you are experiencing and to make an informed decision.

Do I need to say it? We all like to think of ourselves as the best person to correct someone when they are in error. This question allows you to decide if this would be better accomplished by someone else, someone they may trust and listen to. You will also ask whether it even concerns you.

Does it need to be said right now? Something done in the heat of the moment usually ends up causing conflict or hurt. Is this the best time to say something? Could it wait until another time? Reflecting on the urgency of providing unsolicited advice or criticism can help you avoid making a mistake.

Being 100 per cent responsible means controlling how you interact with others. By having a process to guide what you say to or about others will reduce conflict, negative repercussions and personal stress. The less you criticize, condemn or complain about others and circumstances, the more people will accept, like and appreciate you. Developing positive, nurturing and supportive relationships can only increase your chance of living the quality of life you desire.

You Are Responsible for Your Attitude

We all want good results in our life, in our home, at work and with others whom we interact with each day. To ensure this becomes a reality, we need to be responsible for the attitude we develop every moment of the day. Attitude is defined as a way of thinking or feeling about something or someone, typically one that is reflected in a person's behaviour. Your attitude towards life and others is a reflection of who you are. Your attitude tells the world what you expect from others and society in return.

If you have a cheerful and optimistic attitude, it tells everyone you meet that you expect the best from them and the world around you. In life, we tend to live up to our expectations. And others will give us, as far as their attitudes are concerned, what we expect. If you smile and say "good morning" to someone with an honest and welcoming smile, usually they will in turn do the same back. They will be more open to and accepting of you.

Certainly, there are people in the world who are living with and emitting a negative attitude. Their presence can and will affect you and your attitude if you don't keep it in check. When you come across a person like this, you can simply acknowledge and be aware of their attitude. If their negative attitude starts to affect you, then you need to remove yourself from their influence. This may even be a family member and may seem difficult or impossible at the time. This is when responsibility for your happiness needs to be implemented. Be honest and let them know you cannot allow yourself to be around and influenced by such a negative attitude. Remember that we are in total control of our attitude and the attitude we will accept from others.

We determine our attitude each morning when we get up. We do it each morning whether intentionally or not. The problem today is that most people leave the formulation of their attitude to chance. The attitude that you circulate to your family and the world will be reflected back to you. If you start the day cheerful and happy to be living another day of great possibilities, the world will reflect the same cheerful attitude back to you. That is the type of person others like to be around. But if you are gloomy and negative, you will attract the same attitude from others and the world around you.

This is known as cause and effect. Everything we say or do will set in motion a corresponding effect. You and I are responsible for our own lives, and we produce causes all day long. The world will return to us a corresponding effect. That is why each of us determines the quality of our own lives. We get back what we give out.

Each of us has the power and responsibility to shape our own lives. As soon as we begin to shape a positive attitude, our surroundings and experiences will begin to change. Because the world in which we live is a mirror of our attitude, it is time to look into the mirror and discover what our attitude is projecting. Here is a way to determine the attitude you have been transmitting. Would you say that people tend to react to you in a smiling appreciative manner when they meet you? Your answer to that question is a reflection of the attitude you present to others. Our attitude is a reflection of who we are on the inside.

If you want to create a good attitude, you need to develop it like any other ability. This will take time and effort, but the reward far outweighs the struggle required. It requires practice and persistence. To help you get started, try placing a small sign on your bathroom with the word "Attitude" on it. You will see it every morning and be able to start the day off right. You can also place signs in your car or at work where they will remind you to focus on your attitude throughout the day. You will find yourself developing and maintaining an attitude that reflects your life positively, and you will be astonished at the improvement you are experiencing.

Another way to develop an enhancing attitude is to treat every person you come in contact with as the most important person in the world. Here are three reasons to do this. First, most people feel they are the most important person on Earth. Second, this is the way all of us should treat each other. Finally, there is nothing people desire and need more than self-esteem, the feeling that they are important. When they are recognized and feel important and needed, people will give you their respect, commitment and support. Always treat others the same way you want them to treat you, and you will never go wrong.

Another important area in our lives in which our attitude makes a difference is when we start a new activity, especially difficult and unpleasant tasks or projects. Your attitude more than anything will determine if you complete it successfully. Learn to focus only on the positive outcome completing the task will provide. If you allow the negative aspects of anything you need to accomplish attract your focus, you are doomed. Create a positive and supportive attitude and you can overcome any obstacle you encounter. Create an attitude that you can and will achieve the life you desire. To develop this kind of attitude, you need to think, act, talk and conduct yourself like the person you wish to become. When you radiate the attitude of well-being and confidence, the attitude of a person who knows where they are going and how they will get there, you will find all sorts of positive and life-enhancing things happen. Become responsible for your attitude and the world is there to support you.

You Are Responsible for Your Environment
The importance of living in a healthy environment was presented in Chapter Twelve. It is your responsibility to ensure that you are always in a healthy environment. Blaming circumstances and other restrictions for remaining in an unhealthy environment is not an option. But be careful of using your environment as an excuse for other problem areas in your life.

As mentioned in the previous chapter, some people look to their environment as the cause of all their pain rather than focusing on themselves. We all possess within us the ability to achieve what we want. We need to look within ourselves before the environment around us. Here is a true story called *Acres of Diamonds* by Russell Conwell, which illustrates this idea.

It is an account of an African farmer who had heard countless stories about other farmers making lots of money by discovering diamond mines. He was so excited by the stories that he sold his farm and journeyed to find a diamond mine of his own. He spent the rest of his life searching the African landscape in hopes of discovering the rare gems that would bring him riches. After years of fruitless searching and depleting his money, in a state of despair he threw himself from a bridge and drowned.

Meanwhile, the man who had purchased his farm was crossing a stream on the property when he spotted a large shiny stone in the water. Unaware of what he had discovered, he took it home and placed it on his fireplace mantle as a keepsake.

A couple of weeks later, a friend who was visiting spotted the gem on the mantle. He picked up the stone and looked at it closely. Almost faint with shock, he asked the farmer if he knew what he had found. When the farmer responded that he thought it was simply a piece of crystal, his friend told him that he had discovered one of the world's largest diamonds. In a state of disbelief, the farmer told his friend that the creek was full of such stones, maybe not as large as this one but they were all over the creek bed.

It turned out that the farm the first farmer sold so he could go find diamonds turned out to be one of the largest diamond mines on the continent. The moral of this story is that if the first farmer had taken the time to learn about discovering diamonds, he would have first looked around his own environment for clues before going somewhere else to do it.

The same is true in our lives. We each have the responsibility to live in a healthy and supportive environment. We should first investigate our own input and abilities before blaming our environment. Our responsibility is to investigate ourselves before running away to what we believe are greener pastures. I once read that if the other guy's pasture appears to be greener than yours, maybe it is getting better care.

One of the worst things that can happen in a person's life is when they waste it running from one item to another searching for that elusive pot of gold. They never stay with one thing long enough to find it. Ask yourself "am I one of these pot-of-gold jumpers? Or am I willing to accept the responsibility and honestly evaluate my present environment and only make the changes required to succeed?" Only then will you be able to take advantage of the supports and resources available while changing the negative and limiting areas of your personal environment. Your mind is your richest resource. Use it to toughly explore the many possibilities presently available to you before turning to something new.

You Are Responsible for Your Health and Welfare

You are the only one who determines how you feel every moment of the day. It is your responsibility to keep your mind and body in optimal condition. Yes, it is true that people catch the flu and are affected by disease and health issues, both physical and mental. It is how you respond and treat them that is in your control. You are also responsible for what you put into your body and what you subject it to.

Habits like smoking, alcohol, overeating, laziness and drug abuse are all too common in today's society. Most people do not want to be afflicted by their destructive habit but stay with it anyway. They make excuses like "I am addicted, I have tried, or I enjoy it." These excuses are their way of not accepting responsibility for themselves.

Many people have afflictions like diabetes, celiac disease, respiratory issues, tooth decay and many more. When life throws you a curve ball like one of these health problems, how you respond and look after yourself is within your control and your responsibility. Acting like a victim and feeling sorry for yourself is not the responsible way to deal with the situation.

The same is true with mental afflictions. Many people suffer with mental issues but they still thrive in life. They have taken responsibility for their own welfare. For many, giving up and letting others care for them was an option. They chose to live life and the hand they were dealt on their terms.

It is time to stop all the excuses and blaming for your health and destructive habits. It is never too late to become responsible and start to care for yourself. If you smoke, stop; it is that simple. I was a smoker most of my life. I would consume a minimum of a pack a day and two if I was driving or drinking. I had all the excuses.

I had unsuccessfully tried to quit many times and always found a reason or cause to start again. It was only after learning about being 100 per cent responsible for myself that I chose to quit. I threw out my cigarettes and have not had one in over 30 years. Once I committed myself, the rest was easy. Your mind is a powerful tool if you let it work for you.

I have since been able to control other habits and actions I did not even realize I was doing that affected my health. There are many examples of others who have accomplished the same results once they committed themselves to something. Set your focus on the benefits your change will provide rather than what you are giving up. If you use the tools in this book, you are being responsible and will live a happy and healthy life.

You Are Responsible for Your Future

Where you have been and what you have experienced until now is the past. Forget the past and focus on the present and what you want in the future. All you can do is learn from your past mistakes and experiences. Being responsible is doing just that. Learn from the past and move forward with that knowledge assisting you.

If you do not set goals and plan how you will live today and the rest of your life, then outside influences will decide it for you. At the beginning of this book, I explained how important it is to create a vision. In Chapter Fourteen, I will discuss how to achieve that vision through planning and goal setting.

Most people are unwilling to step up and become solely responsible for their future by committing to the ongoing adjustments that are required in their life. Fear of pain and failure can cause them to live in a world of endless uncertainty. By not accepting the responsibility required to live life on their terms, they are always at the mercy of others and random circumstances.

If you are willing to accept the responsibility and the effort it requires to achieve your desires, then you have taken the most difficult step. Only you can create and live the life you desire. Start by accepting the responsibility to create a vision and then a plan to achieve it.

Stop Playing the Blame Game

One of the largest problems in today's society is what I refer to as the victim mentality. It is when someone plays the role of victim by pointing the finger at someone or something outside themselves for things that are going wrong in their own life.

I touched on this earlier in this chapter but now will place more focus on this one life-changing principle. People who have an internal source of control believe that they can influence the events and outcomes in their life. The opposite is true for people with an external source of control. They tend to blame outside forces like other people, circumstances and even fate for everything that happens to them.

Nowadays, more people are living their lives with an external source of control. In several of the examples I gave earlier in this chapter, they are always looking to blame anyone or anything else when things are going wrong in their lives rather than examine their own part.

Basically, you are choosing to have an external source of control anytime you find yourself pointing your finger somewhere else when something is not going right in your life. The problem with this kind of thinking is that it takes away your power. By playing the blame game, you are simply throwing up your hands and saying "I am a victim and there is nothing I can do about it." The moment you blame someone else for how you are feeling or something you are experiencing is the moment you give up your power. By giving your power away, you are making the decision to let life happen to you. You are refusing to take responsibility.

As you might image, this can be a very destructive precedent to set. To be successful in life, you need to become fully responsible for your life. You need to find a way to take control and change your source of control to internal. Even when it seems that the world is out to get you, you need to seize control. That is being 100 per cent responsible for your life.

Bad things are going to happen to you that are outside of your control. The solution is you have to take 100 per cent control of how you react to those situations. You can choose to spiral out of control into a state of anxiety, depression, anger, resentment and hopelessness and pull the covers over your head and give up. Or you can choose to react in a way that finds a positive solution. The choice is totally yours and totally your responsibility.

There are times when you will accept your responsibility and choose to attack a situation or setback head on. Other people may say or do things that are intended to harm you, but ultimately you are the one who decides how those things will affect you. All the outside interference is just noise and you are the one who controls the volume. Therefore, turn it off. Your feelings are yours; don't let others influence them. If you are following your internal source of control, then you will analyze what went wrong and investigate new possibilities that you can implement to get things back on track.

It is also important to keep in mind that your internal source of control is also in play for the positive things that happen in your life. Make sure you keep your source of control internal and give yourself the credit. Do not revert to the external source and credit luck or being at the right place at the right time for your success. You are in control and you set yourself up for the success you are experiencing.

Being 100 per cent responsible for your life means taking control of your personal source of control and making it internal. Start analyzing your current feelings and situation and find out what its current source is and make the changes required to put you back in control of your future.

Staying Responsible

Once you have stepped up and taken responsibility for yourself you must keep it up. Life has a way of distracting us from our desire to stay responsible in many areas of our life. It is when we start to feel comfortable with ourselves that we tend to take all the effort we have invested for granted. Our focus can easily be distracted by others and world events. We must always be aware of this weakness and ensure that we do not slip back into old attitudes and habits. Here are two ways to help you stay on track and not fall victim to circumstance:

Watch for Warning Signs

Nothing in life ever just happens to you. There is almost always a warning of impending problems in front of you. Warnings are telltale signs such as gut feelings, intuition or information that can alert you to pending negative situations and outcomes ahead. You are getting these warnings all the time. You need to become aware of them and be proactive before they start causing problems and result in a negative outcome.

These warnings can come in external forms, for example: your spouse has been out later than normal and less intimate with you lately; you were not able to pay back the money you borrowed as promised; someone gave you a look of disgust; you had to apologize after becoming aggressive. They also can come as internal warnings, for example: a feeling in the pit of your stomach; a feeling of doubt or guilt; a sense of danger. These are all internal warning signs that you need to pay attention to.

In too many cases when we sense our warning signs, we tell ourselves they are not real and we are overreacting. We then go on to talk ourselves out of paying heed to the warning and taking the corrective actions to avoid negative circumstances.

Learn to become open to and aware of your warning signs. These warnings will help to prevent you from saying or doing something that will in the long run cause you distress and pain. Warning signs will also keep you focused on your vision and help you to avoid possible negative consequences.

<u>Regularly Review Your Results</u>

Being 100 per cent responsible means continually reviewing where you are and if you are on track with your vision and goals. In life, we can become so busy and preoccupied that we tend to lose our focus. To ensure you are not backtracking or slipping regarding your responsibilities, you need to review what is and isn't working in your life. Past results don't lie, and the best way to stay on course is to regularly review where you are compared to where you are headed. If you are off course, the responsible action is to get right back on course. There is no time for blame or feeling sorry. Changing your focus back towards your goals is the most responsible action you can take.

Being 100 per cent responsible means watching for life's warnings and continually reviewing where you are to ensure you stay the course. Only then can you avoid life's pitfalls and responsibly live your life.

Summary

We all have ups and downs in our lives, but there is a big difference in how successful and self-sabotaging people handle them. Successful people recognize their mistakes and take responsibility for them. Self-sabotaging people make excuses, avoid being held responsible and blame others for their mistakes and troubles.

Being afraid to accept responsibility for your shortcomings makes you appear untrustworthy and you never learn from your mistakes. Accepting responsibility for you mistakes allows you to learn from them, find a solution and prevent them from ever happening again.

When a responsible person truly wants something, they find a way to get it. Others make excuses. Successful people never let anything get in the way of their goal. Self-sabotaging people allow even the smallest inconvenience to get in the way and stop them. If you find you are making excuses or blaming others or circumstances for not getting what you desire, it is time to search for the real reason and what you are trying to avoid.

I implore you not to continue life like most people who are afraid or unwilling to accept responsibility for what they do, feel and experience each day. They are the ones who find it easier and more satisfying to criticize, condemn and complain and they are the people who allow the world to dictate how their lives transpire. They are quick to blame anyone or anything besides themselves when things go wrong.

You have the power and the responsibility to live a complete and wholesome life on your terms. It is not simply good enough to accept responsibility for certain aspects of your life while letting others randomly control your experiences. Being responsible also means taking control even when it is not convenient or easy. Taking 100 per cent responsibility is accepting the challenge to bear down and take control of all aspects of your being.

You have the power and ability to overcome any obstacle that comes your way. You also have the power and ability to create and live the life you have always desired. It is your choice. Are you willing to accept 100 per cent responsibility, or are you content with how your life is transpiring? It is up to you and only you. I pray that you have the courage and fortitude to accept and do what is required: to step up and become 100 per cent responsible and live the joyful, happy and fulfilling life you deserve and can have.

CHAPTER FOURTEEN

Create a Compelling Future

Design the life you desire

"To accomplish great things we must first dream,
then visualise, then plan... believe... act."
— **Alfred A. Montapert**

- -

In This Chapter
- ➤ It Starts with Goals
- ➤ Break It Down
- ➤ The Ultimate Success Formula
- ➤ Just Lean into It
- ➤ Have a Bucket List
- ➤ Bucket List Exercise
- ➤ Life Goal Exercise
- ➤ Summary

- -

In the beginning chapters of this book, I introduced you to the importance of finding your purpose and mission in life. You then discovered how to create a vision to help you live your purpose and mission. The vision would bring joy, happiness and fulfillment into your life and inspire you to get up every morning and begin the day with passion and determination. It is now time to find out how you can make that vision a reality. It's time to begin the journey towards realizing all your dreams and desires.

To arrive at your vision, you will require a well-developed plan, its immediate implementation and continued evaluation and adjustments. The journey from where you are today to the wonderful life you have envisioned works the same as if you want to travel from where you are to a new location in the world.

To travel from one destination to another, you would usually find a map and then create a plan to get there. As you journey along, you would make the corrections to your plan as circumstances dictated. That is what goals and goal setting is all about. Your goal is the destination, and you create a map and plan to reach it.

If you got into your car and started blindly driving, it is doubtful that you would ever arrive at your destination. Yet, that is what most people do with their life. Without goals and a plan to achieve them, they have no direction for what to do. They have an idea of what they want but they go out daily with nothing to measure their progress nor a fixed plan to guide them. Sometimes they end up driving in circles and experiencing the same unpleasant events they previously experienced and do not know how it happened. With no plan or map, they drift through life not completely sure where they are at any given time. Most are hopelessly lost and hopelessly trying to find their way.

If you want to live the life you have envisioned, then you need to create a plan that will guide you to it. This plan will contain goals and objectives that will allow you to know if you are on target. It is a guide to assist you in reaching your desired destination on time.

In this chapter, I will show you how, by using goal setting, you can create a plan that you will use like a road map to direct and keep you on course towards the life you desire. It will provide markers of your progress and warnings that will help you overcome obstacles that you are bound to encounter along the journey.

It Starts with Goals

Whether you want to change your behaviour, climb the corporate ladder, run a marathon for the first time or simply become a better person, goal setting is a vital part of any effort to improve. Being able to formulate, set and make progress toward goals is a skill that will help you achieve your dreams. Only by setting and meeting realistic goals can you become the happy, successful person you were meant to be. Don't continue to make the same mistakes you've made in the past. Instead of failing to live out your dreams, exceed your own expectations with the tools provided in this book.

What Exactly Is a Goal?

A goal is an idea of the future or desired result that a person or group of people envisions, plans and commits to achieve. People endeavour to complete their goal within a certain time frame. Personal goals can provide long-term direction and short-term motivation. Goals help us to focus on what we want to be or where we want to go with our lives. They are a way of utilizing knowledge and managing time and resources so that you can focus on making the most of your life potential.

By setting clearly defined personal goals, you can measure your achievements and keep sight of your progress. If you fail to achieve at one step, you can reassess your situation and try new approaches. Keeping your life goals clearly defined and updated as your circumstances change and evolve is one of the most powerful ways to keep yourself motivated throughout life.

Attaining your life vision is a motivational goal and comprises many sub-goals and tasks. For example, if part of your life vision statement sees you as a Gold Seal chef owning your own successful Italian restaurant, then your vision or goal consists of two objectives or sub goals that need to be met before the vision can become a reality. The first objective would to become a Gold Seal chef and the second would be to own a successful restaurant. Both of these objectives become goals themselves and they will require several tasks to be completed before they are achieved.

To become a Gold Seal chef, you first need to become a chef. That is your first task. This in itself becomes another sub goal of your vision goal because it requires more than one task to complete it. This sub-goal might require you to find funding, attend culinary school and complete several courses to achieve it. As you can see, your vision is comprised of a series of goals and sub goals that need to be accomplished before you are living your vision.

<u>What Is the Difference between an Idea and a Goal?</u>

An idea is simply something we want or desire, such as I want to be rich or I want to be happy. It is something your mind conceives as pleasurable but does not clearly define. A goal is an idea that is clearly defined, measurable and written down and has a deadline for its achievement.

I will have $500,000 in savings by December 31, 2025. In this example, the $500,000 is a measurable definition of what rich is and a date has been imposed for this to happen. It is hard to assign clear and specific tasks or sub goals to an idea, whereas it is easy for a defined, measurable and time-sensitive goal.

This explains why most people never achieve their New Year's resolutions. They come up with ideas that they believe would bring them pleasure but never commit. "I am going to exercise and lose weight this year" or "I am going to quit smoking" are two ideas that people want and would like to achieve. However, the elements of a goal are not present so they have little chance of success. To succeed in life, you need to transform your ideas into structured goals.

How To Structure a Goal

Goals comprise many factors to be effective. The acronym S.M.A.R.T. is often used to describe five factors required to be considered an actual goal. It must be Specific, Measurable, Attainable, Realistic and Time-sensitive.

I am financially independent and debt-free with $500,000 cash in the bank on September 25, 2024. The above goal is specific (financially independent), measurable (debt-free and $500,000 in cash), attainable and realistic (it makes you reach and takes effort but is not impossible), and time-sensitive (by September 25, 2024). Without all of these components to judge your progress and guide you, you only have an idea.

Goals should always be written down in as much detail as possible. A goal that is not written down is merely an idea or wish. By writing your goal in detail, you are telling your subconscious mind what you want, and it will begin to search for ideas and ways to make your goal become a reality. According to a study done by Gail Matthews at Dominican University, those who wrote down their goals accomplished significantly more than those who did not write down their goals.

Next, a goal should be reviewed regular to help program your mind. The stronger you form the image of what you want in your mind, the harder it will work at achieving your goal. Tell others what it is you want and become accountable for it. By making a public declaration and allowing yourself to be held accountable, you increase the chance of achieving your goal by 20 per cent. The way to live life on your terms is by creating and recording S.M.A.R.T. goals in as much detail as possible and allowing yourself to be held accountable for your goals.

The Real Power of Goals and Goal Setting

I have learned to become a goal-oriented person. Since I started setting goals, my life has improved immensely. Goals give me clarity and perspective both professionally and personally, which is why I take the time to set goals every year. They guide my daily decisions, which brings me closer to rather than further away from my desired outcome. I also discovered that when I am following my goal plan, I have less stress in my life. This is because I can focus on the smaller more accomplishable tasks rather the massive overwhelming ones, which seem extremely difficult or impossible. Even though I have a life vision, I can narrow my focus down to only what I need to do this year. Goal setting has completely changed my life for the better.

I find it interesting how many people shudder at the thought of setting goals. Studies have shown that only three per cent of people set goals, and those people are among the wealthiest and most prosperous people in the world.

Why is it that people don't want to set goals, especially when they know that those who do set goals are in an enviable place? If you ask why, most people will tell you they don't know how to do it or they don't have the time nor the patience necessary. For many, it is the fear of failure or their low self-esteem that stops them.

You have no idea how much you can discover about yourself once you take the time to write your thoughts and your dreams down on a piece of paper. It is a powerful, magical and simple technique. To be all you can be, you must dream of being more. To do all that is possible, you must attempt the impossible.

There are so many things we don't know about ourselves, about life, about what is possible and what is not possible, about what we can and can't do. Most of us choose to believe all the negative and limiting things Hollywood, the media and other people tell us to believe without questioning a single word. It is time to take back control and experience the power of goal setting.

The Proof Is in the Results

Many studies have proven the effectiveness that proper goal setting has provided. In 1979, interviewers asked questions of new graduates from Harvard's MBA Program and found that:

- 84 per cent had no specific goals at all
- 13 per cent had goals but they were not committed to paper
- 3 per cent had clear, written goals and plans to accomplish them

In 1989, researchers again interviewed the graduates of that class. You can guess the results:

- The 13 per cent of the class who had goals were earning, on average, twice as much as the 84 per cent who had no goals at all.
- Even more staggering, the three per cent who had clear, written goals were earning, on average, 10 times as much as the other 97 per cent put together.

By implementing structured and effective goal setting into your daily routine, you are taking advantage of a proven tool that will not only motivate you to achieve your dreams but guide you along the journey. Later in this chapter, you will have the opportunity to complete a goal-setting exercise. I ask you to use this opportunity to set yourself up for success by committing yourself to fully completing the exercise.

Break It Down

As you begin to write down your life goals, some of them may seem overwhelming and forbidding. This is because you are looking at the goal from the outside as one massive entity rather than a group of smaller, more attainable action steps. Once you have clearly defined your goals, written them down and assign a timeline for their completion. Then you will be able to break them down into smaller actionable steps. These actionable steps or tasks will become your road map to success. They will simplify your life and assist you in becoming more productive.

How To Break Down a Goal

There are several ways that you can break down your goal into actionable steps; here are five suggested way:

Ask someone who has done it: Find someone who has achieved the goal you desire and ask them for advice and the steps they took that brought them their success. Their experience, setbacks and strategies can save you much time and heartache. Who better to learn from than someone who has already experienced the trials and tribulations associated with the endeavour? You can also research books and manuals or take courses that will guide you, breaking any goal down into a workable plan.

Make a list: You can use the list process to help identify what needs to be accomplished for your goal to become a reality. Take a piece of paper and write your goal in the most complete detail you can at the top of the page. Next, below the goal make a list of all the items you can think of that would be required to complete the goal. Do not try to rationalize the items you think must be done. The items do not have to be in any order—simply list them. Once you have completed the list, you will be able to use the information to create a workable plan of action.

Mind mapping: Many people use a process called mind mapping. Mind mapping is a highly effective tool for getting information in and out of your brain. Mind mapping is a creative and logical means of note-taking and note-making that literally maps out your ideas.

All mind maps have some elements in common. They have a natural organizational structure that radiates from the centre and use lines, symbols, words, colours and images according to simple, brain-friendly concepts. Mind mapping converts a long list of varied information into a colourful, memorable and highly organized diagram that works in line with your brain's natural way of doing things.

One simple way to understand a mind map is by comparing it to a map of a city. The city centre represents the main idea; the main roads leading from the centre represent the key thoughts in your thinking process; the secondary roads or branches represent your secondary thoughts, and so on. Special images or shapes can represent landmarks of interest or particularly relevant ideas.

The great feature about mind mapping is that you can put your ideas down in any order as soon as they pop into your head. You are not constrained by thinking in order. Simply throw out any and all ideas, then worry about reorganizing them later. A mind map for goal setting is a great tool for brainstorming your wishes and desires.

To create a mind map for goal setting, all you need is a large piece of clean paper. Make sure there are no lines on it, as that will impose a structure on your thinking, which you don't want.

In the centre of the page, draw a circle and write your vision or main goal in it in capital letters. This is the key thought for the mind map. Now, draw lines radiating out from this circle, and at the end of each one of lines, write the name of something that must be done to achieve your goal. Under each of these sub goals, list anything that needs to be done to complete the sub-task. All the information you require to formulate a plan to achieve your vision or goal is now in front of you.

Create a to-do list: Once you have listed all the tasks and action steps required to achieve your goal, it is time to engage them. The first step is to assign each of them a completion date and then place them in the order they need to be completed. When you are finished, you will notice that many of the steps can be done at the same time. It is now time to prioritize them in order of their importance. Each day, you should choose a minimum of five of your tasks from the list to accomplish. You now have a road map to success that you can follow. It important that you review and update this list weekly as circumstances change and you want to be prepared for them and respond accordingly.

Eat That Frog: When you look at your daily list of five items, there is a tendency to avoid a difficult task and choose an easier one first. This is what is known as procrastination, or the desire to avoid difficult or unpleasing tasks. In his book *Eat That Frog! 21 Great Ways to Stop Procrastinating and Get More Done in Less Time*, Brian Tracy tells us how to avoid procrastination and how to effectively complete all our tasks and action steps on time. He advises you to pick the one large and daunting task or action from your list of five tasks and action steps. Consider this your biggest ugly frog. Why not eat it first? Because you know you eventually must eat this big ugly frog, eating it first can only empower you. Unfortunately, most of us do just the opposite and leave the biggest ugly frog for last. We hope it will go away or somehow become easier. We do everything we can to avoid it. The problem is we end up spending our day thinking about or dreading it. Brian also adds that when you do eat the big ugly frog first, you feel a sense of accomplishment, pride and motivation to deal will all the less difficult things on your list that you need to accomplish.

Plan Your Day the Night Before

When breaking down goals, an extremely powerful tool is to plan your next day just before you go to sleep. This helps you gain more control of your life and increases your productivity. These are two good reasons to make this tool a nightly routine in your life.

By choosing the top five tasks from your to-do list, you set your mind in motion to find ways to help you complete them. As you sleep, your mind works on ideas that will come to you the next day as you are working on your tasks. It is like you were up all night working on solutions to your tasks.

Also, by selecting your tasks and creating a game plan the night before, you can start your day immediately. You know exactly what you are going to do and when. You are gathering the required resources and support from the start. By noon, you will have accomplished a great deal without the stress of deciding what to do next. You are in control and that is far more effective that running blindly through the day.

The Ultimate Success Formula

An excellent tool I learned from Tony Robbins is a process he refers to as the Ultimate Success Formula. As soon as I discovered this life-changing formula, I implemented it into my daily routine and have never looked back. This one process has helped me gain clarity, motivation and the power to create and achieve life-enhancing goals. It alone is the reason I am where I am today.

The Ultimate Success Formula

Regardless of your goal, Tony Robbins believes achieving it is 80 per cent psychology and 20 per cent mechanics. Success and life are hard when you don't focus on your psychology or mindset. Here are the five steps:

1. **Know your outcome:** Be specific about what you want. As I discussed earlier, you need to know exactly what you want. You must be specific because if you are not, then you are not able to judge your progress or know when you have reached your destination. Once I became specific about what I wanted—so specific that I could visualize every detail of my goal in my mind—only then did I start to realize positive results in my life.

2. **Know your why:** When you know your why, the how's will work themselves out. This is a very important step. I had many goals in the past for which my why was weak. My why turned out to be what I thought would make me happy. Take money for an example. Like most people, I believed money would bring me happiness. This is one of the biggest misleading beliefs out in the world today. Don't get me wrong, money can help in the pursuit of happiness, but it can't buy it. It is not the money that provides the happiness but the things it can purchase. The problem is that if you are not sure on the why of the item that money gets you, then you are no better off. It all

comes down to the why. If you know what it is that you are receiving from your goal, then you are on the right track. You are then able to decide if the effort is worth the reward you anticipate. When you know exactly what the goal will provide you and it is something you truly desire, then it becomes the fuel that will drive you when things get tough.

3. **Take massive action**: Tony always preached that you do not leave the scene of a goal setting without first taking action. You need to build up momentum. By taking immediate action, you set in motion the action. You need to turn that into massive action if you want to succeed. Simply sitting around hoping things will transpire or work out for you will only lead to failure and pain. You must take charge, and action followed by repeated action is the only way to succeed. No one said it would be easy, but if your why is strong enough, then the action will follow.

4. **Know what is working and what is not:** You need to assess your progress. If you want to lose weight and body fat, you need to measure before you start, such as each Monday. Based on your results, you can review what you have done and decide if changes are required. The definition of insanity is doing the same thing over and over and expecting a different result. You need to have a way to regularly measure your results and learn if what you are doing is working or not.

5. **Change your approach:** Based upon your assessment of your progress, you may need to work on some new strategies or beliefs. If you have hit a plateau or find yourself spiralling downhill, this is the time to ask for help. Spiralling often happens because we missed our opportunity to assess and missed the plateau that happened before the spiral.

If you run each of your goals through this five-step process, then you are setting yourself up for success.

Just Lean into It

Most people journey through life with self-imposed limitations. They hold themselves back with negative images they have formed about themselves and have not let go of. They live their lives obstructed by their own subconsciously formed comfort zone. Their inaccurate beliefs, self-doubt and guilt overpower their good intentions every time they attempt to achieve a goal. Eventually, their attitude becomes "why even try," and they quit before they start.

It is time to get out of your limiting comfort zone, change your behaviour and create momentum. By starting now, you will begin to form a path that will appear clearer as you journey along it. Successful people have discovered that instead of using willpower to help them move forward, they need to become proactive and commit themselves to the process of just do it and give it your best. When they do, the path to follow becomes much clearer, and they will ultimately reach their goal.

Get Out of Your Comfort Zone

Many of us are reluctant to move out of our comfort zones. After all, it's comfortable in there. Our comfort zone is familiar. We know the thoughts and feelings that reside in that zone. We know the kind of life that exists there.

Sometimes, we're not even that comfortable in our comfort zone. But we still stay there. We worry that things outside our comfort zone will be worse and we experience the fear of the unknown. We also stay in our comfort zone because it provides safety from being too vulnerable. Think of a comfort zone as a bubble: it feels protective. But it also might be claustrophobic, because it prevents change and growth. Leaving our comfort zone gives us a better understanding of who we are and what we like when we expose ourselves to new experiences. Plus, it's through trying new things and taking risks that we develop resilience. We mainly grow through our mistakes, as much as they sting.

What does leaving your comfort zone look like? Of course, it's different for different people, because each of us defines our comfort zone in different ways. Here are some examples of leaving your comfort zone: having a conversation you'd rather avoid; doing things alone, such as eating dinner at a restaurant; putting yourself in a new situation by signing up for a new class or going somewhere you've never been; letting go of harmful relationships; and communicating with people you don't know.

A tip for leaving your comfort zone would be to rethink the part that feels frightening. Identify what feels uncomfortable to you and decide to view it in a way that feels exciting or adventurous. That is, try not to get stuck on how intimidating something is. Instead, focus on how excited and proud you'll feel after you do it. Use that to motivate you. Here are four tips for leaving your comfort zone:

> **Give it a try:** Remind yourself that you're simply giving this new situation a try. If you don't like it, you can always stop doing it.

> **Devise a plan:** Having a plan helps you leave your comfort zone slowly, and it still feels like it's within your control. If you want to take a solo trip to South America but you're worried about spending that much time by yourself, your plan could be going to dinner alone, followed by a solo weekend getaway. You could also research solo travel and try to prepare yourself for the types of situations that might come up. You could add talking to other people who've travelled alone.

Celebrate: Brainstorming ways you'll celebrate leaving your comfort zone is another way to motivate yourself.

Seek support: Talk about what you'd like to do with your friends. Ask them to join you. For example, if you've been feeling bored and want to change up your fitness routine, ask a friend to try out a new fitness class with you. That way you don't have to do it on your own. You also can seek support from books or travel groups.

When you learn to get out of your comfort zone, you open yourself to endless possibilities. Learning to understand what your comfort zone is and how it came to be is the first step. You can then use rationalization to help you expand it and eliminate limiting aspects of it.

Change Your Behaviour

For most of my life, I felt very uncomfortable with people who wanted to hug. I would do anything I could to avoid it. I did not even like hugging my own mother. I am not sure where this unease developed or how it became a part of my comfort zone. When I started my diaconal formation and people discovered I was going to become a deacon, they would approach me and want to hug me. My comfort zone was to shake their hand but theirs was to hug. I began to react slowly by reaching around and giving them a pat on the back. The more I did this, the more comfortable I started to feel, whereas today I approach others and give them a hug. I am no longer uncomfortable with the process and in fact find it quite empowering. This complete change in my comfort zone began with a change in behaviour. Instead of avoiding a request for a hug, I started to respond. The change in my comfort zone resulted.

If you want to be able to change your comfort zone, it begins with a change in behaviour. It may be a small change at first, but the results are phenomenal. Acknowledge that it leaves you uneasy and then commit to it and change your behaviour in some way. This will allow you to experience new things and enhance your life.

It was uncomfortable when I first reached out to give a hug. I would stand a short distance and pat them on the back, but it was a beginning. Eventually, it became natural and gradually I turned my hug into a proper embrace. That is all it takes. A small change in behaviour can lead to a lifetime of joy and happiness. It can move you from fear of the unknown to a feeling of security.

Create Momentum

When you honestly let yourself go and just lean into it, miraculous things will start to happen. You will set in motion a momentum that can and will change your entire life. By creating momentum, you are releasing an unseen energy that will bring you more opportunities, more resources and the people who can help you at the right time. As your momentum builds, so does your motivation to move forward. Momentum gives you the desire and ability to overcome any obstacle that appears in your path.

Sometimes to create momentum you need to start a project or opportunity without seeing the complete path you must take. Too often in life people have a dream or goal they desperately want to achieve but because they cannot see a clear path to it, they do not even start. It is time to end this life-limiting affliction and use momentum to get what you want. You will always find a way if it is important to you. All it takes is seizing upon the momentum you are building to carry you through. As you build momentum, your path will start to become clear. One of the secrets of success is to build momentum and trust that you will find a way to succeed.

Have a Bucket List

There are many things a person wants to experience in life. Each person has a unique list of the things they would like to experience, do, learn, visit or own in their lifetime. Yet, most people go to their eternal rest achieving only a few of these goals. In fact, most people are hard pressed to list everything they want from life. It is no wonder they do not experience them at some point in their life if they do not know what it is they desire.

We have discussed goals in the form of life achievement up till now. Here, I want you to think beyond how you are going to live your life to what you want to achieve while you are here. I want you to list all the things you can think of that you desire to experience, learn, have or do in your life. The sky is the limit. If you know what it is you want, then your mind will get to work to get it for you.

Bucket List Exercise

I want you to take a piece of paper and make a list of 101 things you want to achieve in your life. As you write your list, do not judge whether you are able to have, visit, experience or do these desires. Simply list them. Remember, the how will work itself out. List anything you can think of and do not stop until you have at least 101 items on your list.

Once you have completed the list, I want you to review it every week. Commit the list to memory, if possible. Put your mind to work so that it can find ways for theses desires to become a reality. Then, every time you complete one of these goals, draw a line through it and thank yourself for achieving another one of your bucket list desires.

You will be surprised at how many of the items on your list you do complete. The bucket list is a way to bring meaning to your life when you are in a funk. Review what you have done and what you would still like to do, and it will move you away from your funk into a state of desire and gratitude. From there, the sky is the limit.

Life Goal Exercise

In Chapter Three, you created and recorded a life vision statement. This statement was a summary of what your envisioned future would look like and why you desired your vision. This statement was a summary of the visions and reasons you produced and wrote down for each of your seven life areas.

It is now time to create a plan to help you journey towards realizing and living these visions. You are going to create a road map to success that you can follow and journey your way to the destination of your vision.

First, I want you to look back at your vision entries and transfer each individual vision and reason to a sheet of paper following the format of the form below. Write one for each of these life areas: Career/Business, Financial, Lifestyle, Relationships, Personal Development, Health and Fitness, and Contribution.

Next, I want you to list anything you believe has to happen or be done for your vision to become a reality. Do not judge whether you can do it or not; simply list what is required in any order. Spent at least 15 minutes brainstorming ideas for each vision.

These are the goals you need to achieve to live your vision. Now, go through each list, and using a number or letter system, list the order in which the things need to be done on the left of each entry.

On the right of each entry, enter a date you will complete this task by.

Take your highest priority goal and write it on the sheet. Make sure to write the date you want to achieve it by on the right of it.

Now, list any tasks or events that need to be done to accomplish this goal. As before, prioritize and date each task.

Career/Business
My vision:

_____
_____
_____

Why living this vision would make me feel happy and fulfilled:

_____
_____
_____

What goals need to be completed to meet this vision?

_____
_____
_____
_____
_____

First goal:

_____
_____

Tasks to achieve my goal:

_____
_____
_____
_____

You now have seven separate road maps to follow, stay focused and stay on target.

I want you to take your top goal from each life area and start to work on completing the tasks you have assigned to each one in order. By following this plan, you can move ahead in the direction of your final destination.

Your plan can be used to keep track of your progress. Make sure you are following your timeline and don't stray off course. You will come across some roadblocks along the way. By following your plan, you will be able to identify when they happen and be in a position to recalculate and make the required adjustments to find a new course to follow.

Once you complete one task, move on to the next one. And when you reach a goal, do the same and move on to the next one.

Summary

To be successful, happy and fulfilled in life you need to know exactly what it is you want and why you want it. If your why is not strong enough to achieve your want, then you need to understand why and adjust your why to compel you. Once you know what you want and have a strong enough why, then you require a deadline and plan on how you will achieve it. There is no other way. Life does not just happen the way you want it to. You need to take control and guide all aspects of your life towards the results you desire.

In this chapter, I explained how you can create a compelling future and as Nike says "Just Do It." So far you have discovered your purpose, mission and a vison on how you wish to live your life. You now also have the tools to implement your vision. You should now have a compelling future that will motivate and guide you to live the life you have always desired. Use the power of goal setting and the tools that go with it to live and experience life on your terms and truly achieve your dreams.

CHAPTER FIFTEEN

Believe It Is Possible

Trust in yourself

"Never let life impede on your ability to manifest your dreams.
Dig deeper into your dreams and deeper into yourself and
believe that anything is possible, and make it happen."
— **Corin Nemec**

- -

In This Chapter
- ➢ Do You Believe in Yourself?
- ➢ Believe It's Possible
- ➢ Train Yourself To Believe in Yourself
- ➢ Summary

- -

One of the first quotes that I ever heard and implemented into my
life was "What the mind can conceive and believe it can achieve,"
coined by W. Clement Stone. When I first heard it, I was skeptical.
I became hung up on the words "believe it."

At the time, I had extremely low self-esteem. I did not believe
that I could be or do anything important in my life. As a result, I

did what I thought would impress other people or give me instant pleasure. I was constantly seeking approval, validation and things that made me feel good.

This resulted in a life of surrender and acceptance. My dreams and desires were merely that, dreams and desires. But Mr. Stone's quote intrigued me just the same. I knew that in the past, any time I set my mind on something, I achieved it. I thought, "If I was able to believe in those instances then, why do I not believe in myself now?" This led me to seek out the answers.

When I discovered the mechanics of self-belief and esteem, the answers became clear. I was then able to use the tools I had discovered. Learning how to believe in myself subsequently helped introduce endless new possibilities into my life. At the beginning, I found this difficult to do, but nonetheless I continued and committed myself. By learning the whys and the tools to overcome them, I was able to open myself up to a variety of new possibilities.

Throughout our lives, we have all been conditioned to doubt ourselves. We are deluded daily with negative and limiting information. It is no wonder so many people live a life of doubt and fear of failure. If you come to understand and acknowledge these limiting beliefs, you will be able to retrain yourself and eliminate all your fears and self-doubt. Only then will you be able to develop the self-esteem and self-confidence you require to succeed. Without change, you will continue to experience life the way you do now.

Everything you have accomplished or acquired in your life is a result of either an empowering or limiting belief in yourself or your belief whether it was possible. In this chapter, I want to help you discover how to build a strong belief in yourself and in the goals you desire to pursue. Then, you will be able to achieve what you conceive and believe.

Do You Believe in Yourself?

This question is not meant to patronize you. Rather, it's meant to empower you. If you have self-doubt, great! That means that you are human. We all have moments in life when we need to believe in ourselves a little more. Sometimes we get knocked down by life, and it takes away our faith in who we are and what we can achieve. However, it's during your weakest moments that you need to dig deep and remind yourself how strong you truly are.

When you think about it, nothing is impossible, but our minds try to tell us otherwise. People come from nothing every single day and go on to achieve great feats in life. Why? They have developed an unwavering belief in their capabilities. Who you believe you are is who you end up becoming.

People get into trouble when they allow other peoples' criticisms and judgments to define who they are. You cannot control what other people think. I learned this the hard way when I was younger, but I learned it nonetheless. As my life transpired, I held the mistaken belief that I was not loved. I felt I had nothing to offer others, so I needed to do outrageous things to get attention. I had to stand out.

In order to facilitate this, I built up a wall around myself and did things to garner attention to the point where I did not care what type of attention I received as long as I received attention. This was my mechanism to avoid experiencing hurt or pain. I carried on my life as if others did not impact me, but the bare truth is that they did. What I didn't believe then, but I do now, is that I can be liked for who I am and I can also achieve anything I can conceive. Today, I totally believe in myself and am confident that any goal I conceive I can achieve. You also can begin to believe in yourself.

When we think about what we are capable of, we never think big enough. We look at others and we believe that somehow they have something we don't and that perhaps they were always destined for more. We tell ourselves that we don't have it in us to live that way and to take the action that they do. We worry that we're not brave enough to make the decisions needed to live from a place of truth. Or worse, we fear we have nothing of value to offer.

These are all stories to keep us small and playing safe. We have all these fears bubbling away inside us: the fear of failing, being seen, being rejected, being judged or even criticized for what we believe in. Instead of facing them head on, we choose to run and hide, and in doing so we deprive the world of our gifts!

Maybe you're someone who fears success itself, because who would you then have to be? What would have to change in your life? What would you no longer tolerate? Who would you lovingly release and let go of? Even when change is for the best, it's still scary. No one enjoys difficult conversations or potentially hurting someone's feelings, and this can stop many people from fulfilling their potential. But, do you want to dim your light for the sake of another? Is their happiness more important than your own?

It's time to stop limiting yourself. You are so much stronger than you know, and whatever is thrown at you, I know you'll deal with it. Plus, you always have me in your corner for support!

If you can see and feel the dream in your mind, then it is possible. Know that you have so much to give and share, and the world is waiting for you and only you. We are all special and unique expressions of the divine, and someone needs your talents and skills, with your unique voice and story. No one else will do. It's time to step up, to believe in yourself and to dream big!

Remember, the only thing stopping you from achieving the dream is you. Do you want to waste a few more years blaming things outside yourself, only to have to face the cold, hard reality that it was you all along? If you want this year to be your year, then you need to commit to yourself and your dreams now. Stop putting things off until you feel more ready or the time is perfect. I guarantee there will never be a right time, because your ego will always find something else to focus on to keep you safe. Decide that you are ready, and this is your time. Decide that you are going to impact the world with your unique gifts, and you will change lives. Decide that you are ready to share your story and truth and know that the world will hear and embrace it.

It's time to decide to start believing in yourself and what is possible for your life. Choose to face your inner demons and take the action required to finally start creating the life you want to live. Believing in yourself is a choice you can make anytime.

It is now time for you to choose to believe in yourself. Start by asking yourself "why don't I fully believe in myself? Why do I feel I cannot do something that I wish I could do?" Notice the self-doubt start to creep in. "I will never complete something that big, I can't control myself, I am not smart enough or my past won't let me." These are a few of the self-doubting thoughts that begin to appear. Self-doubt and fear of making mistakes cause you to not believe in yourself. These doubts come from other people's expectations of us and sometimes even their criticism of us when we've made mistakes. Accepting these self-doubts is a choice you decided to make.

You are the only one who can decide whether to accept these self-doubts or not. They are not fact unless you choose to accept them as fact. The problem is that up until now you abdicated your choice and decided to accept without question this limiting and destructive information. It is now time to take responsibility and start making informed choices about the information you accept and your abilities.

When self-doubt raises its ugly face, you need to start questioning why. Simply questioning the doubts sets in motion your reasoning, and you can make an informed choice from all the information not others' opinions. Questioning your self-doubt will help you make empowering choices and life decisions. Choose to believe in yourself because you are worth it.

Believe It's Possible

As I mentioned earlier, I am now able to achieve anything I conceive because I now believe anything is possible. But to arrive at this point, I first had to believe that change is possible. When I observe myself and others, it seems that the crucial first step to making change or improvement in behaviour or lifestyle resides first in the belief that change is possible. I often hear people make statements like these: "Oh, I could never live without cheese. There is no way I could run a marathon. I just don't see myself going out and not having a drink. I could never jump out of a plane." How can they ever expect to change with such limiting beliefs?

It's not that people can't change; it is that they don't want to change at all or they don't want to change badly enough. Let's all be more honest and say statements like these instead: "I don't want to live without cheese. I don't want to run a marathon. I don't want to go out and not drink. I don't want to be a skydiver." Then examine if you're ok with those choices and their consequences.

Clarity and self-honesty are keys to integrity and integral living. Individual mindset and heart-set rooted in what we believe is possible leads to satisfactory results and the attainment of goals. Our perception is our reality, and if we think change is possible, then it is possible. Conversely, if we don't think change is possible, it will not be possible. Sometimes, we scapegoat possibility to protect lack of desire or willingness to start the change process.

Once we can believe that change is possible, we need to believe that anything we want to become, achieve or have is possible. Is anything really possible? Yes! The problem is that people have what is known as a confirmation bias, which I introduced in Chapter Six. To reiterate, this means that if people want to believe something, then they look for proof they are right and ignore the proof they are wrong. They do not understand the difference between the improbable and the impossible.

I want to show you why anything is possible if it is probable. If there is a million-to-one probability of you jumping a train on your motorbike and if you try it a million times, you will succeed at least once. Though it is improbable that you will successfully jump the train your first attempt, it is possible. This is an example of why anything is possible if you understand the difference between improbable and impossible. Understanding probability is the first step to understanding the reasons why anything is possible.

How improbable was it that humans could fly or travel to the moon and back? How improbable was it that someone could be heard from the opposite side of the world as clearly as if they were right beside you? These are a few examples of events thought impossible but which became a reality. No matter how improbable or impossible your goal may seem, it can become a reality.

Anything is possible if you have a big enough why and the desire to achieve it. Just look to the Wright brothers, NASA, Alexander Graham Bell and the many others throughout history who turned the impossible into a reality.

When you truly believe in yourself and develop a big enough why, you too can believe it is possible and turn the impossible into the probable. You can achieve any goal you conceive because you will believe it is possible if you work hard and long enough to attain it.

Train Yourself To Believe in Yourself

To do well in life, you must believe in yourself. You are the one person you can truly rely on. Your belief about yourself and your abilities reflect in your personal success and happiness. When you lack confidence in yourself, others pick up on that and don't take you seriously, and in turn your confidence can shrink even more.

Belief in yourself opens the doors of opportunity to your dreams and aspirations. It allows you to live your truth and be your best self. You are an important and integral part of life as much as anyone and anything else. You have a purpose! When you believe in yourself, the ability to follow your passions and live your purpose is available. You are allowing good things to come to you, and your belief in yourself allows you to act on those opportunities.

But in this often highly competitive and demanding society we live in, we can feel small, unworthy and far from confident.

That doesn't mean you can't believe in yourself. It takes specific skills and habits that must be consistently practised. Here are five ways to train yourself to believe in yourself:

Reflect on Your Past Successes

If you're in an emotional rut, use the tools from your past and get yourself out. Here's an exercise: vividly remember a time when you wildly succeeded! You rocked it! You exceeded your own expectation. Put yourself there and feel the excitement and pride you had inside. Now, remember you can do it again.

It's healthy to use the past to your advantage. Too often we easily recall what has hurt us, but we can just as easily allow the past to help propel us. If you need a bigger boost, repeat the exercise.

Seek Positive External Validation

Every day, we are subconsciously seeking validation, essentially for love in some form. That level of validation depends upon the attitude of the people around us. If we surround ourselves with positive people who care about us, cherish our strengths and help us be uplifted, we will flourish. However, if we are around people with negative, limiting beliefs, we can become surrounded in a negative environment, not providing ourselves with the fertile ground we need to grow.

Happy, confident, successful people credit others. We all need positive encouragement. That can be a good friend, family member or mentor.

Transform Your Self-Talk

We create who we are every day by our daily beliefs and self-talk. Our words are essentially affirmation. It's important that we talk to ourselves with love and kindness. We deserve our own compliments. For some, that can be incredibly difficult. We can complement and love others, but love ourselves? It seems egotistical, but it's not.

You deserve your love and appreciation more than anyone else. Shine your light and love towards every area you feel needs improvement. Embrace your flaws. But doesn't that mean you're accepting and allowing them to be there? Actually, loving your flaws releases them and allows them to become whole and well again. If you are having a hard time, switch your focus to another area and come back to it later. This practice can be achieved easier through daily personal affirmations and mirror work.

Give Your Fears Less Credit and Give Yourself More

Fear is merely false evidence appearing real. Its worry set on fire. It holds you back from believing in yourself more than anything else. It's an illusion. Realizing that your fear is not real is the first step, which can actually be hard to do, so when you do you are well on your way.

Transcend the fear with action and do not hesitate. As the Latin proverb says, "Carpe diem!"

You are capable of much more than you believe. When you conquer a fear, you allow for more of your true self to shine. Keep up the momentum and declare to conquer a few fears in a specific amount of time, such as one a month. In a year, you'll look back and feel like a completely new you.

Celebrate the Positive

Your everyday attitude affects how you treat yourself and others. Strive to be an optimist and see the good in the world. Focus on what you love about yourself and your strengths.

Celebrate who you are and the good people you have in your life. Feel gratitude for everything going right and all the blessings on the way. A positive attitude is the quickest way to believing in yourself. It bypasses everything else and gets right to the end goal: happiness, love, success and belief in yourself.

Add these five concepts to your daily routine and in no time your belief in yourself will grow and empower you to become all that you can and want to become in life.

Summary

In this chapter, I have discussed the importance that believing in yourself plays in living a happy and successful life. If you do not believe in yourself or your goals, how are you ever expected to develop self-respect and develop a winning mental attitude towards success? If you want any chance at implementing positive change into your life, it is imperative that you develop a strong and sincere belief in yourself and your abilities.

I have often heard the term "fake it till you make it" used to help people overcome their low self-esteem and lack of confidence. I encourage you to do this by acting as if you have already succeeded in reaching your goals and by implementing the tools I have provided you in this chapter. It may feel silly or beneath you to start, but change requires sacrifice and commitment. Commit today to yourself and to someone you regard and trust that you will do whatever is required to help yourself. Become a person who not only believes in themselves but resonates their belief and solid self-esteem to anyone they meet.

Remember to keep believing in yourself no matter what others say about you. They are the ones who have low esteem and try to build themselves up by putting others down. Don't become a victim of their low self-esteem; show them what someone who truly believes in themselves can do. You will then be on the way to living a joyful, happy and fulfilling life.

CHAPTER SIXTEEN

Program Yourself for Success

Train yourself to succeed

"Programming your mind with positive thoughts each
day will go a long way to keep you from allowing
external criticism to derail your dreams."
— **Ken Poirot**

- -

In This Chapter
- ➤ The Power of Visualization
- ➤ Engage the Law of Attraction
- ➤ Law of Attraction Exercise
- ➤ Use Positive Affirmations
- ➤ Talk to Yourself as a Winner
- ➤ Act as If
- ➤ Reject Rejection
- ➤ Overcome Your Fears
- ➤ Summary

- -

It's a fact that the human subconscious mind has the power to make people's dreams come true. That's because the subconscious mind stores and processes everything we see, say, do and think. If we input positive thoughts into our mind, the subconscious goes about turning those thoughts into reality. Of course, the opposite is also true: if we program our subconscious mind with negative thoughts, it turns them into reality too.

The mind is the seat of thought. It is divided into two main sections. These are the conscious and the subconscious mind. The conscious mind actively performs tasks such as calculations, logical comparisons as well as the active direction of our bodies. On the other hand, the subconscious part of the mind controls functions in your body that are supposed to happen automatically. Examples of such functions are the heart beat and breathing processes. Dr. Bruce Lipton, a biologist and expert on subconscious beliefs and their effects on our genes, said, "The major problem is that the people are aware of their conscious beliefs and behaviours, but not of subconscious beliefs and behaviors. Most people don't even acknowledge that their subconscious mind is at play, when the fact is that the subconscious mind is a million times more powerful than the conscious mind and that we operate 95 to 99% of our lives from our subconscious programs. Your subconscious beliefs are either working for you or against you, but the truth is that you are not controlling your life, because your subconscious mind supersedes all conscious control. There may be an invisible subconscious program sabotaging your life."

Your subconscious mind stores information such as your personal values, beliefs, memories, skills, life experiences, circumstances as well as all the images that you have ever seen in your life. It also can trigger emotions automatically and does not have the ability to tell the difference between what is real and what is fictional. As such, it has a significant effect on our lives.

Yet, your subconscious mind can easily be manipulated. You can train your subconscious mind such that it will help you to attract exactly what you desire in life. In this chapter, you will learn techniques on how to reprogram your subconscious mind for greatness and success.

The Power of Visualization

Visualization is the technique of focusing your imagination on behaviours or events you'd like to have occur in your life. Advocates suggest creating a detailed picture of what one desires and then visualizing it repeatedly, using all your senses. What do you see? What do you feel? What do you hear? What does it smell like?

The practice is based on the idea that your body and mind are connected. By providing positive pictures, creative imagery and self-suggestion, visualization can change emotions that subsequently have a physical effect on the body.

Psychologist and author Gay Hendricks believes that visualization is one of the most powerful tools for change. "Many people are propelled by events of the past, but visualization is an act of projecting the present into the future," said Hendricks. "Visualization changes the dynamics of personal change by pulling the person toward a visualized happier, healthier and fulfilling future."

You've probably heard the phrase "the mind is a terrible thing to waste." But it's also a powerful tool to effect change. Many people turn to visualization to help them move past obstacles (internal and external) in their lives, relax and relieve stress, resolve or cope with chronic pain, heal themselves emotionally and physically, or accomplish goals such as losing weight or quitting smoking. Athletes use it to help them perform better, therapists use it to help patients heal from trauma, and experts conduct visualization seminars designed to help people realize their dreams.

In his book *The Success Principles*, Jack Canfield states that visualization is the act of creating compelling and vivid pictures in your mind, and it may be the most underutilized success tool that you possess because it accelerates the achievement of any success in three powerful ways.

First, visualization activates the creative powers of your subconscious mind. It also focuses your brain by activating your reticular activating system (RAS) to notice available resources that were always there but previously unnoticed. And finally, through the Law of Attraction, visualization magnetizes and attracts to you the people, resources and opportunities you need to achieve your goals.

By visualizing in your mind a clear and vivid picture of you believing in yourself and your goals, you are setting in motion a powerful process that will strengthen your beliefs and how you view anything in the future.

When I first implemented the power of visualizing myself as a strong, successful person who gets what I want, miraculous things started to happen. Not only did ideas, people, resources and support start to appear in my life, but I began to like who I was becoming.

There are several ways to use visualization to help program your mind for success. Think about this: everything we do begins as a thought. Every action, every word, every human creation exists first in our imagination. The ability to see things before they happen is what enables us to pursue our dreams and ultimately achieve them. In fact, the better we visualize the future we want, the better our chances to make it happen.

Training the Mind Is Training the Body

Your brain cannot differentiate well between real action and mental action. Research shows that thinking about an action— even while your body is at rest—will fire the neural pathways in your brain as if you were doing it.

To see this for yourself, hold a piece of string and let it dangle. Then, keeping your hand as still as you can, imagine twirling the string around. Most likely, the string will begin to move ever so slightly.

The good news is that mental training can improve almost all our skills and fast-track us towards our goals. For instance, many psychologists and life coaches recommend mental rehearsal for all sorts of things. Usually it is social or work-related, for example, to enhance assertiveness, smooth out an interview or a meeting, or even to enhance a date.

Athletes at the highest level are also encouraged to use visualization to improve their technique, motivation and drive. When interviewing Olympic gold medalists, researchers discovered that several winners used visualization, not just for the sport technique, but also to capture the feeling of being awarded a medal.

Five Applied Visualization Techniques

How do we develop and apply the powerful skill of visualization? Here I present five basic techniques in order of difficulty. Do them in order, moving on to the next one only when you have mastered the first. You can take as many days as you like to get good at each level; there is no rush.

Technique Number 1: Find a photograph and take your time to analyze it. Memorize every detail you can. Then simply close your eyes and try to re-create it in your mind. Bring in as much as you can: the colours, the birds in the sky, the freckles on the skin—whatever is there. Open your eyes to get more detail, if you must. Remember, this is not a test: do it until you get good at it.

Technique Number 2: For this one, we're going three-dimensional. This time pick up a small object: perhaps your pen or your keys. Again, analyze all the details and memorize it. Take your time. Now, close your eyes and see the object mentally. The challenge here is to start rotating it. See every detail but from all angles. If you feel comfortable, begin to bring in some surroundings. Place it on an imaginary table. Shine a few lights on it and imagine the shadows flickering.

Technique Number 3: This technique builds on the second one and can be hard for some people, although others will find it very easy. This time re-create your little object but with your eyes open. See it in the real world, right in front of you. Again, move it around, rotate it and play with it. See how it interacts with the objects in front of you. Imagine it resting on your keyboard, casting a shadow on your mouse or knocking over your coffee cup.

Technique Number 4: This is where things start to get fun. This time, we're bringing you into the picture. Think of a pleasant location. I like to use my favourite beach. Now, imagine yourself in it. It's important to be in the scene, not just thinking of it. Bring in your other senses one by one. What can you hear? Are the leaves rustling? Are there people talking in the background? What about the sense of touch? Can you feel the sand you are standing on? What about smell? Can you imagine eating ice cream and feeling it slide down your throat? Again, make sure that you are in the scene, not merely thinking of it. Make this mental movie as strong, vibrant and detailed as you can.

Technique Number 5: In the final technique, we're going to make things a bit livelier. Bring up the mental location from the previous exercise. Now, begin moving around and interacting with things. Pick up a rock. Sit on a bench. Run in the water. Roll around in the sand. Then, bring in someone else. Perhaps you could bring in a lover and then choreograph a dance with them. Or you could imagine a friend. Hold a conversation with them. Imagine them smiling as you tell them a joke. Now, imagine them slapping you on the shoulder playfully. What does that feel like?

Detail and realism are important. The reason we emphasize detail and realism is simply because practice doesn't make perfect. As you might have heard, only perfect practice makes perfect.

If I asked you to imagine the execution of your goals, whether it be doing well in a business meeting, or a date or sports, you probably saw yourself doing it perfectly straight away. You win big, you look cool, and everyone falls in love with you. This feels good and can increase motivation but, to put it bluntly, it's mostly a waste of time.

Realism is the most important consideration in visualization. Soldiers train in almost exactly the same gear they are going to wear in combat. None of them got good by playing shooting games on the computer or by playing paintball.

It is the same with mental training. Everything must be as realistic as possible. Until I understood the power of visualization, my mental imagery had merely been fantasies and I had been wasting my time. But when I began visualizing properly, I found that I was able to imagine a lot of possible mistakes before I actually made them, and all this while I was sitting on the couch.

Did that mean I failed? No, it meant I succeeded. From then on, my mental training began working for me because I overcame a lot of my fears through visualization and avoided a lot of mistakes in the process.

Applying Visualization to Your Goals

Now, what if we're not dealing with a physical skill? What if you had set a goal for something like money, a new career or a holiday?

Visualization applies in much the same way. Here are four tips for applying it to your goals:

1. **Focus on the positive.** A common mistake is focusing on the opposite of what you want. When I wanted to lose weight, I initially made the mistake of posting pictures of

my fat belly all over my room, thinking it was motivating me. But that was the wrong way. By focusing on my fat, I was keeping the fat there. I should have been visualizing the stomach I wanted.

2. **Have it, don't want it.** Think of something you really, really want. Now, do you have it? Probably not. Most often, wanting is the opposite of having. When you visualize, don't think about wanting something, see yourself as already having it.

3. **Be consistent.** You must work hard on this. Your mind is a muscle, just like your body. The top bodybuilders didn't get to where they are by working out for two minutes a day. They worked hard for it. Make your goal your burning obsession, a passion and purpose in life.

4. **Be specific.** Most people have vague goals. They vaguely want to be rich, or they want to travel somewhere nice. Where? "Oh, never thought about it much," they say. It's like getting into a car with a vague goal of wanting to buy something. It's not going to happen, right? You want to have a specific goal: I'm going to the supermarket to buy myself some shampoo and a toothbrush. It is the same with your goals. Set each goal in as much detail as you can: a specific amount of money, a specific outcome from a meeting, whatever it is.

Visualization is a very powerful tool for helping to achieve your goals. I strongly recommend you start using this powerful tool today. Don't worry if your mind starts fighting it at first. Keep doing it and those doubts will start to disappear, and you will feel the strength of possibility start to take over. It is not hard to do, but the rewards are tremendous.

Engage the Law of Attraction

Simply put, the Law of Attraction is the ability to attract into our lives whatever we are focusing on. It is believed that regardless of age, nationality or religious belief, we are all susceptible to the laws which govern the universe, including the Law of Attraction. The Law of Attraction uses the power of the mind to translate whatever is in our thoughts and materialize them into reality. In basic terms, all thoughts turn into things eventually. If you focus on negative doom and gloom, you will remain under that cloud. If you focus on positive thoughts and have goals that you aim to achieve, you will find a way to achieve them with massive action.

The Law of Attraction is working in your life whether you're aware of it or not. And it may explain why you are attracting the things in your life that you do. Here is everything you need to know about it.

While the Law of Attraction is getting quite a bit of publicity these days, the concept has been around for centuries and has been known, and used successfully, by great minds throughout history. According to books like *The Secret* by Rhonda Byrne, there's evidence that the Law of Attraction was used by Beethoven, Einstein and even Jesus, but you've also used it in your own life whether you're aware of it or not! This is because the Law of Attraction works whether or not you're aware of it. The main reason for its current popularity is that if you're aware that you're using the Law of Attraction, you can control what you attract into your life.

Basically, the Law of Attraction works like this: you create your own reality. What you focus on and what you think about is what you draw into your life. What you believe will happen in your life is what does happen.

However this isn't as simple as it seems, or everyone would have the lives that they want naturally. For example, people who are in debt and continually tell themselves "I need more money" don't find more money. They continue to attract "need more money" because that is the reality that they create.

Many people wonder why this works, and there is more than one explanation. The two main schools of thoughts go along these lines:

- **The spiritual explanation:** Many people believe that the Law of Attraction works by aligning God or the universe with our wishes. We are all made of energy, and our energy operates at different frequencies. We can change our frequency of energy with positive thoughts, especially gratitude for what we already have. By using grateful, positive thoughts and feelings and by focusing on our dreams, rather than our frustrations, we can change the frequency of our energy, and the Law of Attraction brings positive things into our lives. What we attract depends on where and how we focus our attention, but we must believe that it's already ours or soon will be.

- **The traditional scientific explanation:** If you're one who needs things to be a little easier to prove, there is also a different explanation for how the Law of Attraction works. By focusing on attaining a new reality and by believing it is possible, we tend to take more risks, notice more opportunities and open ourselves up to new possibilities. Conversely, when we don't believe that something is in the realm of possibilities for us, we tend to let opportunities pass by unnoticed. When we believe we don't deserve good things, we behave in ways that sabotage our chances at happiness. By changing our self-talk and feelings about life, we reverse the negative patterns in our lives and create more positive, productive and healthy ones. One good thing leads to another, and the direction of a life can shift from a downward spiral to an upward ascent.

Whatever the underlying reason, reams of anecdotal evidence confirm that the Law of Attraction works. For those science-minded folks out there, research does seem to support the positive effects of the Law of Attraction as well. For example, research on optimism shows that optimists enjoy better health, greater happiness and more success in life. (The traits of optimists are that they focus their thoughts on their successes and mentally minimize their failures.)

The best way to use the Law of Attraction is to realize that you will get exactly what you give your greatest amount of thought to. Everything that you are living right now, you attracted into your life: the good, the bad and the ugly. Most people do not like to hear this. I didn't like hearing it. But once you understand the Law of Attraction and learn how to use it to your benefit, you will be able to think the thoughts that will help you to live the life that you desire and no longer will you attract the bad and ugly things into your life experience.

If you truly believe that everything will work out, then it will. If you believe you will get sick, then you will call sickness into your life. If you believe that you will be wealthy, then you will have the money that you desire. If you believe that you will be poor, then it will be hard for you to attract riches into your life.

There is a huge difference between the way a rich person and a poor person thinks. Think of a person who you know who is struggling and constantly complaining about how broke they are. Have you seen any changes in their financial status? Think of a successful person. Let's say Bill Gates, the guy who helped create Microsoft. Do you think that he walked around saying how broke he was and that he will never have money? No, he had to have been very confident in his skills to attract money in order to be the success that he is today.

Some of the most successful people in the world believe and practise the Law of Attraction. For example, Oprah Winfrey, one of the most successful women in the world, attracted the part of Sofia that she wanted so badly in the 1985 popular movie *The Color Purple*. Oprah explained that she used visualization by acting as if she had the part before she was even considered for the role.

Wealthy people believe that they will always have money, so they are always thinking of innovative ways to create more of it. Be confident in yourself. Know that you can have anything that you can possibly think of.

All you must do is believe in yourself, and the universe will believe in you. With the help of the Law of Attraction, you will get exactly what you want and desire. The key to deliberate creation is to get happy and be happy in the knowing that good things will come to you. If you are sick, know that your body knows how to heal itself.

The Law of Attraction states that "like attracts like," so if you are feeling miserable, you will attract miserable people and circumstances into your life. Have you ever started off the day on the wrong foot? Say, you got out of bed one morning and you bump your toe really hard. Then as you are getting ready for work, you realize that you cannot find your other shoe. Then you say to yourself "this is going to be a bad day," which causes you to start looking for other bad things to happen. Guess what? Just as you imagined, nothing but bad things show up all day long.

Now, picture if you would have stopped your negative thoughts from the time you bumped your toe. Imagine if you would have laughed it off and said "this day is going to be a great day." You would have stopped looking for other negative things to occur, thereby cancelling the creation of negative things into your life existence.

Here is an example of a Law of Attraction story that caused me to create a negative circumstance into my life.

One day as I was driving to work, a car ran the red light and entered the intersection. The car was about two inches away from hitting my car. I then said to myself, "Oh my gosh, these people are going to kill me." And sure enough, as I was driving, I kept seeing more and more evidence of crazy people on the road.

While on my way home from work, I was still thinking about my crazy morning ride and all these crazy people on the road and a car suddenly changed lanes, causing me to immediately merge into the emergency lane to keep from being hit. I didn't realize it then, but because of my negative thinking, I attracted these events into my existences.

Now when I get into my car, I always intend on a safe, smooth ride to and from my destination. And I have been blessed with a carefree, easy ride every single day and it has been great. As I stated before, like attracts like, so whatever you are giving your thoughts to, you will attract into your life. You may as well deliberately create good things.

We must realize that we all use the Law of Attraction in our everyday lives, whether we realize it or not. We attract our life circumstances from the time we wake up to the time we go to bed.

And the best way to remember this is to know that life is reflected back to you according to the way you think and feel. If you feel good, you will attract good-feeling people and things into your life. If you are feeling bad, then you will attract negative or bad-feeling things and people into your life.

And always appreciate, appreciate, appreciate. When you appreciate all that you have right now, you will be able to keep those things and even more good things will appear in your life. If you have a roof over your head, be thankful. If you can put food on your table, be thankful. If you can put clothes on your back, be thankful. The universe loves gratitude and appreciation. Be thankful for both big and the small things that you have in your life right now.

The way to tell if you are allowing what you desire to come into your life is the feeling "no resistance." No resistance means that you are letting go of whatever it is that is holding you back from allowing your manifestations to come into your life.

For example, some people ask for more money, but they don't feel they are worthy. Not feeling worthy is resistance. Some people want more money, but they concentrate on the stack of bills that are piling up. That's resistance.

In order not to resist, you should focus on something that feels good to you. It could be your cat or your dog. It could be a newborn baby or a wonderful song you just heard on the radio. It could be a great gift or compliment that you just received.

Law of Attraction Exercise

Follow these three steps to create what you want using the Law of Attraction:

Step 1. Ask a command to the universe. Get a piece of paper and write down how you would like your life to be. You can say things like "I am so happy and thankful that I have _____." Your list can be as long as you want. You must write your list in the present tense, like you have what you are asking for right now. You do not have to ask more than once. Once you give your command to the universe, this starts the creative process and you can now move on to Step 2.

Step 2. Believe. You have to believe that whatever you are asking for already belongs to you. You must believe that you have whatever you are asking for right now. When you are trying to deliberately create with the Law of Attraction, you must see the things that you want as yours now! You must act the part: see yourself in the house that you want or car that you want to drive. The universe will create the circumstance, people or events that are needed in order for you to attract whatever you desire into your life.

Step 3. Receive. The last step is to receive. Get into the feeling of already having whatever it is that you desire. Once you feel very good about having what you want and desire, you are sending good feelings or vibrations out into the universe, which will give you enough power to manifest what you want into your life. Don't get caught up in the where, when and how your desires will come to you; the universe will make a way. Just feel it and your wants and desires will manifest.

For example, if you would like to create more money in your bank account, first you must ask. Write down the amount you would like to create. Then, you must believe that you already have the money that you want and desire. Do whatever it takes to convince yourself that you have the money that you desire. Talk about the things that you are going to buy and the places where you are going to vacation.

Then you must feel like you already received the money that you are asking for. Really feel like you have the money that you desire. Start by thanking the Universe for allowing you to have all the money that you want and desire at your disposal to do as you please.

Once you master all three of these steps, you will receive whatever you need in order to create the money that you desire. You probably won't even realize the action that you have taken in order to complete the process because it will not feel like hard work; it will feel like inspired action.

When you deliberately apply the Law of Attraction to your life, it doesn't matter what you use to feel good. The key is to take your attention away from what you feel is going wrong in your life, and once you feel good, you can now think about how you want your life to be. You need to do this as much as possible until feeling good is natural to you. You must focus on the good-feeling thoughts and not concentrate on the manifestation. And once you feel good and have no resistance, your manifestations will have no choice but to come into your existence. Start attracting joy, happiness, abundance and love into your life today by employing the Law of Attraction.

Use Positive Affirmations

"I'm never going to be able to do this job; I'm just not smart enough."

"Why does my boss want me to present at the trade show? I'm a terrible public speaker, and I'll just embarrass myself."

"I wish I could stick up for myself at work. In every meeting, I let the others walk over my ideas. I'm never going to get ahead."

Many of us have negative thoughts like these, sometimes frequently. When we think like this, our confidence, mood and outlook can become negative, too. The problem with negative thoughts is that they can become self-fulfilling prophecies. We talk ourselves into believing that we're not good enough. As a result, these thoughts drag down our personal lives, our relationships and our careers. However, if we deliberately do the opposite and use affirmations and positive thoughts about ourselves, the effect can be just as powerful but far more helpful.

What Are Affirmations and Do They Work?

Affirmations are positive statements that can help you to challenge and overcome self-sabotaging and negative thoughts. When you repeat them often and believe in them, you can start to make positive changes. You might consider affirmations to be unrealistic "wishful thinking." But try looking at positive affirmations this way: many of us do repetitive exercises to improve our physical health, and affirmations are like exercises for our mind and outlook. These positive mental repetitions can reprogram our thinking patterns so that, over time, we begin to think and act differently.

For example, evidence suggests that affirmations can help you to perform better at work. According to researchers, spending a few minutes thinking about your best qualities before a high-pressure meeting, for example, a performance review, can calm your nerves, increase your confidence and improve your chances of a successful outcome.

Self-affirmation may also help to mitigate the effects of stress. In one study, a short affirmation exercise boosted the problem-solving abilities of "chronically stressed" subjects to the same level as those with low stress. What's more, affirmations have been used to successfully treat people with low self-esteem, depression and other mental health conditions. And they have been shown to stimulate the areas in our brains that make us more likely to affect positive changes regarding our health.

This latter study suggests that a stronger sense of self-worth makes you more likely to improve your own well-being. For example, if you're worried that you eat too much and don't get enough exercise, using affirmations to remind yourself of your values can spur you on to change your behaviour.

How To Use Positive Affirmations

You can use affirmations in any situation in which you'd like to see a positive change take place in your life. These might include times when you want to:

- Raise your confidence before presentations or important meetings
- Control negative feelings such as frustration, anger or impatience
- Improve your self-esteem

- Finish projects you've started
- Improve your productivity
- Overcome a bad habit.

Affirmations may be more effective when you pair them with other positive thinking and goal-setting techniques. For instance, affirmations work particularly well alongside visualization. Instead of merely picturing the change you'd like to manifest, you can also write it down or say it aloud using a positive affirmation.

Affirmations are also useful when setting personal goals. Once you've identified the goals you'd like to achieve, affirmative statements can help you to keep yourself motivated in order to achieve them.

The power of affirmations lies in repeating them to yourself regularly. It's useful to recite your affirmations several times a day (have them pop up in your notifications!). You also need to repeat your affirmations as soon as you engage in any negative thought or behaviour that you want to overcome.

How To Write an Affirmation Statement

Affirmation statements usually target a specific area, behaviour or belief that you're struggling with. The following five points can help you to write the affirmation statement that best fits your needs:

- **Think about the areas of your life that you'd like to change.** For instance, do you wish that you had more patience or deeper relationships with your friends and colleagues? Or would you like a more productive workday? Write down several areas or behaviours that you'd like to work on. Be sure that they are compatible with your core values and the things that most matter to you, so that you'll feel genuinely motivated to achieve them.

- **Be sure that your affirmation is credible and achievable.**
Base it on a realistic assessment of the facts. For instance, imagine that you're unhappy with the level of pay that you currently receive. You could use affirmations to raise your confidence to ask for a raise.

  However, it probably wouldn't be wise to affirm to yourself that you're going to double your salary. For most people and most organizations, doubling what you're earning in one go isn't feasible. Keep it realistic! After all, affirmations are not magic spells. If you can't believe in them, it's unlikely they'll impact your life.

- **Turn negatives into positives.** If you are struggling with negative self-talk, write down the persistent thoughts or beliefs that are bothering you. Then, choose an affirmation that is the opposite of that thought and belief.

  For example, if you habitually think, "I'm not talented enough to progress in my career," turn this around and write a positive affirmation such as "I am a skilled and experienced professional."

- **Write your affirmation in the present tense.** Write and speak your affirmation as if it's already happening. This helps you to believe that the statement is true right now. For instance, "I am well-prepared and well-rehearsed, and I can give a great presentation" would be a great affirmation to use if you feel nervous speaking in front of a group.

- **Say it with feeling.** Affirmations can be more effective when they carry emotional weight. You need to want this change to happen, so every affirmation that you choose to repeat should be a phrase that's meaningful to you. For example, if you're worried about a new project that you've been tasked with, you could tell yourself, "I am really excited to take on new challenges."

Examples of Affirmations

By definition, your affirmation will be personal to you and specific to what you want to achieve or change, but the following examples may provide some inspiration:

- I have plenty of creativity for this project.
- My work will be recognized in a positive way by my boss and colleagues.
- I can do this!
- My team respects and values my opinion.
- I am successful.
- I am honest in my life and my work.
- I like completing tasks and projects on time.
- I'm grateful for the job I have.
- I enjoy working with my team.
- I'm bringing a positive attitude to work every day.
- I am excellent at what I do.
- I am generous.
- I am happy.
- I will be a leader in my organization.

Benefits of Using Positive Affirmations Every Day

There are many benefits of using positive affirmations for success throughout your day. Using uplifting affirmations each day can make your daily thoughts become more positive and reduce negativity from seeping into your brain. Positive affirmations, such as ones for success and money, can also encourage and motivate you towards a better life.

Many people use daily affirmations for success because they help keep things in perspective in the stressful world we live in.

We easily lose sight of how big and small problems really are. A recent study shows that optimistic and happy people have healthier hearts. Daily affirmations can help you stay more positive.

As you begin to implement positive affirmations into your life, others take note and you will begin to notice that you are also helping those around you without even trying. This in turn helps keep you focused and in a constant state of gratitude. When you practise using positive affirmations for happiness, success and fulfillment every day, they not only help keep you surrounded by the things you want in your life but are also known to bring about an abundance of blessings and gifts into your life.

Talk to Yourself Like a Winner

If you want to develop a strong belief in yourself and your goals, you need to tell it to yourself on a regular basis. From the first moment that you wake up in the morning, you have a choice about how your day is going to flow. You can either bombard your mind with negative thoughts about who you are or you can think empowering and uplifting thoughts that motivate you to achieve more. Which path sounds better? Unfortunately, many people don't think that they have a choice to begin with. They assume that self-deprecation is, and will always be, a part of who they are.

The fact of the matter is that nobody is born with low self-worth. You come into this world with a positive, "can-do" outlook. Unfortunately, the media and people come along and fill your mind with negative thinking, so much so, that you stop believing in yourself. You start to take on self-defeating beliefs that weren't even yours. These beliefs become your thoughts, which then become the words that you speak. It's fair to say that negative self-talk can drastically affect your confidence and self-esteem. When you think the worst about yourself, that's exactly what you end up creating in your life.

The good news is that, with positive self-talk, you can overwrite that negative voice that lives inside your head. Your inner critic can't survive on positivity. When events happen in your life that are viewed as negative, positive self-talk swoops in and reframes the situations, so that you can find the good amidst the bad. When you talk to yourself as if you are a winner, you embody that truth. The good news is that this has always been your natural state. Somewhere along the way, you may have lost yourself, but you can always get that positive person back.

Much of the time when we talk to ourselves about ourselves, we are more critical than we should be. This is a common problem and could become a roadblock for you. To help, try to talk to yourself like you would a friend. We say things to ourselves that we would never say to a friend. If you treat your self-talk this way, you will find yourself being less critical and more supporting. Become your own friend and learn to tell yourself you believe in yourself daily.

Belief is an attitude, and if you tell yourself that you believe in yourself and your goals on a regular basis, you will reinforce it into your mind strong enough to overcome any negativity or obstacle that comes your way. You will also start to attract ideas to support your beliefs and goals. Successful people all tell themselves they are winners and relay the attitude of a winner every day of their lives.

Act as If

Another great tool I found effective in changing my belief in myself and what I could accomplish is this: Act as If. The idea is that if you act as if you are already having what you desire, you will be drawn towards believing and achieving it. "Acting as if" is about believing in things that don't currently exist and for which there may not be much evidence for. This is about living a "faith-based" life, not an "evidence-based" life. The term "faith-based" often gets used in a political, social or moral context when talking about initiatives or organizations that relate to the church or some specific organized religion. However, being a faith-based person, while it can and often does encompass our religious beliefs and our spiritual practices, it is even broader than this.

When we choose to live with a strong faith in things not seen, not proven, and not guaranteed, we tap into the power of the possible and we supersede the literal and predictable. It means you begin to think, talk, dress, act and feel like the person you want to become. When you do this, it sends powerful commands to your subconscious mind to create ways to achieve what it is you desire. If you want to be a successful executive, then you would wear a smart business suit and carry yourself like a successful executive would. You learn to talk and do the things they do. By "acting as if," you program your reticular activating system (RAS) to look for anything you need to become who it is you are acting like. It also sends a message out to the world that this is who you see yourself to be.

Without realizing it, I used to do this process many years ago in my sales career. I always dressed in a nice suit and tie and carried a professional-looking briefcase with me. When I met with clients, I acted as if I were the best person to service their needs. This worked and I started to believe and feel I was the person I was presenting. The mind is a wonderful and powerful thing. You can easily program it to reinforce anything you feed into it.

If you are not sure how the person you want to become acts, then find someone you know who already is like the person you want to become. Watch how they act and present themselves. You could also ask them how they think and feel about who they are. If you do not know someone personally, then research it. The news and social media are full of examples you can draw from. Learn where these successful people get their self-esteem from and mirror it in your own life.

If you want to be a person who believes in themselves and who can achieve any goal, then set your mind and start to act as if you are already that person. This tool goes hand in hand with visualization, which I explained earlier in this chapter. The tool "act as if" can reprogram your mind, helping you totally believe in yourself and achieve the impossible. Start acting "as if" today and in no time at all you will become that person.

Reject Rejection

If you want any chance of living a life of joy, success and fulfillment, then you will have to learn to deal with rejection. Rejection is a natural part of life and affects us all. It is the actions of others and we have no control over it.

I am sure you can recall many times in your life when you experienced rejection and the resulting negative feelings. You were not chosen, you were not invited, or your invitation was turned down. You did not get the job you wanted, or your idea was laughed at. Whatever it was, it probably left you feeling disgraced, unwanted, embarrassed and hurt.

Rejection is simply a concept we place in our minds. If you want to succeed, you need to control and eliminate the negative thoughts you place in your mind as a result of being rejected. We tell ourselves the things we feel are real, but are they real? Our life did not get any worse because of what happened. Suppose you asked someone out on a date and they refused. Are you any worse off than before you asked? The answer is no. You did not have a date before you asked and you do not have one after you asked. What hurts are the things you tell yourself because of the rejection. If you tell yourself "I knew I wasn't good enough," then you have lost. You have lost self-respect and caused yourself pain and doubt about yourself. Your negative self-talk may even prevent you from asking anyone else out. If your response was "boy, did they miss out on a great opportunity," then how would that make you feel?

It is what we tell ourselves about the experience that can either limit us or enhance us. There are many examples of people in the world who have experienced repeated rejection and then gone on to great success. They did not let their negative self-talk continue and carried on until they got what they wanted.

One of the lessons I learned early in my sales career was that every rejection I received brought me one step closer to a yes. That is how you need to deal with rejection in your life. In *The Success Principles*, Jack Canfield presents a tool he terms "Just Say 'Next.' " He recommends getting used to the idea that there is going to be a lot of rejection in our lives. The secret to success is not to give up. When you are rejected, simply say "next" and keep on asking.

Stop allowing your self-talk about rejection to control how you feel and act. Learn to become one of the thousands of people who use rejection to become more and more determined and simply say "next, it is their loss." You will find it an empowering and rewarding way to live your life.

Overcome Your Fears

One of the most limiting factors in your life today is fear. It is fear—whether real or imagined—that has the power to stop you dead in your tracks. Fear is responsible for so many people not reaching their fullest potential.

Fear is natural and needed in our lives. It is fear that warns us of impending danger and keeps us safe. Whenever we think about trying something new, stepping out of our comfort zone or putting ourselves out there, we experience fear. Unfortunately, most people allow that fear to stop them from taking action and reaching their dreams. Successful people do exactly the opposite. They face their fears and use them to safely guide their decisions and actions. They have learned that fear needs to be acknowledged, understood and experienced. Successful people do not let fear limit them; they let it enhance their lives.

Fear should be a signal to us to stay alert and be cautious. We need to acknowledge fear for what it is and not let it stop us from acting. Many people will do anything to avoid the uncomfortable feeling of fear. In doing so, they run the risk of never accomplishing great things in life. Most great things in life require some sort of risk. It is also important to remember that, when taking a risk, by its very nature, things don't always work out. Failure and loss are always possible when there is a touch of risk involved. It is that failure or loss that should help you to become stronger not defeat you. In life, you cannot succeed if you don't try. Do not let the risk of failure stop you from succeeding.

Not all risk is real. Many people develop a risk in their heads that does not really exist. This fear (False Evidence Appearing Real) is responsible for so many people's lack of joy, success and fulfillment in life. This self-generated fear appears real, even though it is a fear of the future and is not happening now. Therefore, it has no real substance and arises when the subconscious is threatened, which makes you cling to the known and familiar. Such fear creates untold worry, apprehension, nervous disorders and even paranoia. Our immediate response is to stop any thought or action that could make this fear become a reality. If you push away, deny or ignore fear, it will hold you captive and keep you emotionally frozen, unable to move forward. The best way to handle this type of fear is to question it. What is it that you are afraid of and why? Could the situation turn out differently? Questions like these will help you break the fear down and see it is not real. It will help you to move forward towards your objective with confidence.

Another way to release your fear is to replace your vision of fear by focusing on the results you will receive from accomplishing your objective. If you are afraid to fly, stop focusing on the vision of your fear that is resonating in your mind, like the plane crashing. Instead, create a vision of you sitting around the yard with all your family enjoying the delicious barbecue and good weather.

If you truly want to succeed in life, you need to take control of your fears and not let them blindly dictate your decisions, actions and life experiences. Use questions and common sense and allow fear to strengthen and guide you to living your dreams.

Summary

As with building muscle, the more we "work out" certain neural pathways, the stronger they become. Robust pathways become your favoured psychological "highways." You can generate more happiness, calm and kindness in your life simply by practising these methods.

Throughout your life, you have unwittingly used this technique to program negative emotions, but now you take control and reprogram your mind with positive and life-enhancing information. Many of you have known something intellectually but failed to apply that wisdom. You knew jealousy would push your partner away, but you still get angry when they talk to the opposite sex.

When judgment or negativity comes up, it means your internal dialogue is off. Thankfully, there is a simple fix. Your subconscious mind works more through feeling than language. By leveraging strong emotion, you can create a direct line to the operating instructions of your subconscious.

Tony Robbins said, "Your mind is the key to success. And if you want to live the life you desire, then it's time to decide, to commit and to resolve. It's not what we *can* do in life that makes a difference—it's what we *will* do. And there's no better time to take back control of your mind and set your sights on something better right now."

In this chapter, you have received several tools to help you reprogram your subconscious. It is now time to start implementing them into your life.

CHAPTER SEVENTEEN

Take Massive Action

Pursue your goals with integrity

> "You don't have to be great to start, but
> you do have to start to be great."
> — **Zig Ziglar**

In This Chapter
- ➢ Ask for What You Want
- ➢ Create and Implement an Action Plan
- ➢ Transcend Your Limiting Beliefs
- ➢ Eliminate Negative Self-Talk
- ➢ Be Willing To Pay the Price
- ➢ Practise Persistence
- ➢ Change What Isn't Working
- ➢ Clean Up Your Past Mistakes
- ➢ Create a Breakthrough Goal
- ➢ Turn Your Decisions into Actions
- ➢ Summary

You could read all the self-help books in the world and have all the good intentions of achieving success, but unless you take massive action on the knowledge you gain, you're better off reading fairy tales! Reading is an important first step to making the necessary changes in your life; however, the changes can only be made once you actually take action.

When you keep reading and reading and you don't do anything with what you are learning, it's a form of procrastination. Making massive action a discipline in your life will set in motion steps that move you towards your goals and desires. Massive action will help break you through the obstacles you are sure to encounter along the journey and assist you in generating the kind of success you are truly capable of.

When I discussed the Ultimate Success Formula in Chapter Fourteen, it was made abundantly clear that to have any chance at succeeding, you need to take massive action. That is exactly what this chapter is designed to help you do. Here, you will discover many tools and processes to help you act and become the person you desire to be. But you need to take action, massive action. Please do not simply read the information I am providing but start to use it. Do not leave a chapter without taking one immediate action and implement something you learned from it to help you realize your goals and desires.

Ask for What You Want

The world is full of people living their dreams simply because they asked for what they desired. They knew what it is they wanted or needed and went out and asked for it. Yet, so many people today never ask for the things they desire. They find asking, which is one of the most important success principles available to everyone, challenging. Their lack of asking holds them back and, in most cases, they become frustrated with themselves for their lack of courage and action.

People invent many excuses that prevent them from asking for what they want. Looking needy, foolish or stupid are some of the excuses they create in their minds. But the biggest one is the fear of rejection. They are afraid of and expect to hear the word "no."

Nobody likes to be rejected so they go out of their way to avoid it, even to their own detriment or loss. The problem is they are actually rejecting themselves by not asking. By not asking, you are not giving the other person a choice. You are saying "no" for them even if they had no intention of saying "no" in the first place.

You should never assume others are going to automatically say "no." Always step out and take the risk. The worst thing that can happen is they do say "no." You have lost nothing, but you did provide yourself a chance to get what it was you wanted because you asked. You only lose when you say "no" for them.

How To Ask for Anything You Want

Here is a simple process to help you get what you desire by asking for it. Start by asking as if you expect to get it. Have no doubt in your mind that you can have it and you are determined to get it. Always assume you can have it. Do not let doubt weaken your belief.

Make sure you are asking the person who can say "yes." Many times, people have accepted a "no" from someone who did not have the final say. Be sure you are asking the right person and be specific about what it is you want. If you want more money, say how much it is you want, or you may be surprised at what you receive. Tell the other person exactly what it is that you want.

Finally, ask repeatedly. Do not accept "no" for an answer. A study by Herbert True at Notre Dame University found that 44 per cent of sales people quit after the first "no" they received, 24 per cent stop after the second "no," 14 per cent after the third "no" and 12 per cent after the fourth "no." This means that 94 per cent of salespeople have given up by being told "no" four times. It was also discovered that 60 per cent of the yeses come after the fourth "no." That means that 94 per cent of sales people miss out on 60 per cent of the sales. Successful sales people are persistent because most "noes" eventually become a "yes."

If you can teach yourself to ask for what you want and not be afraid of hearing "no" or letting it deter you, you will have a far better chance of getting what you desire in life. This is one process I have added into my life and now I almost always get a "yes" where there were only "noes." Here is a recent example of how I used this principle to get what I wanted.

While I was writing this book, my wife and I were on a holiday in Mexico and we went out to celebrate our 29th anniversary. We had done the same thing one year earlier and were treated to a private table on the beach at a fabulous restaurant. The evening was arranged by a hotel employee who we had befriended over the years of staying at the resort he worked for.

We had enjoyed the evening so much that my wife asked if we could do it again this year. Our friend had accepted a new job out of town and was no longer there to arrange a table for us.

I went to the restaurant early in the day and requested the same setup as we had the year before. The lady at the booking stand said they didn't provide that service there. I questioned her, even showing her photos from the previous year. After her fifth "no," I asked to speak to her manager or someone who could speak better English. She responded that she was the only one available at that time. I did not accept this "no," so I persisted until she finally called the head waiter who could speak better English but gave the same "no" she did. After four more "noes" from him I persisted, and he went to the manager. After a short conversation with the manager and showing him the photos of what I wanted, he agreed and told the others to set it up. That night they provided us an even better experience than we had the year before.

Because I asked specifically for what I wanted and did not accept "no" for an answer, I ended up receiving even more than I requested and had a very happy and appreciative wife. You have nothing to lose and everything to gain by persistently asking for the things you want in life. To be successful, you must take risks and face possible rejection. When you ask for what you want and follow the process outlined above you, will get a lot more "yeses" and fulfillment in your life.

Create and Implement an Action Plan

A personal action plan is a method of application that individuals choose in order to achieve one or more personal or professional goals. Individuals usually write down action plans to more easily follow the series of steps that it takes for these plans to come into fruition. Personal action plans are also called personal goal plans or life plans.

Personal action plans are composed of three main elements. The first element is a list of the specific steps that must be taken for an individual to achieve their goals. The second element is the time factor that the individual uses to motivate themselves to achieve the goal on or before a certain date. The third element is listing the resources available to help the individual realize their goals.

For example, an individual who wants to get a better job first describes the type of job that they desire and then lists ways to uncover one and the action steps required to obtain one. Then, they choose a date, possibly six months to one year, during which they want to secure their new job. Next, they enlist the help of others, such as career counsellors, friends or family members already working in their chosen field, to help them uncover ways to get interviews at the types of companies that hire people to fill their dream job.

Individuals must figure in unexpected circumstances and events as part of their personal action plans to be successful. When individuals plan for bumps in the road, these occurrences do not hinder their progress or cause them to lose sight of their goals.

Have you ever gone on a holiday with no or little planning? I did, and instead of having an adventurous and spontaneous journey, I ended up being frustrated because I needed to find everything during the journey. It is hard to fully enjoy the trip if you constantly need to think about where to sleep, what to eat and where to go.

It is much easier to travel when you have at least some big-picture vision and an idea of where you want to go, as well as a basic plan of the things you want to do. It's even easier if you have a more detailed plan.

It is the same with the journey of life. Many people live life with no or little planning, so it is no surprise when they end up being frustrated or asking themselves "How did I end up here?" That's why it is important to prepare a plan in advance. Jim Rohn, a renowned entrepreneur, author and motivational speaker, once said, "I find it fascinating that most people plan their vacations with better care than they plan their lives. Perhaps that is because escape is easier than change."

If you don't think and plan, you can easily end up being angry, frustrated and not satisfied with your life. There are other benefits of having a personal development plan. If you ever find yourself feeling lost in life, you can look at your plan and remind yourself where you want to go. A personal development plan is your guideline for life.

By "developing" your future, you will get a better sense of control over your life and you will make better decisions along the way. If you are a driver and you want to make your journey more pleasurable, you need to know where you are going and how you will get there. Good preparation decreases the risk of getting lost or things going wrong with your journey. It's the same with a personal development plan: it increases possibilities that your life will go in the right direction.

A personal development plan helps you to structure your thinking. We constantly plan and think in our head, but very often we miss important details and we don't create a realistic strategy to realize that plan. That's why many "plans" just exist as dreams. A personal development plan is a process that consists of defining what is important to you, what you want to achieve, what strengths you already have that help to achieve your goals, and what you need to improve and develop with time.

If you like the idea of having a personal development plan, you are probably asking yourself "where do I start?" Once you have decided and know exactly what it is you want from life, it is time to create and set into motion exactly how you are going to get it. If you completed the goal-setting exercise in Chapter Fourteen, you have the information you require to do this. When you are developing or designing something new, it's usually not finished overnight. That's why you need to be prepared and recognize that every important plan will take time before it's realized.

Below is a personal development plan process to help you structure your thinking and create a strategic plan for achieving your goals.

If you want to achieve anything important, you need to take time to make a detailed plan.

There are some important things to consider when creating a personal development plan. Here are nine steps that can help you to create a good personal development plan:

1. Define your goals
2. Prioritize
3. Set a deadline
4. Understand your strengths
5. Recognize opportunities and threats
6. Develop new skills
7. Take action
8. Get support
9. Measure progress

Define Your Goals

What is important to you? Which new skills do you want to acquire? Which achievements would make you happier? Do you have any unfulfilled dreams that you are now ready to accomplish? Do you want to move ahead to the next stage in your career? Do you want to get a better job?

The first step is to define goals that are important to you. It can be something related to your career or something that will enrich or improve your personal life (like lose weight, start a new hobby or activity, or learn a new language).

Step 1. Write down 5 to 10 goals that are important for you to achieve.

Prioritize

Out of all goals you wrote down, which one is the most important? This is your key goal that will be your focus. Maybe you want a career change or you want to achieve a desired physical shape or acquire some new skills. Are there any transferable skills (skills that you can transfer to different areas of your life) that would be important for your success? For example, if you improve speaking skills, the result can be more confidence, better relationships and communication with others, and even business success (such as more successful negotiations and more sales).

The purpose of a personal development plan is to help you expand your knowledge, develop new skills or improve important areas of life.

Step 2. Take a good look at your list and select one goal that is the most important to you and you will work on first.

Set a Deadline

If you have a goal but don't know when you want to achieve it, chances are it will never happen. Also, if you are planning to achieve a big success in a very short period, again, chances are it will not happen. When planning, you need to be realistic, specific and make good assumptions time-wise.

Rather than saying "I want to be a millionaire someday," it's better to plan to double your income this year. How long will it take you to achieve your goal? Once you have a realistic time frame for your goal, it's important to commit that you will indeed do it. Be serious about it. If you are not the one who is taking your plan seriously, nobody else will either.

Instead of focusing on problems and obstacles that could happen, think about how great you will feel when it's done. You can also define how you will reward yourself when you manage to achieve your goal.

Step 3. Set a deadline.

<u>Understand Your Strengths</u>

Everyone in the world is good at something and has above-average skills or strengths in some specific areas. Even if you are not a talented singer, actor or artist, you can still be a good parent, excellent listener or a caring person. What are your key strengths?

If you are not sure about the answer, then ask your friends and family. Ask them "what do you think are my biggest strengths?" Maybe you will be surprised with their answers. Your key strengths are ones that make you unique and special. No one can ever take them from you.

It's very important for your confidence to be aware of your strengths. Are you well-organized, patient, persistent, outgoing, intelligent, brave, a fast learner, talented, open-minded?

Step 4. Once you understand what your strengths are, write down which of these strengths can help you to achieve your goal.

<u>Recognize Opportunities and Threats</u>

Your current behaviours and habits can either support or not support you in achieving your goal. Which of your habits or actions are threats to your goal achievement? These are the things you need to stop doing. For example, if your goal is to live 100 years, then you need to stop smoking, stop buying junk food, stop worrying about things, etc. Write down at least five things that you commit you will stop doing.

On the other hand, there are some new actions that are opportunities for you to achieve goals much easier. What actions can you choose to start doing that will help you to achieve your goal?

If you want to save more money, then you can start managing your money, you can start writing down your expenses, you can start spending less, etc. Write down five things you commit to start doing.

Step 5. Create a start doing and stop doing list.

START DOING	STOP DOING
1.	1.
2.	2.
3.	3.
4.	4.
5.	5.

Develop New Skills

A personal development plan is a plan for how to get from the place you are now to the place you want to be. If you want to get something, you will need to give something in return.

For example, if your goal is to move ahead to the next stage in your career, you will have to learn new skills. If you want to start your own business, you will have to learn about marketing, sales, entrepreneurship, finances, etc.

A quote by Brian Tracy in *Eat That Frog!* is "For everything you want in life, there is a price you must pay, in full and in advance. Decide what you really want and then determine the price you'll have to pay to achieve it. Remember, to achieve something you've never achieved before—you must do something you have never done before. You must become someone whom you have never been before. Whatever you want, you'll have to pay a price measured in terms of: sacrifice, time, effort, and personal discipline. Decide what it is and start paying that price today."

In other words, to achieve something you have never achieved before, you need to develop skills you have never had before and start working on those skills as soon as possible. Which skills or knowledge will help you to achieve your goal?

Step 6. Write down the list of the skills you need to develop that will help you achieve your goal.

Take Action

If you want to achieve a big goal, there will be many actions you will need to take.

Step 7. Write down at least 3 to 5 most important actions you will need to take within your defined time frame.

Get Support

Who can help you achieve your goals faster? For example, if you want to change your career, you can consider talking with a career adviser; if you want to lose weight, you can have a fitness coach; if you want to improve your finances, you can talk with a financial adviser.

Step 8. List anyone who you can think of who would be able to help you to achieve your goal.

Measure Your Progress

The best motivator to stay persistent in achieving goals is your own progress. Even if it is a little progress, it is still something. It is important to recognize that you are moving forward and to write down things that you are doing well. If something is not going well, what can you do differently?

If something is not going well, you need to change or improve the strategies you are using. By doing the same things, you will be getting the same results. If you want better results, you need to change something.

Step 9. Write down things that you need to improve and define new strategies you will try. Your responsibility is to make things work for you.

What's working well (my accomplishments)	What do I need to change (improve)

This nine-step Personal Development Plan process will help you to create a detailed plan for the goals that are the most important to you.

A personal development plan is a very powerful method to assess your life, define what is really important for you and start working on things that matter the most. Often in our life, we are so busy with our day-to-day activities that we rarely have time for important thinking and planning. Exercises like this can help you to get more clarity about goals that are the most important to you and to create realistic strategies for how you will achieve them. I suggest that you now act and create a new personal development plan for your life and then take the first step required towards its fulfillment.

Transcend Your Limiting Beliefs

As I brought to your attention earlier, many of us have beliefs that limit our success, whether they are beliefs about our own capabilities, beliefs about what it takes to succeed, beliefs about how we should relate with other people, or even common myths that modern-day science or studies have long since refuted. Moving beyond your limiting beliefs is a critical first step toward becoming successful. You can learn how to identify those beliefs that are limiting you and then replace them with positive ones that support your success.

How To Overcome Any Limiting Belief

Here is a simple but powerful four-step process you can use to transform any limiting belief into an empowering belief:

1. Identify a limiting belief that you want to change. Start by making a list of any beliefs you have that might be limiting you.
2. Determine how the belief limits you.
3. Decide how you want to be, act or feel.
4. Create a turnaround statement that affirms or gives you permission to be, act or feel this new way.

Remember, all your inner dialogue and outer conversation should be aimed at getting you to where you want to be. It is vital to keep replacing any thought or belief that is keeping you from achieving your goals with an empowering thought or belief that will take you closer to your goals. Use the following template to turn any limiting belief into an empowering belief:

1. My negative or limiting belief is ...
2. The way it limits me is ...
3. The way I want to be, act or feel is ...
4. My turnaround statement that affirms or gives me permission to do this is ...

Taking massive action includes eliminating your limiting beliefs. Once you have addressed your limiting belief, created a new belief and your turnaround statement, you will need to implant it into your subconscious mind through constant repetition several times a day for a minimum of 30 days. It is now time to act on your limiting beliefs and turn them into enhancing ones.

Eliminate Negative Self-Talk

We all have an inner critic. At times, this little voice can be helpful and keep us motivated toward goals, like when this critic reminds us that what we're about to eat isn't healthy or what we're about to do may not be wise. However, this little voice can often be more harmful than helpful, particularly when it gets into the realm of excessive negativity.

This is known as negative self-talk, and it can surely bring us down. Negative self-talk is something that most of us experience from time to time, and it comes in many forms. It also creates significant stress, not only to us but to those around us if we're not careful. Here's what you need to know about negative self-talk and its effects on your body, your mind, your life and your loved ones.

Can you remember a time in your life when you had an idea or desire to do something only to mentally talk yourself out of it? Your mind would come up with all sorts of reasons that would stop you without even trying. Thoughts like "I can't do this, I'm not smart enough, it is unrealistic or who am I kidding?" are a few of the negative self-talk scripts that run through people's minds when contemplating something new. Most of this is controlled by the subconscious automatically. At no time did you question these thoughts; you accept them as gospel and let them make your decisions for you.

Many people have missed out on great opportunities and advancements in their life because of their negative self-talk. It is also responsible for people's fears and decisions that keep them stuck in a life of despair. Negative self-talk can affect us in some damaging ways.

Studies have linked negative self-talk with higher levels of stress and lower levels of self-esteem. This can lead to decreased motivation as well as greater feelings of helplessness. This type of critical inner dialogue has even been linked to depression, so it's definitely something to fix.

Those who find themselves frequently engaging in negative self-talk tend to be more stressed. This is in large part due to the fact that their reality is altered to create an experience where they don't have the ability to reach the goals they've set for themselves. This is due to a lowered ability to see opportunities around them as well as a decreased tendency to capitalize on these opportunities. This means that the heightened perception of stress is due to mere perception and the changes in behaviour that come from them. The following are additional negative consequences of negative self-talk:

- **Limited thinking.** You tell yourself you can't do something, and the more you hear it, the more you believe it.

- **Perfectionism.** You begin to believe that "great" isn't as good as "perfect" and that perfection is unattainable. In contrast, mere high achievers tend to do better than their perfectionistic counterparts because they generally are less stressed and are happy with a job well-done rather than picking it apart and zeroing in on what could have been better.

- **Feelings of depression.** Some research has shown that negative self-talk can lead to an exacerbation of feelings of depression. If left unchecked, this could be quite damaging.

- **Relationship challenges.** Whether the constant self-criticism makes you seem needy and insecure or you turn your negative self-talk into more general negative habits that bother others, a lack of communication and even a "playful" amount of criticism can take a toll.

One of the most obvious drawbacks of negative self-talk is that it's not positive. This sounds simplistic, but research has shown that positive self-talk is a great predictor of success.

For example, one study on athletes compared four different types of self-talk: instructional: where athletes remind themselves of specific things to do to play better; motivational: self-talk that keeps people on-task; positive; and negative. The research found that positive self-talk was the greatest predictor of success. People didn't need to remind themselves how to do something as much as they needed to tell themselves that they are doing something great and that others notice it as well.

How To Minimize Negative Self-Talk

There are different ways to reduce negative self-talk in your daily life. Here are eleven:

Catch Your Critic

Learn to notice when you're being self-critical so you can begin to stop. For example, notice when you say things to yourself that you wouldn't say to a good friend or a child.

Remember that Thoughts and Feelings Aren't Always Reality

Thinking negative things about yourself may feel like astute observations, but your thoughts and feelings about yourself can definitely not be considered accurate information. Your thoughts can be skewed like everyone else's, subject to biases and the influence of your moods.

Give Your Inner Critic a Nickname

There was once a *Saturday Night Live* character known as "Debbie Downer." She would find the negative in any situation. If your inner critic has this dubious skill as well, you can tell yourself, "Debbie Downer is doing her thing again."

When you think of your inner critic as a force outside of yourself and even give it a goofy nickname, it's easier to realize that you don't have to agree, and it becomes less threatening and easier to see how ridiculous some of your critical thoughts can be.

Contain Your Negativity

If you find yourself engaging in negative self-talk, contain the damage that a critical inner voice can cause by only allowing it to criticize certain things in your life or be negative for only an hour in your day. This puts a limit on how much negativity can come from the situation.

Change Negativity to Neutrality

When engaging in negative self-talk, you may be able to catch yourself, but it can sometimes be difficult to force yourself to stop a train of thought in its tracks. It's often far easier to change the intensity of your language. "I can't stand this" becomes "This is challenging," or "I hate ..." becomes "I don't like ..." and even "I don't prefer ...." When your self-talk uses more gentle language, much of its negative power is muted as well.

Cross-Examine Your Inner Critic

One of the damaging aspects of negative self-talk is that it often goes unchallenged. After all, if it's a running commentary going on in your head, others may not be aware of what you're saying to yourself and thus can't tell you how wrong you are. It's far better to catch your negative self-talk and ask yourself how true it is. Most of the negative self-talk is an exaggeration, and calling yourself on this can help to take away the damaging influence of negative self-talk.

Think like a Friend

When our inner critic is at its worst, it can sound like our worst enemy. Often, we'll say things to ourselves in our heads that we'd never say to a friend. Why not reverse this? When you catch yourself speaking negatively in your head, make it a point to imagine yourself saying this to a treasured friend. If you know you

Achieve Your Dreams

wouldn't say it this way, think of how you'd share your thoughts with a good friend or what you'd like a good friend to say to you. This is a great way to shift your self-talk in general.

Shift Your Perspective

Sometimes looking at things in the long term can help you to realize that you may be placing too great an emphasis on something. For example, you may ask yourself if something you're upset by will truly matter in five or 10 years. Another way to shift perspective is to imagine that you are panning out and looking at your problems from a great distance. Even thinking of the world as a globe and of yourself as a tiny, tiny person on this globe can remind you that most of your worries aren't as big as they seem. This can often minimize the negativity, fear and urgency in negative self-talk.

Say It Out Loud

Sometimes when you catch yourself thinking negative thoughts in your mind, simply saying them aloud can help. Telling a trusted friend what you're thinking about can often lead to a good laugh and shine a light on how ridiculous some of our negative self-talk can be. Other times, it can at least bring support. Even saying some negative self-talk phrases under your breath can remind you how unreasonable and unrealistic they sound and remind you to give yourself a break.

Stop That Thought

For some, simply stopping negative thoughts in their tracks can be helpful. This, unsurprisingly, is known as "thought-stopping" and can take the form of snapping a rubber band on your wrist, visualizing a stop sign or simply changing to another thought when a negative train of thought enters your mind. This can be helpful with repetitive or extremely critical thoughts like, "I'm no good" or "I'll never be able to do this," for example.

Replace the Bad with Some Good

This is one of the best routes to combatting negative self-talk: replace it with something better. Take a negative thought and change it to something encouraging and accurate. Repeat until you find yourself needing to do it less and less often. This works well with most bad habits: replacing unhealthy food with healthy food, for example, and it's a great way to develop a more positive way of thinking about yourself and about life.

By eliminating your negative self-talk and replacing it with positive self-talk, you are enhancing your chance at success. You will reduce the stress you feel in life and will be motivated to forge ahead when obstacles cross your path. If you change your self-talk scripts, you will change your life.

Be Willing To Pay the Price

We all want the beautiful, loving wife or strong, loyal husband, the luxurious home, the sweet, pimped-out ride and the lean, hard physique of an awakened warrior or goddess. We all want to achieve financial prosperity, raise happy, healthy children, or start our own lucrative business doing what we love. We all want to travel this beautiful paradise of a planet, attain spiritual enlightenment and most importantly find happiness and contentment in life.

We all want it (or our own version of it), yet only a small percentage of us will ever make it our reality. Why do you think that is? Is it because the gods are cruel and enjoy tormenting us humans for their own entertainment? Is it because the one per cent secretly control and hoard all the country's wealth and refuse to share? Is it because we are cursed by our fate and can never rise above the waterline of mediocrity?

No, no and no again! The cold, hard truth of the matter is that we are simply too lazy and cheap to pay the price of victory. What's worse is that many of us have developed a sense of entitlement in which we unrealistically expect to receive the good things in life without actually having to give anything in return. We think that it should all be handed to us just for being born.

Well, I've got some shocking news for you. In order to live the dream life, to have it all and be successful in your career and relationships, you must be willing to pay the true price of victory. Unfortunately, we've all been taught that the price of victory is a lot of seriously demanding, finger-crunching, bone-jarring, mind-numbing, muscle-straining, sweat-producing hard work. And hard work is the last thing anyone in the world wants to do.

Most people want to avoid hard work at all costs, yet what they are failing to realize is that nothing worth having comes without substantial effort. If you want to live the dream life, you must be prepared to do the work that each of your goals requires. You must be willing to put in the sweat and blood equity by which the high price of victory is paid.

But I have good news for you. The pain of paying the price is only temporary and the benefits last forever. Yes, you may have to study hard or miss out on great times with your friends for a while but the benefits you will receive from your education will last a lifetime and you will be in a far better position to enjoy it.

Take Olympic athletes for example. These men and woman spend several years of painstaking repetitious practice to one day win the gold medal. When they do end up on the podium, all their short-term pain is forgotten as they accept the medal, which they will cherish for a lifetime as well as all the perks that go with it.

Think of a time when you truly wanted something and worked hard to achieve it. In many cases, you had to temporarily sacrifice to get what you desired. Was not the result worth all the short-term pain? Were you not glad you were willing to pay the price?

I remember how concerned I was when I realized the effort, sacrifice and commitment it would require to complete my four years of formation to become a deacon. I had asked myself more than once if I was willing to commit myself and do what was required to be worthy, deserving and capable of such an honour.

Four years might seem a long time in the present, but it is only a fraction of our time here on Earth. Though those four years seemed to last forever, the price I paid is nothing to the blessings I have received over the years because of it.

Once you have made the decision to pay the price required to achieve whatever it is you desire, you will receive the strength to put into action a plan of sustained effort to complete it. You will find yourself discovering whatever is required of you, even if it seems difficult or impossible at the time.

But for you to truly make the decision to pay the price, you need to know what the price is. You are the only one who can determine if the price asked of you is worth the reward you will receive.

The first step is to investigate everything that will be required of you to achieve the result you desire. Only then will you have the information you need to make a commitment to pay the price. You will have weighed the price of what is required to the result you will receive or experience. When you are fully informed and willing to pay the price, you will develop whatever is required to achieve your desires.

If you believe in yourself and have dedication and pride—and never quit—you'll be a winner. The price of victory is high but so are the rewards. Taking action means being willing to pay the price.

Practise Persistence

If you want to be successful in life, you will need to become persistent in the pursuit of your goals. High achievers are always persistent in their endeavours. They simply refuse to give up. Even when it looks hopeless, winners keep on trying. No matter how hard your path may seem, you must be persistent and find a way to keep moving towards your goal. The longer you persist, the more likely you are to be successful.

The problem is most people tend to give up just before they cross the finish line. They either come across an obstacle they had not planned for or they stop in fear of failure. They have no self confidence that they can finish what they started or that something is better than nothing.

I watch a lot of football and have always been frustrated when a team strategically marches the ball all the way down the field to the one-yard line and, after stumbling a bit, are facing a third down, but they give up on scoring a touchdown and settle for a field goal. Instead of getting seven points they get three, and at the end they lose the game by only a couple of points, points they could have had if they were persistent and did not give up and settle. They wasted all their hard work moving the ball against the defence and getting so close to their goal of a touchdown only to quit so close and not believe in themselves to find a way to achieve their goal. How many times have you given up in life just before the finish line only to try and justify it to yourself and others? Winners don't quit, and if things don't work out on the first try, they are persistent and try again until they do achieve what it is they truly desire.

To achieve more of your desires, you must become persistent even when you are faced with unforeseen obstacles or setbacks, which you could not have expected or prepared for. Successful people continue forward and find ways to overcome obstacles and anything that gets in their way.

For every roadblock, there is an alternative course of action that you need to find. Whenever you encounter an obstacle or run into a roadblock, you need to step back and brainstorm for ideas on how to move forward. Do not let fear or doubt stop you. If you want to succeed, you will find a way. Brainstorm at least three ways you can overcome your obstacle and get back on track towards your destination. There are always a number of possibilities if you are persistent and search for them. Always be solution-oriented in your thinking and persevere until you find a way that works.

Like the Jedi Master Yoda said, "Try not. Do. Or do not. There is no try." Take the master's advice and become more persistent in everything you do. You will be surprised and pleased with the results you will begin to experience. Become one of the high achievers in the world by regularly implementing the tool of persistence in your life.

Change What Isn't Working

We have all had the experience of realizing that something in our lives is not working. This knowledge can come as a sudden realization or a nagging feeling of doubt that grows stronger, waking us up to the fact that something needs to change.

Some people tend to act rashly and make sweeping changes before even understanding what the problem is. Other people fear change, so they live with the uncomfortable awareness that something needs to shift but won't do anything about it. Between these two extreme responses lies a middle way that can help us powerfully and gracefully change what isn't working in our lives. The first step is remembering that your life is made up of many beliefs, values and habits. Changing any one of these can change other areas in your life. Because of this, small changes can often have a big effect in your life, whereas at other times you may realize that much bigger changes are necessary. The only way to know for sure is to take the time to rationally understand the problem.

Examine your life as an entirety—your work, your relationships, where you live—and determine what specifically is not functioning the way you would like. Once you have acknowledged and understand the problem, write it down on a piece of paper. For example, "I am not happy with my relationship" or "I don't like my apartment." The next step is to figure out the adjustment you would like to make and how you can go about making this change. If you are unhappy with your relationship because you spend too much or not enough time with your partner, you may want to discuss this problem with them and come up with a compromise. On the other hand, if you realize your relationship is not working to such a degree that it needs to end, begin working through that process. Writing down the truth can be a powerful catalyst for change. The key to making changes that work is to accept the necessity of change as part of life. As we change, we may find it necessary to fine-tune our relationships, work and living situations. Our lives are living, breathing entities that reflect our dynamic selves.

Remember the Ultimate Success Formula: after reviewing your progress towards any goal you need to change what isn't working. Do not be like so many people who put on blinders when things are not working out and continue to do more of the same thing hoping for a better result.

When things are not working out according to your goal or vision, then change is required in one of two possible ways. You need to change either how you feel or what you are doing, your behaviour. You need to determine if the problem is the feeling you have associated to a situation or an action that was taken that caused the problem. Only then will you be able to be able to properly examine the situation and implement corrective change.

If you are feeling badly about something, you need to determine if the feeling is the result of something you misunderstood, something you did yourself or outside powers or another person's actions. If it is something outside your control, like the actions of someone else that is interfering with your efforts, you need to determine if it is even possible to change the situation.

It is important to remember that you cannot always change the world around you or other people. You can try and influence change, but you cannot force change. If you determine that the outside force cannot be changed, then all you have left is to change your direction and how you feel about it.

One of the best ways to get results is to change your approach. You can change yourself faster than you can change other people. This gives you incredible flexibility in any situation. Your ability to change your thinking, feeling and doing is the key to changing your lot in life or changing the results you get.

Let's say you had a heated argument with your partner. You were left feeling upset, minimalized and hurt. The argument was over your partner not doing something you asked them to do. After some heated discussion, your partner replied that they were too busy and were not able to get it done. Your partner asked, "If it was so important to you, then why didn't you do it yourself?" Then they walk out of the room, ending the discussion with the last word.

If your vision of marriage is a couple working in loving harmony and sacrificing for each other every day, there is a conflict. Because this situation did not match your vision, you need to ask yourself why. Was it something you did, something they did, unrealistic expectations or a mixture of all? Once you have looked at the whole picture, you will be able to determine what needs to be changed to make and feel everything right. Only then will you be in a position to implement the corrective change required.

When you know the corrective change you want to implement, then you need to act and set the change in motion. As you move forward, you need to be prepared to change your approach whenever the actions you are taking are not receiving your desired results. As soon as you set in motion your commitment to achieving what it is you are after, the how will expose itself.

Clean Up Your Past Mistakes

It was deemed to be the greatest moment in Tom's life. A musician turned entrepreneur, Tom had been dreaming about it for ages and now all his dreams were coming true. Seven long years of struggle, disappointments, failures and heartburns had borne fruit at last. He was on the verge of getting the biggest contract of his entrepreneurial career from a top production company. His happiness was beyond words.

Then, the unexpected happened. The organization pulled back its offer, citing "not forthcoming." On further plodding for details, Joe found out that the organization did a background check to verify his credentials and had stumbled upon one of his most embarrassing life failures during his early days.

They discovered that as a young adult Tom was involved in a gang that was responsible for a robbery and death of an innocent child. Even though Tom was not directly involved in the robbery, he was implicated by association and spent time in a young offender's penal institution. The event had resulted in a great deal of hostile publicity. Tom had "conveniently" hidden away this fact and unfortunately it came back to haunt his future.

Tom's biggest mistake here was that he did not handle his past failures, the "skeletons in his closet," in the right way. If he had been forthcoming and highlighted what he had done to make up for his poor decisions and reputation of the past, events may have turned out differently for him. We are all humans and humans make mistakes. However, some of the mistakes or blunders we make refuse to go away and end up as "skeletons in our closets." We try our best to hide these skeletons from public glare. But that never proves to be a good idea in the long run.

The only permanent way is to take out these skeletons and vanquish them once and for all so that they do not haunt us again. And here is how we can do it.

Turn Over a New Leaf

Turning over a new leaf is the most foolproof way to remove past errors but not easy to implement. You move ahead from the worst chapter of your life into a brand-new book. For example, you change your profession or your business so that your past becomes irrelevant for the present. Such a move is easier when you have just started out or are quite young to shoulder the risk. As you grow older, doing a U-turn and transforming completely becomes even more difficult. Sometimes there is also a stigma of "escapism" or "cowardice" associated with this move, but if you can justify and succeed, why care what the world thinks?

Don't Let Sleeping Dogs Lie

Ignoring our past errors is the simplest and yet the most dangerous. You are leaving a big chunk of your success to fate and hope that the sleeping dog does not wake up. Sometimes (as we have seen in Tom's case), it becomes too late to make amends. This option should be tried only when you are sure that the discovery will not lead to any adverse effects. If there is even a slight chance of adverse effects, it is better to confront the demon, rather than push it under the carpet.

Confront the Demons

This is the bravest path possible when we are not in a position to correct the past. Rather than waiting for the demon to rear its ugly head, we confront the demon with all our might and smartness. We go all out to change the perceptions and improve ourselves visibly beyond the mistakes made. We do not hide the mistake, but rather make it a benchmark from which we learn, improve and succeed for the better. Initially, the going will be hard in this case, but once people get to know about your qualities, your past will soon be forgotten.

Go Back and Make Amends

It requires a lot of guts to admit a mistake, and it requires extraordinary grit to go back and rectify that mistake. People who adopt this method not only are brave and courageous but are destined for greatness. Such people never sit quietly till they get an opportunity to go back and rectify their mistakes. This might not always be possible and at times can prove excruciatingly painful, both physically and emotionally. They might also be called foolish or weirdos by many, but from their point of view, this is the only way to lead a more satisfying life.

The Past Was a Mistake

The past can only be treated as a mistake if your present is impressive. Success may be a poor teacher but a powerful intoxicant. People around you can become impressed by how far you have come in your success, such that they can forgive your past. You can proudly use your efforts and life improvements to show how much you have given to overcome your past mistakes. You can even use your past mistakes to teach a lesson or two to those who are interested. Always remember that your hard work and effort to improve and make up for past failures can be a tool to support you.

Bringing It All Together

The bottom line is if you want a happier life, bring those skeletons out of the closet. Mistakes of the past should never be pushed under the carpet or forgotten. They require careful detailing and attention to ensure that they are conquered and subjugated once and for all. Do not allow them to be impediments to your future success.

Create a Breakthrough Goal

Is there something you would like to achieve that would change your life? Possibly you want to own your own restaurant, write a best-selling book or become a pilot. A breakthrough goal is something that if accomplished would drastically change your life. It's a goal so big that the idea of reaching it would motivate you even through the toughest of times and it would change your whole life.

In his book *The Success Principles*, Jack Canfield states that most of our goals represent incremental improvements in our lives. They are like short offensive plays that lead you down the field towards a touchdown. A breakthrough goal is like a 50-yard pass leading to a touchdown in one play. These accomplishments are a quantum leap in your life, such as becoming a self-employed chef, winning the Masters Golf Tournament, getting married or graduating from university. This one goal would direct the rest of your life.

I had a breakthrough goal like this several years ago. My goal was to become an ordained Deacon in the Catholic Church. This was a goal that would completely turn my life upside down and lead me into unchartered waters. I truly believed that I was being called by the Lord to become a servant of Christ. My whole being was focused on doing whatever was required of me to make this goal become a reality. It fuelled me to overcome many obstacles I previously believed were impossible to overcome. At the beginning, the idea of me being a servant in the church was preposterous. I was completely opposite to what I needed to become.

What is your breakthrough goal? Is there something you have always wanted to achieve or do that would completely change the direction of your life? Grab it. Don't judge it and talk yourself out of it. Make it your breakthrough goal and create massive action towards this goal by writing out a statement of what it would look like when you have accomplished it. Feel what it would be like as you complete it.

You will now have the power to write out a list of everything you would have to accomplish to get there. With this information, you could create a plan on how you are going to accomplish your breakthrough goal. You will then create a timeline for when you will accomplish it and take the first step towards this life-changing event.

That is taking massive action towards your future. By choosing and planning your breakthrough goal, you will receive the motivation and fortitude required to achieve all the short- and long-term goals required to achieve your dreams. Your future is in your hands and I believe in you. Go forth and become the success you were created to become.

Turn Your Decisions into Actions

I have a simple math question for you. Five frogs are sitting on a log. Four of the frogs decide to jump off. How many frogs are left on the log? Did you answer one? Wrong, the correct answer is there are still five frogs sitting on the log. This is because there is a difference between deciding and doing. Deciding takes thought where doing requires action. Decision is not the same thing as action. We often confuse it as such, but deciding to become a millionaire is entirely different from actually doing what it takes to become one.

For a decision to mean anything, you must start taking action towards it. This concept may sound simple, yet most people never move beyond deciding to and begin doing. They are not in the habit of taking action. That is why most people do not accomplish all they could be accomplishing in their lives. By getting into the habit of putting ideas and decisions into action, you are in a better position to achieve the results you desire.

How many times have you heard the following statements, or perhaps even said them yourself?

- I've decided to change my career!
- I've decided to write a book!
- I've decided to quit drinking!
- I've decided to start a business!
- I've decided to leave my spouse!
- I've decided to exercise more!
- I've decided this is my year!

All these statements are noble decisions to make, and I'm not discounting the process it takes to get there. But once the decision is reached, it's only the beginning. Deciding to do something doesn't make it happen. It doesn't automatically equip you with everything you need for success.

Once the decision is made, that's when the real work comes in: the planning, the allocation of resources, the dedication of time, the intelligent risk-taking and the unshakable commitment to the decision. We don't always know the needed action to see our decision come to fruition. All too often, we make a mild attempt at action only to find it's not what we thought it would be. And the decision we so laboured to reach goes to waste. We become the frog who made the decision to jump, dipped his toe over the side, but never took the leap. It requires planning and commitment to turn a decision into reality.

Believe me, I know. I decided a long time ago that I was going to write a book. And guess what? That decision was only a thought for years because I never acted. It's only been in the past six months or so that I've taken the action to make it happen. It's slow going, I assure you. But I now feel like I'm getting somewhere.

It's worthwhile mentioning here too that sometimes, once the action starts, you realize the decision isn't what you want any longer. And that's OK. Maybe our little frog loves his log. Maybe he takes the leap and decides the new environment is not for him. Once again, that decision on its own accomplishes nothing. He now must take action to rectify the situation.

I know how hard it is to make decisions about life and work. We pour a lot of time and mental energy into the process. But don't let all that effort go to waste through inaction. Let your decision be your jumping off point—your catalyst for action.

Remember, you can always jump back on the log. But if you never jump, you will not experience the fruition and possible benefits of your decision. Taking massive action means acting on your decisions. Start today by choosing a decision you have made and take action to begin the process of achieving it. Even if you merely plan what you need to do. This action will set into motion more actions and the momentum to succeed, and make your decision become a reality.

Summary

Every individual in this world wants a comfortable life; they want smooth relationships; they want enough money so they can live comfortably and have their own house and car as well as enough money to enjoy their yearly or monthly vacations. Everyone has their dreams and desires of how they would like their life to transpire. But to have a dream and desire isn't enough. To have this kind of life the most important thing that is required is action and plenty of it. Taking action will lead you to what you have always desired.

Generating action on your decisions doesn't always have to be difficult. It is usually the first step towards your success journey that can seem difficult, because that first step will move you out of your comfort zone. But once you start and set your decision into motion, you will become more comfortable as you journey along.

Even if you begin by taking small baby steps towards your goals, the most important action is that you take that first step. By taking action and that first step, you will be setting into motion all the items required to achieve your dream and vision. No matter how knowledgeable and intelligent you are, if you do not put into action that knowledge, you will never experience the success and accomplishments you are capable of.

In this chapter, you have been shown several ways to address your desires and put them into action. If you adopt these principles and start to take massive action towards your goals, you are increasing the chance of them becoming a reality in your life. Massive action sets into motion all that is required to assist you to advance along the journey. You are the only one who has the power and can set action into motion in your life. Understanding what you have learned in this chapter should entice you to start today to take some small action towards the life you desire and deserve.

CHAPTER EIGHTEEN

Reach Out for Help

Don't go it alone

"The most important thing I think we need to remember
is that we're a work in progress. Do not be ashamed or
afraid to ask for help. That's what I did. I asked for help."
— **Carnie Wilson**

In This Chapter
- ➤ Ask for Feedback
- ➤ Get an Accountability Partner or Life Coach
- ➤ Have a Mentor
- ➤ Mentor Exercise
- ➤ Join a Mastermind Group
- ➤ Summary

Successful people are people who get things done. The question is
how do they get things done in today's tumultuous world? They
step up and take risks, they think big, and they make and execute

well-thought-out plans. There's something else they do that most people don't think about: successful people ask for help.

If you look at any successful person, they will invariably have a go-to person or even a network of people behind the scenes who help them solve problems and plan their life for optimal success. They have mentors, well-wishers and a range of people and groups who support them.

Asking for help is not a weakness but a strength. And it is as relevant in our personal lives as it is in the workplace. Asking for help makes sense for so many reasons. Projects get done quicker as we ask people who are more experienced than we are to advise us on the solution or path. Things get done in a better and smarter way. Asking for help allows you to get out of the stress and mess more quickly when the problem has hindered you in any way.

Also, think back to the times you may have helped out another person. How did it make you feel? What did you gain? We often lose sight of the big picture when we get caught up in our own microscopic views of things. When it comes to asking for help, we can get in our own way. Instead of realizing that we are giving others an opportunity to feel good about themselves, we think incorrectly that asking for help means we are a burden.

We also get in our own way when we assume asking for help means something about us when it doesn't. Our ego gets in the way. We may think asking for help means we are weak, inadequate, less desirable, helpless, inferior or any other derogatory label that comes to mind.

The reality is that asking for help does not indicate anything about us; it simply means we need help in a specific situation at a specific time. It is not a reflection of our character, intelligence, competence or desirability. It is actually a sign of strength and wisdom to seek out help when you need it.

Next time you need help, have the confidence to ask for it, knowing that it can truly benefit you both. Everybody gains! Keep in mind the giver is gaining a boost to their confidence, knowing they are a good person and receiving the good feelings that come from that, and the recipient gets the help they need.

If you want to achieve and live your dreams, you need to learn to ask for, accept and provide others help. You should develop your ability to ask and allow others to help you get what you desire and do the same for them. In this chapter, I will introduce ways you can accomplish this so that you can experience success in your life.

Ask for Feedback

What exactly is feedback? We hear the term all the time, but do we truly know what it is and why it is so important? The term "feedback" is used to describe the helpful information or criticism about a prior action or behaviour from an individual that is communicated to another individual (or a group) who can use that information to adjust and improve current and future actions and behaviours.

Who would dispute the idea that feedback is a good thing? All of us can benefit from feedback. Both common sense and research make it clear that feedback and opportunities to use that feedback help to improve and enhance an individual, group, business or organization, and that information can be used to make better informed decisions. It also allows us to build and maintain communication with others.

Effective feedback, both positive and negative, is very helpful. Feedback is valuable information that will be used to make important decisions. Top performers are at the top because they consistently search for ways to make their best even better. For top performers, continuous improvement is not merely a showy catchphrase. It's a true focus based on feedback from across sources such as family, friends, a coach, a mentor and others who have an interest in the person's success.

Top performers not only are good at accepting feedback but deliberately ask for feedback. And they know that feedback is helpful when it highlights weaknesses as well as strengths. They understand that effective feedback has benefits for the giver and the receiver.

Feedback is a critical component of growth and development. We all have life and performance blind spots, and learning to take advantage of feedback in all areas of our life will help us to grow and better our chances at success. A tool to help implement feedback into our lives is to become A.W.A.R.E.: Ask for feedback, Watch your emotions, Ask questions for clarity, Reach out for suggestions, and engage your talent.

By asking for feedback, you are showing that you truly want to improve yourself while at the same time telling the other party that you respect their opinion. When you ask for feedback, you are exposing yourself to positive and negative insights that you can use to process and help you make informed decisions for the future based on events that have transpired.

When you receive feedback, whether asked for or freely given, you need to be in control of your emotions. It is important not to react in a defensive manner when negative feedback has been received, in the same way you should not let positive feedback cause you to become egotistic.

Feedback is information for you to process. You should learn from feedback what is working and what is not so you can make informed decisions in the future. By allowing you emotions to cloud your judgement, you are doing more harm than good.

Some people will provide hurtful negative feedback on occasions. Keep your composure and take into account the source of the feedback. Reacting in defence of yourself or cursing the person providing the feedback can only be counterproductive and could cause relationship rifts. No matter who gave the feedback and what it consisted of, thank the person for their feedback and let them know you will consider it. Leave it at that for the moment. You can evaluate it later and, if the feedback was helpful, you can go back and thank the person again.

After you have carefully reviewed the feedback, make sure to clarify any questions or concerns you have with the person who provided it. Too many times a misunderstanding has caused good feedback to be ignored. Fully understanding what the person meant with their feedback is vital for it to be used effectively. Never assume what they meant when not clear. Always clarify and be sure.

After reviewing someone's feedback, if you are not sure what to do, be sure to reach out to them or other people you trust for suggestions to help you move forward. Many times the answer is right there in front of your nose but you cannot see it. Hearing it from someone else makes it clear. When you are truly stuck for ideas, others may provide the necessary information to help you develop a strategy.

Once you fully understand the feedback and have an idea of how you want to proceed, you need to engage your talents and ability to implement and carry out your new strategy. By taking action, you are using feedback and past experiences to help propel you forward.

Most successful people happily use feedback to help themselves change and improve on a daily basis. Feedback is a powerful tool if you learn how to use it properly and not allow it to cause you suffering or embarrassment.

Get an Accountability Partner or Life Coach

We all have those nagging voices in the back of our head reminding us of the things we wanted to do, or were supposed to do, but we simply didn't get around to yet. Not getting them done frustrates us, but we don't seem to get any closer to completing the projects or tasks.

Often, they are things we have wanted to get done for ages but some reason we are no closer today than we were a year ago. It might be losing some weight, stopping a nasty habit, exercising more, doing more business development, upgrading your website, writing a book, getting your accounts in order and so on. For most of us, the list of things we want to do but aren't getting done tends to be a long one.

If you can relate, perhaps it's time to get yourself an accountability partner or life coach. This person will hold you accountable for getting things done, meeting your deadlines and achieving the goals you set yourself.

Being accountable to someone means you stand in integrity, keep your word and honour your commitments. But you do this knowing someone's got your back. And that someone is your accountability partner or life coach.

Accountability Partner

Your accountability partner or life coach will lift you up when you're down, help you celebrate your wins, keep you on track and mirror back to you the highest version of yourself possible. Plus, aren't you more likely to follow through with something and achieve your goals if you know that someone is cheering for you and wants you to succeed just as much as you do?

Together you can achieve so much more than you can on your own. Don't isolate yourself in a cocoon. Invest your energy in an accountability partner or life coach who will ride the waves with you. Supporting and stretching is what coaching is all about. Accountability is the difference between believing the impossible and achieving the impossible. Your accountability partner or life coach will help you turn the impossible into the possible.

You may be wondering "what is the difference between an accountability partner and a life coach?" I will now explain the difference for you beginning with an accountability partner.

An accountability partner is a trusted companion who helps you make progress toward a commitment you have made. They hold you accountable to the goals and changes you tell them you are trying to accomplish.

Helpful accountability partners are kind, gentle and gracious. They encourage, challenge and remind you of your goal. They are free of personal interest in your success or failure—other than wanting to see you succeed. Excellent accountability partners are trustworthy, dependable, willing and committed to helping you. They communicate clearly, directly, honestly and respectfully. Good partners ask difficult questions when appropriate and make critical but helpful observations. They are trusted friends who keep matters appropriately confidential.

Your accountability partner should expect growing successes along with reasonable failures. They will help you brainstorm solutions if you get stuck. And finally, a good accountability partner refuses to accept excuses or let you get away with doing less than you agreed to pursue.

Your accountability partner's main purpose is to keep you on course towards your goal. They are not there to tell you what to do or instruct you along the way. If you require more direct input, help and direction, then you should look into getting a life coach.

Life Coach

A life coach is a professional who helps you reach a goal or make a change in your life. They help you to get out of your head and start taking action in the areas of your life that you wish to change. A life coach guides you through the process by asking questions that help you evaluate and decide which steps to take in order to reach your goal or make an important change. Then they play the important roles of motivator, strategist and accountability partner.

Their purpose is to help you reach your goal in the most efficient, effective and rewarding way possible. Life coaches are more than simply a counsellor or consultant, they step you through the achievement process from the beginning to the end, from the planning stage all the way through the execution stages.

You would never expect someone to become a successful athlete without the help of an experienced coach. Just as athletes rely on a coach to guide, support and keep them accountable along their growth to success, so do most successful people. If you ask anyone who has become successful in their life, you will hear how coaching from someone with life experience helped them along the way. If you truly want to enhance your chance at achieving your dreams, I would strongly suggest you find a life coach to get you started and guide you along your journey.

Regardless if you are trying to implement a complete change in your life, achieve a personal or business goal or simply find yourself, a personal life coach can help. A personal life coach will help you to define your values, vision, mission, purpose and goals. They will help you develop the plan and action steps required to achieve what you desire. They help you sort through opportunities and focus on your top priorities. With their guidance and support, you will be able to achieve a greater balance in your life while achieving the goals you have set for yourself.

A life coach is a source of motivation and inspiration that gives you the push you need to reach your full potential. You might hire a life coach for similar reasons that you would hire a personal trainer. You may already be fit, but you have specific goals for which you need more guidance and pushing to accomplish. Or maybe you are overweight or feeling sluggish and know you need motivation and encouragement from outside of yourself to make a significant change.

Life coaches are like personal trainers for your life goals. They have the professional training and mindset that are needed to coach you towards your dream life. They are with you every step of the way, helping you find ways to stay on track and motivated to accomplish those goals and so much more. Where there is a lack of focus and direction in the workplace or in your personal life, a life coach is helpful for tackling that problem and helping you rethink and re-evaluate where you are heading.

Depending on the situation you are currently in, it is vital that you seek out and find an accountability partner of life coach right away. While I was working with prisoners in an institution that did not have access to a professional life coach, I encouraged them to find someone they could trust to be their accountability partner.

I saw tremendous positive change in their lives of those inmates who did find an accountability partner. I was even able to find some of them life coaches to assist them upon their release. All the prisoners I worked with that took advantage of this powerful tool changed their lives to become happy and contributing members of the community. If you implement this tool into your efforts, you will benefit from the results, I assure you. Take massive action and go out and find an accountability partner or life coach today.

Have a Mentor

Tony Robbins said, "If you want to be successful, find someone that has achieved the results you want and copy what they do and you'll achieve the same results." That person is a mentor and you should have one or more of them in your life.

The Merriam-Webster online dictionary defines a mentor as "a trusted counselor or guide." Wouldn't it be wonderful to be surrounded by others who want to help you work toward and accomplish your goals? We all could use a few good mentors with us along our path through life.

The problem is you already have mentors and do not realize it. The problem is that they are people who have and are experiencing exactly the opposite of what it is you desire. It is from these default mentors that you obtain information on how to live. Their mentorship works because all you have to do is look at the results you are experiencing compared to their lives.

It is now time for you to take control and replace the negative mentors you have accumulated throughout the years and purposefully seek out new empowering mentors who will lead you to your goals rather than away from them. Empowering mentors have the experience and a successful track record to draw from.

A good mentor can give you advice and inspiration that will completely change your future. They'll give you easy shortcuts that will help you get on the right path again quickly. They'll even be a role model and a guide whom you can follow.

Mentors are not only the professional people you usually think of, like teachers and coaches, but also everyday people in our lives. For example, some of your current mentors include your friends, family members, neighbours and colleagues.

Mentors can positively influence you and even change your long-term future. That one tip from an older cousin or that one moment of inspiration from your friend can totally change your life's direction by influencing your attitude, thoughts, beliefs and behaviour.

Mentors are everywhere, if you're only willing to see them. They are your siblings, significant others, grandparents, business professionals and acquaintances, to name a few. Keep your eyes open and make sure they are empowering and not limiting you.

A Mentor Is . . .

A friend. Like any friendship, mentors and mentees do fun things together. They also teach each other, help each other and are honest with each other. And sometimes they might want to have conversations about things that make them feel worried or upset.

A role model. Mentors try to set a good example for how to live. Mentors are not perfect people. Your mentor will do their best to share with you what they're good at, and they should be honest about mistakes they have made or things they are not good at doing.

A listener you can trust. You may say things to your mentor that you don't feel comfortable saying to anyone else. Sometimes you may tell your mentor about your hopes, dreams or fears. Other times you may reveal mistakes you've made. Mentors have your best interests in mind and try to be supportive of you, regardless of what you confide in them.

Someone who is proud of you. Your mentor should be able to see all the talents you have and help you learn and grow. They can help you take actions that make a positive difference to others in your family, neighbourhood, school or community.

Someone who has already achieved what it is you desire. Imagine having a book in which you can find the exact recipe for succeeding in any area of life. The recipe can be for anything, from building a successful career, starting a profitable business or getting six pack abs in a few months to finding the love of your life or anything else you want.

Imagine having a step-by-step guide in your hand that tells you how to achieve your goals with the least amount of effort, including all the secrets, shortcuts and pitfalls. An outstanding mentor is someone who already achieved what you want and has faced all the obstacles. They are the closest you can get to that kind of guide.

A Mentor Is Not …

A mentor to your family. Their role is to provide special attention to you. While getting to know your family can help them understand you better, their energy and attention should be focused on you.

A social worker or doctor. When you tell something to your mentor or they think something is going on in your life, they may need to ask for help from other people in order to help you. This is because some problems you face may be complicated, and your mentor might need professional help in order to be the best mentor for you.

A "fixer." Your mentor is not trying to change you or make you "better." Of course, their support can help you overcome hurdles in your life. But don't forget that you have gifts and talents;

you have a lot to offer the world. Your mentor's job is to help you build and use those gifts and talents to make a difference in your life and in the lives of others.

Having a mentor relationship is the best way for you to get your life moving and reach your goals as fast as possible. It will provide you with many advantages. Mentoring is a brain to pick, an ear to listen and a push in the right direction. A mentor can help to shorten your learning curve, open your mind to new ideas and possibilities, identify opportunities and advise on how to promote yourself.

<u>Finding a Mentor</u>

For many people, finding a mentor seems like a daunting task. They have no idea where to begin. There are a few steps in the process of acquiring a mentor that I will explain to you. As you move through these steps, know that developing a mentor/mentee relationships should feel as easy and enjoyable as developing a new friendship. Approaching the process with this mentality makes all the difference.

The first step in locating a mentor is to know exactly what it is you are looking for and from a mentor. Are you seeking guidance on how to overcome an addiction, wanting to start a business, trying to develop a mutual romantic relationship or wanting to know how to cook? There are many areas in one's life where the guidance and support of a mentor would be a great asset.

Also note that you do not have to restrict yourself to only one mentor. You can have more than one mentor assisting you with different areas of your life. However, I suggest you have only one mentor in the beginning who will help you focus in your most needed area of growth or change.

Once you know what you are looking for, you need to define what attributes and experience the mentor should possess that will assist and inspire you. You want to look for someone who has successfully reached the goal you are pursuing. If you want to overcome an addiction, then you would look for someone who has done just that and is now living a successful, respected and happy life. Do not look to someone who is well on their way to success but set your eyes on someone who has done it. They are in the best position to guide and inspire you. They have experienced most of the things you will be exposed to and have learned how to deal with them. Choose someone whom you admire for what they have achieved, someone who inspires you and is living a similar lifestyle to the one you want.

Do not judge whether the person would want anything to do with you. You do not know what other people are thinking. Do not allow fear or your judgment to stop you, as you are doing yourself and them a disservice. You would be surprised at the high-profile people out there who have been more than happy to assist someone they have never met. Not all people are willing to become a mentor, so you should not limit your choices.

Mentor Exercise

Write down all the attributes your mentor must have, including any quality that you desire to have or learn.

_____

_____

_____

Next make a list of the possible candidates you can think of who possess these attributes. You can also ask others for suggestions that you can add to your list.

Enter their names below.

_____

_____

_____

Now prioritize your list starting with the person you prefer the most and on down. Place a number by each name.

You are now ready to move on to the next step. It's time to contact your prospective mentor to determine if they are interested and would be a good fit. Before you contact them, make sure you research the person. Check books, social media and public information available about them. Get to know what they have accomplished, including hobbies and any unique information about them. This will give you something to talk about besides your needs. People love it when they know someone has taken the time to learn about them. This is a great relationship starter. You may even want to read the book *How to Win Friends and Influence People* by Dale Carnegie.

Start by contacting the first person on the list. Depending on their location and availability, the best way is to make a personal phone call. This might be difficult and take many attempts but be persistent, the reward is well worth the effort. If a personal call is not possible, you can use email or write a letter and mail to them marked "personal and confidential."

During your call, you should start by introducing yourself and stating the purpose of the call. Then explain why you have chosen them. Finally, ask to meet them. Offer to take them out for lunch to meet. Remember Ask, Ask, Ask. If they agree, then set a date, time and location to meet. If not, move on to the next name. Remember, every "no" brings you closer to a "yes." You have lost nothing and gained valuable experience.

Before you meet with your prospective mentor, you should write down what it is you want from them and what you are willing to provide in return. As to what you want, you are requesting their advice, guidance, expertise, time and friendship. You are offering your appreciation, dedication and commitment.

During your initial meeting, you will want to explain clearly what it is you are requesting of them and then ask them what it is they expect of you. If you agree to their expectations, make sure it is something you are able and willing to do. Remember to treat the meeting as two people trying to build a mutual friendship. You know that friendships don't develop from a single email or a 10-minute introduction. Instead, they develop slowly through continued interaction. Building a strong relationship is about offering praise, asking for advice and discussing your ideas over time.

Online resources as well as organizations are available to help people locate a mentor. Feel free to gain more knowledge and assistance before you start. Finding a mentor and building a mentor/mentee relationship may seem like an overwhelming task and it is. But a good mentor can and will change your life for the better and lead you successfully towards achieving your goals and dreams.

Finally, after you've gotten a mentor and your relationship is solidified, make sure to remember these times when you're down the road. Someday someone will be asking for your help. Remember when you felt lost, and don't let your success and busy schedule keep you from offering the helping hand you needed at one point in your life. Mentoring not only grows the mentee, but it grows the mentor as well.

Join a Mastermind Group

Your environment is everything. The people in it will make or break your success. That's why all of the most successful people throughout history have deliberately surrounded themselves with others who inspire them to become the best versions of themselves. If you want to achieve more success in your life, then you must do the same.

You need to surround yourself with people who inspire you, lift you up when you fall, challenge you to become more, help raise your standard and believe in your ability to achieve your wildest dreams. The best way to create this empowering environment is by creating or joining a mastermind group.

We have all heard the saying that "two heads are better than one." What if instead of two heads there were four, five or six heads together? That's even more productive, right? That is the premise of a mastermind group, when four to six people come together for the purpose of problem-solving, brainstorming, networking, encouraging and motivating each other in their life endeavours.

Mastermind groups have been in existence since before the turn of the 20th century. The concept of the mastermind group was first introduced by Napoleon Hill in his legendary book *Think and Grow Rich*. They are one of the most powerful tools for success ever used. Most of the successful people over the past 100 years acknowledge being part of a mastermind group as a contributing factor in their success both in business and personally.

The idea of a mastermind group is that more can be seen and achieved in less time when several individuals work together. A mastermind group is made up of individuals who meet together on a regular basis to share their experiences, ideas, thoughts, information, feedback, connections and resources. Being involved in a mastermind group opens your eyes to many ideas and opportunities that alone you may have missed. Mastermind groups are people who come from many types of backgrounds. Most groups comprise individuals from the same profession or life situation while some have a variety of business and life experience backgrounds.

The group as a whole can focus on specific business and life issues or be open to different topics, depending on the desire and needs of its members. But for the group to be effective, they must all be on the same page, trust each other to talk openly and hold the confidentiality of the group sacred. It is the trust and confidentially of the group members that allow for the openness and understanding needed to make their discussions honest and forthcoming.

Mastermind groups should consist of four to six committed members. They should meet regularly, such as weekly, biweekly or monthly but not longer. The meetings should be short so as to avoid them becoming a social event. Each meeting should have a topic agreed upon by the group and members assigned to enlighten the group on the topic.

At the beginning of the meeting, each member should give an update on their life since the last meeting and end with any concerns they may have at the time. After the opening round, a discussion about the chosen topic should be led by the member who researched the topic. Next, time should allow for each member to provide feedback on the topic or the information mentioned by the members at the start of the meeting.

Finally before the meeting ends, the next date, time, location and topic should be chosen along with one or two members who will prepare a briefing on the topic.

If possible, it is vital for all members to be present at all meetings and to provide equal input. Keeping the same members is also extremely important to the group's success. Mastermind groups will provide you with extra insight on a wide array of topics and will be a great resource to make new connections and access the resources required to become successful.

The benefits of a mastermind group are obvious. In addition to answering specific questions about challenges in your business or personal life, a mastermind can offer you:

> **Accountability.** You're going to write an e-book or launch a new campaign, eh? Well, when you tell others whose job it is to help keep you accountable, you'll find that extra bit of motivation to get something done that you don't have when you don't have accountability partners.

Camaraderie. Life isn't always a rose garden. It's hard, and often we simply need someone to talk to, not always someone like our family or friends. Interestingly, it's in these sorts of "venting" sessions that some creative solutions are discovered.

New ideas. You never know what ideas will birth from the cross-pollination of like-minded people sharing their triumphs and disappointments. Because you are in a safe and trusted environment, you allow yourself to be a bit more daring and vulnerable with your brainstorming.

Now that you understand the benefits of being part of a mastermind group, you may want to join one, but don't know where to start looking for one. Mastermind groups are everywhere; you just need to know where to find them. Be sure you know what you're looking for in a group before trying to find one to join. For instance:

- Do you want to meet in person or is meeting by phone or video chat acceptable?
- Do you need to meet in the evening or is a day-time meeting better?
- What topic areas do you want the group to focus on?
- Do you want to be held accountable for getting actions done and reporting back to the group, or do you want something more casual?
- Do you want a group that focuses on pure brainstorming, problem-solving and decision-making, or should there be an education element to the group as well?

Here are six ways to become part of a mastermind group:

1. Start a group of your own. It's easier than you think, and you can hand-select the people you want to brainstorm with. This way you get to choose the dates, times, locations and topic areas that work best for you. You're bound to find friends and colleagues who are searching, too.

2. See if there are any local mastermind groups by checking online. You can search within a radius of your postal code to find local mastermind groups on many topics. Then contact the group organizer and find out if the group is still meeting and if they're taking new members.

3. Use a "Find a Mastermind Group" service, which lists people who have existing mastermind groups and are looking for new members. Read the descriptions to see which group is right for you, then email the facilitator to set up time to talk on the phone about their group.

4. Talk with colleagues. Ask your connections via email, Facebook, Twitter and LinkedIn if they know of any existing groups looking for new members or any new groups that are forming. Telephone colleagues and friends and let them know you're looking. Ask co-workers. They might be in a mastermind group right now and would know if the group is a good match for you. Or search through their network of friends and colleagues and they can spread the word about what you're looking for.

5. Check with your favourite mentors, teachers and writers. They often have mastermind groups, which are often not advertised. If they don't have groups themselves, they may know of others who do.

6. Check with your local professional organizations, including trade groups, chambers of commerce, religious groups, networking groups and schools. Anywhere that

groups of people regularly meet together are the most likely to have mastermind groups.

Look around and you'll be surprised how many groups there are. Then interview the facilitator and some of the other members of the group to determine if the group is a good match for you. Ask if you can attend one meeting to get a feel for the group and how it's run. You'll love being part of a mastermind group! Add this powerful tool to your life war chest and you will be on your way to success and happiness.

Summary

Life in today's society can be extremely complicated to manoeuvre through. There are so many distractions around to sway us off our intended path that it is no wonder people become lost and frustrated. Most people try and face life on their own because of lack of trust in others, selfish pride or fear of change and the unknown. They struggle from day to day, passing up assistance that could quickly help them become more focused and overcome the obstacles that are interfering with progress, happiness and success.

In this chapter, I have explained that there are knowledgeable, experienced and valuable people resources out there to assist you through your struggles. All you need to do is identify which roadblock is stopping you from seeking and asking these people for help.

Learn to put your pride, fear and trust issues aside and reach out to grab a hold of the available lifelines available to you. Reach out to others and let them help you to create a clearer purpose, vision, plan and focus in your life. Allow them to benefit personally by assisting and watching you grow and become the success you were always meant to be.

There are many people who want you to succeed and would be more than willing to help you do it. All that is required is for you to take action and reach out to them. When you do, you will be amazed with the results and extremely happy you did.

You can try to go it alone, convinced that you are strong enough to reach success through your own effort. Some people have lived their life this way and gone on to success. But were they truly happy? Rather than go through the struggles of life alone, why don't you allow others to help you carry the burdens life can impose on you?

By reaching out for help, you will reach your goals in a quicker fashion and you will have the moral support required to get through those difficult days. Reach out today and live the successful and fulfilling life you have always desired in a quicker more focused manner. Use the tools introduced above to help you along your journey in life.

CHAPTER NINETEEN

Ensure Continued Success

Keep on learning and growing

"Success is a process that continues, not a status that you reach. If you are alive, there are lessons to be learned."
— **Denis Waitley**

In This Chapter
➤ Begin and End Each Day Right
➤ Commit to an Hour of Power
➤ Continuous Self Development
➤ Engaging A Support Team
➤ Summary

If you want to improve any aspect of your life, you must be totally committed and take consistent action. You must increase your personal standards and beliefs to improve the quality of your life. If you want ongoing success in your life, then you need to commit to Constant And Never-ending Improvement (CANI). With CANI, your life becomes better by gradual improvements in each area of your life. CANI expands who you are and how you live. Growth comes from improvement that enhances the quality of your life. Imagine what will happen if every day you would improve one thing in each area of your life in a small way? Little things may not seem like a lot but they can mean everything!

The more you improve, the better you feel and the more you are able help yourself and other people. When you commit to CANI, you will consistently grow and expand in all areas of your life: spiritually, mentally, emotionally, physically and financially. You will feel and enjoy a deep sense of well-being, happiness, joy and satisfaction. This type of growth only comes from a commitment to Constant And Never-ending Improvement.

Long-term change requires practising a new pattern for at least 21 days. Then, this new pattern becomes a habit. The little things that you do each day in all areas of your life may start out as small and consistent improvements, and then they create massive change. In this chapter, I will show you how you can employ CANI in your life and become all you can be.

Begin and End Each Day Right

Aristotle once said, "We are what we repeatedly do. Excellence, then, is not an act, but a habit." If you learn to repeatedly start and end your day in a positive and constructive manner, you are setting yourself up for success. The beginning and end of your day are powerful times that can set you up to challenge whatever you face or hold you back from attaining the things in life you desire.

How To Begin Your Day

You begin by reflecting on the morning ritual that you set up for yourself. Let's say you start the morning in a frenzy and you continually hit your snooze alarm, skip breakfast and rush out the door. Does the rest of your day reflect that mood of chaos? The tone of your morning will determine the tone of your day, so it's time to start planning accordingly.

When you form healthy habitual behaviours for the morning, you set your day up for success. Whether you are aware of them or not, you operate under habits (both good and bad) all the time. They are an integral part of your daily existence. Part of developing a healthy habit is to become intentional with it. Most habits are formed because they are easy or along the path of least resistance. If you want to cultivate positive habits, then you may need to put some intentional effort into forming them until they become second nature.

This is particularly true with morning habits. What you cultivate in the morning influences how you feel, act and think during the rest of your day. Here are some simple habits that you can add into your morning routine to ensure you are feeling, acting and thinking at your highest potential for the rest of your day and days ahead.

Begin the Day with Gratitude

The first thing you should do each morning even before you get out of bed is to start your day with gratitude. This starts the day off positively so as to produce a better daily life experience. Take a moment to list at least three things that you are grateful for in your life.

Gratitude is one of the most powerful human emotions, but most of us don't do enough to harness it. In fact, it's easy to get out of the habit of feeling grateful for much of anything at all. If you haven't given much thought lately to all the good things in your life, it might be time to change that by training yourself to choose a grateful mindset over a negative one.

Adopting a morning gratitude practice can make a huge difference in your overall mood and outlook on life. When you take the time to practise gratitude intentionally every day, a grateful mindset will become a habit and you might find that your life improves dramatically. Being thankful for what you have helps you to shed any negativity you're carrying around and open yourself up to the positive side of life.

Stay Unplugged

If the first thing you do when you wake up is check your phone for emails, texts or social media updates, you are doing yourself a large disservice. You are immediately cultivating a reactive mindset instead of a proactive one. Doing this will cause you to start your day in a defensive state, rather than a place of inner peace and control. Try remaining detached from technology for the first hour of your day so you can begin your day with present-moment awareness and a positive focus.

Move Quickly

Don't allow the thought of laziness or lack of motivation set in when you wake up. After you have practised your gratitude, quickly jump out of bed yelling "yes, what another lovely day to be alive." As you do this, clap your hands together. This will wake you up both mentally and physically.

Don't fall into the trap of wanting to stay in bed for just a few more minutes. This will only program your mind to regret having to get up and begin the day. It will sour your mood and restrict your productivity. By taking charge before laziness can overpower your mind, you will start your day off in the right frame of mind.

Take Time To Look and Feel Good

Putting time and effort into your appearance helps build self-confidence. When you feel "put together," it is one less thing to worry about throughout your day. Shower, wash your face, brush your teeth, floss, comb your hair, apply lotion, dress to impress and follow any other hygiene or grooming habits that make you feel good about yourself.

This may involve picking out or ironing your clothes the night before, especially if you are short on time in the morning. Do whatever makes you feel like you are taking care of your health, looking presentable and feeling confident.

Make Your Bed

This may seem minor, unimportant, unnecessary or a waste of time, but making your bed is a simple action you can take in the morning that makes you start your day feeling like you have accomplished something—and what better tone to set than a sense of pride and accomplishment? Taking charge and completing simple tasks will give you the foundation to take on more and more throughout the day.

Review Your To-Do List

Take a few minutes to think about your to-do list for tomorrow. Then prioritize your day's list and write down three to five of the most important ones. Rank your list in order of priority to make sure you tackle the most pressing ones first. Doing this reduces the stress of trying to decide what needs to be done next.

Writing down your to-dos instead of keeping them floating around in your mind helps clear mental chatter. You also give yourself a sense of purpose each day when you know what you need to get done. And there is something satisfying about crossing off tasks on your list—it cultivates a sense of accomplishment.

Have a Daily Hour of Power

I recommend that you add a daily hour of power to your morning routine. This is a process that will help build a healthy mental and physical life. You will learn about this powerful tool in the next part of this chapter.

Unfortunately, we often rush through our mornings and start our days disorganized, hurried and stressed. When stress builds up, it's almost impossible to start the day with a good attitude. Your goal is to start each new day with a solid head on your shoulders, low stress and a feeling of optimism. It isn't easy to do, but it's one of the greatest things you can do for yourself.

How To End Your Day

Now, let us investigate how you should end your day. It's a period of time that's important for your personal development, whether you realize it or not. It's as important as the morning routine. A day that's started well should also end well. And the way to do it is simple and the benefits are amazing. How you end your day may be similar to how you started it, but its effects work on your mind throughout the night subconsciously preparing you for the next day.

How do you feel at the end of your day? Are you stressed? Do you fall peacefully asleep or do you need to distract yourself with mindless television or social media to fall asleep? A few changes to your bedtime routine can help you feel positive, have a good sleep and get tomorrow off to a great start. A great day begins the night before, thus ending your day well is key to setting up your next day with success.

Try adding some of these suggestions to your nightly routine:

Let It Go and Accept Yourself

In order to be ready for the next day with all its opportunities, challenges and surprises, you'll need to let go of what was today. Let go of all the things you did, didn't do, forgot to do and failed to do. Breathe deeply and let things be as they are now. Let go of all your disappointments, little arguments, people that annoyed you, doubts, negative thoughts, judging and comparing.

Also, forgive. Forgive all those who insulted you, made you feel bad or didn't behave the way you expected. Forgive yourself for making mistakes, not being brave enough, missing a chance or not being honest with yourself.

Accept yourself for who you are and the way things turned out. Understand that everything is perfect just the way it is and things are just fine. Realize that you did your best. Feel how everything bad and negative is leaving your body and you don't feel exhausted anymore. Let in freedom, peace and joy.

<u>Be Grateful and Optimistic</u>
Thank the Lord for this day. It was a gift. Appreciate all the chances you had, the nice meals, the opportunity to be with your loved ones, your comfortable place and the ability to do things you love. Not everyone has all this. Notice it and be grateful.

Look forward to tomorrow. Envision how tomorrow is going to be amazing, new and exciting. Think about the special opportunities and events that you are going to experience. Every day is a new opportunity to learn, love and experience life to its fullest. Being grateful and optimistic provides your subconscious positive ideas to focus on and process while you sleep.

<u>Plan for Tomorrow</u>
The last thing you probably want to think about just before falling asleep are all the things you need to get done tomorrow. Who wants the stress of another busy day keeping them awake at night? You think, "I just want some peace and quiet. Leave my problems for tomorrow to deal with them." These thoughts are real and prevent many people from thinking about tomorrow tonight. I would like to tell you how these thoughts are misleading and can limit your productivity.

By taking the time just before you go to bed to plan what you want to accomplish the next day, you are increasing your chance of experiencing a successful day immensely. If you take the time to list the things that you want to get done the next day, you are opening your subconscious mind and allowing it to work on solutions to your desires all night while you sleep.

You see, the subconscious mind does not sleep. Thus, while you are in dreamland, your subconscious mind is quietly working to solve any task you present it. If you don't give it anything to work on, then it will draw from your past and find ways to make it again become a reality.

By feeding your subconscious what you want to accomplish, you have a head start on finding shortcuts and solutions for your goals. Rather than spend the morning trying to think of ways to accomplish what it is you are trying to do, much of that work was done while you were sleeping.

These are some of the best ways to end your days—no matter how bad or good your day was. If you practise them, they will soon become a habit. And your life will become simpler, easier, more pleasant and joyful. There's no better feeling than leaving all that burden each night and waking with enthusiasm and confidence the next day, starting your day with freedom, wisdom and happiness.

Commit to an Hour of Power

Have you ever looked at how you spend the first hour of your day? Did you know that most productive and successful people have a power-hour routine during which they connect with themselves, both mind and body, before starting their day? The power hour allows you to get charged up to live your best life each and every day and it also keeps you on track to achieve your life goals.

I must say that before creating my own power hour, I was like most people. I would grab a coffee and waste my time looking at Facebook, emails and newspapers before starting my day. However, when I started reading, exercising and meditating, my entire morning routine changed. Instead of lazily feeding my mind with useless and negative information, I was now feeding it and my body the positive and strengthening sources required to produce a healthy, enjoyable and productive day.

To help me get the best out of each day, I now start every morning by reading something empowering for 20 minutes. I then do my prayer, meditation and visualization session for 10 minutes, before finishing the hour by walking outside or on the treadmill. This usually sets a great tone for my day, and I notice the difference on the mornings when for some reason I don't take the time to complete my hour of power.

This routine works best for me; however, you can customize your own power hour in the way that will serve you best. For you, it might be spending quality time with your kids before rushing them off to school, exercising, writing a few pages of your book, doing yoga, reading a few pages of a self-development book, going for a walk or simply sitting quietly enjoying a few cups of coffee or tea.

You can use your 60 minutes to do one activity or you can divide it into two or three blocks. One day, you may read for 60 minutes, another day you may prefer to do 20 minutes of reading, 20 minutes of exercise and 20 minutes of meditation. You can do all three at once or with breaks. It doesn't matter: stay flexible and be sure you do it. Limit yourself to a maximum of three activities. You want to be making 10 steps in one direction, not one step in 10 different directions.

You can make the power hour your own, but most importantly it's supposed to "empower and uplift" you. It's important that you stay away from the news, whether on television, the internet or the radio. You might not notice it, but the news is rarely joyous, and your subconscious mind picks up on all this negativity and it gets trapped inside your body and creates mental havoc.

Successful people have all found ways to hone their focus, break the habit of procrastination and become a master of good habits in their lives, all of which will largely determine whether you are ultimately successful or not. Adding the hour of power into your daily morning routine is one more way to ensure your success.

It is important to exercise both your mind and body on a daily basis. When ignored, the mind and body can deteriorate and inflict stress and problems in your life. If we don't keep our bodies healthy with good food and exercise, then our business and personal lives will suffer. I think it's great to plan to go to the gym in the evening after work. But if most folks were to be honest, it doesn't always get done at the end of a long, tiring day. Start the day off with something simple like walking or some other type of exercise and then it will be a bonus if you get your gym time in at the end of the day.

Lifelong learning is one of the traits all successful people share. Spending merely 20 minutes each morning reading educational or inspirational books or listening to CDs is all it takes. You can also add meditation and prayer. Ask yourself what you need to learn or do today. Do you need inspiration to get you out of your funk or do you want to educate your mind today? Whatever the answer is, start each day off with some brain food.

Try this concept of the power hour for a week, and I guarantee that you'll have achieved more than you thought possible because you'll have done it all with energy, focus and conviction. Though it may seem challenging at first, habits take time to develop and in no time your hour of power will become a natural part of your day.

In fact, if you miss engaging your hour of power one day, you will feel at a loss. Make every effort to complete your hour of power daily. Even when what appears to be a very important issue arises, make sure to commit to this important part of your day.

If you go on holidays, don't stop your daily effort. When you take time away from a habit, it weakens it and it may become hard to motivate yourself. Your hour of power is important to your success and happiness. Do not take it for granted but cherish it.

Continuous Self Development

Nowadays, many people believe that learning only happens in schools. Once we graduate from high school or college, the learning ends. We have occupational-specific learning, but there is often no attempt to increase our knowledge in other fields of interest. We become stagnant.

For many of us, the school days represent a time in our lives when we were forced to learn. We are placed into a system to prepare us for life. We must read books, we must learn information, and we must pass tests on subjects that we have no interest in or will never use again in our lives. When we leave school, we are often ready to set learning in the rear-view mirror and finally enter the "real world." I strongly believe that it is important to separate our school-based learning from continuous self-development.

Continuous self-development should be focused on areas of your life that you want to improve, whether this is fitness, increasing the number of books you read, practising gratitude, learning to play an instrument or learning to become less reactive. There should always be an aspect of ourselves that we are trying to better or else we may never evolve past our 20-year-old selves.

If you aren't actively looking to learn new things, there are reasons why you might want to rethink your strategy. Self-growth is key for us to live fulfilling lives and to have a successful career. Here are four reasons to learn new information:

<u>You Will Become Happier</u>

Learning is tough and can be frustrating. This is especially true when we are taking on new sports, changing our thoughts and actions, or pushing our brain to the limits trying to learn code. Although the task is hard, nothing is greater than your accomplishment. For highly challenging goals like learning to write software, it is an amazing feeling when your code works bug-free. When we play sports, beating our personal records gives a high like none other.

Several studies have shown that the more ambitious goals we set, the happier we are. When we decide our own goals, our happiness is not reliant on others. We pick how many hours we practise, and we take ownership over what we achieve. Personal development is a way to guarantee us serenity from within.

You'll Become Irreplaceable to Others

The person who can adapt the most wins. This is a piece of advice I learned reading about fighter pilots in the air force. It is not about the strength of the plane, but instead it's the ability to react to different situations that makes a fighter pilot. The best fighter pilots can adjust to more circumstances than the norm, making them much deadlier.

This same idea can be applied to our value in our organizations. If you can only sell your product, you are limited by your contribution. If you can sell, build and run operations, now you've become irreplaceable.

You'll Stay Humble

When we are looking to learn as much as possible, there's less of a chance that you will come off as arrogant. True charmers don't make themselves look smart, they make others look smart. And when people see that you are trying to learn from them, it makes liking you that much easier.

Every interaction you have is a chance to learn something. One of the recent ways I've learned this is through watching TED talks. What I love about these short speeches is that you can learn so much about subjects you thought you'd have no interest in. But by keeping an open mind, you discover patterns in how people present their talks that you can learn from. It shows you that no matter whom you meet, there is always something valuable to learn from the encounter.

You'll Become a Great Coach

The only way to mastery is through teaching. One of the best feelings in the world is teaching others what you've learned. Not only will it affect the person you're teaching, but they in turn will teach others.

As a leader in an organization, you need to make learning a part of your culture. A way to start this is by teaching others what you've learned over time. You want to become such a great teacher that your company can run itself without you there. When you've achieved that, you've truly accomplished the state of mastery.

There are three different kinds of education that you can acquire, either deliberately or in a random fashion. These three kinds of learning are maintenance learning, growth learning and shock learning, and I'll go into each one below.

Maintenance Learning

Maintenance learning means you are keeping current with your field. This keeps you on pace and prevents you from falling behind. Many people think that reading an occasional book and keeping current with blogs and newsletters is the equivalent of adding to their education. This is not the case.

Maintenance learning is the same as checking the stock market reports each day to find out the prices of various stocks and securities. This information does not add to your knowledge of the companies, the market or the investment potential of a particular stock.

Maintenance learning is absolutely essential. It's similar to light physical exercise that keeps you at a particular level of fitness. It won't increase your level of fitness or improve your conditioning in any way, but it will keep you in shape.

Growth Learning

This is the kind of learning that adds knowledge and skills to your repertoire that you did not have before. Growth learning helps you expand your mind. You're acquiring information that you didn't have that enables you to do things that you could not do previously. Some of the very best thinkers in the world today are producing some of the very best material and ideas that you can use for continuous education and to help you expand your mind.

You can find this information by doing a quick search online. You can discover great ideas by listening to podcasts, reading blogs and reading books. You can discover incredible information without having to buy anything at all.

<u>Shock Learning</u>

Shock learning is learning that contradicts or reverses a piece of knowledge or understanding that you already have. Shock learning can be extremely valuable if you act upon it. The primary sources of innovation in life and an organization are the unexpected successes or the unexpected failures, something that happens that is completely inconsistent with the expectations of what should have happened.

This "shock" can give you insights that can enable you to either take advantage of a major change in the world or guard against a serious reversal. Unfortunately, most people are creatures of habit. When something happens that is completely unexpected, they choose to ignore it in favour of the old information with which they are more comfortable. Don't be afraid of change. Always change and adapt.

Dedicate yourself to continuous education and self-development, as knowledge is the primary source of value in our world today. Your ability to expand your mind and devote yourself to lifelong learning is the key to breaking any success barriers that may be in front of you.

Engaging a Support Team

You have all heard the myth of the self-made man. I call it a myth because we all know no one makes it on their own. When we achieve success or accomplish our goals, we do so through the support of or assistance from others.

As you fulfill your dreams and achieve success, it stands that you will have a circle of support from friends, family and acquaintances. But each of your supporters will have different talents, skills, interests and abilities to contribute to your quest to accomplish the goals you have in mind.

Finding a group of people who know about your life and are able to support and encourage you is important. It means that you are not alone as you make your journey. It makes it easier for you, as the more that people understand your situation and your coping strategies, the more supportive they can be. They can help to keep you on track.

Try to share relevant information about your successes and failures with members of your life support group. If people in your support group don't know what you are going through and how you are trying to cope, then it is difficult for them to support you. Remember, that it does not mean that you have to tell each member of your support group everything. Only share what you are comfortable sharing at the moment. As your relationship matures, the sharing of your feelings and situation will become easier.

In the previous chapter, I discussed some of the different types of supports you should implement into your life. Think about the places where you spend the most time. This might be home, school, work, sports clubs, community groups or with friends. Within these places are people whom you can trust. This could include family members, teachers, business professionals, coaches, health professionals and best friends.

It would be helpful to have at least one person in each of these places who has some understanding of you and your goals. These people are then in a better position to support and encourage you along the way. They can also help you consider whether anything you are doing can be changed to help you better succeed. For example, telling a trusted person about your successes and challenges in coping with goals means they can support and encourage you when you next face difficult situations. Together, you might be able to plan for challenging situations by developing a coping plan.

As soon as you begin to implement asking for help in your life, your mindset will shift, your priorities will change and you will gain the ability to focus on enhancing your life more fully.

Sometimes small tweaks are all that are needed to move you in the right direction. Build a strong and supportive team and you will not fail.

Summary

The importance of self-improvement often goes unnoticed. We are conveniently brushing our shortcomings under the carpet, refusing to face them or are happily being ignorant. The truth is you cannot run away from yourself. The farther you run, the deeper a hole you dig because there will come a time when all those unresolved emotions will surface, leaving you overwhelmed.

It is time for you to become more self-aware, observing your thoughts, emotions and responses and deciding to make self-improvement an integral part of your life. Similar to the way learning should never stop, the same applies for self-improvement. The idea should be to focus on continuous self-development at every stage in our life and become better versions of ourselves.

Self-improvement lets you identify your personal strengths and play on them. From relationships to careers, knowing your strengths is important for every sphere of your life. It gives you a better understanding of what you are seeking and where you are likely to thrive and excel. It helps you set life goals and make them happen. After all, you can only achieve what you want when you know what you want.

The goal of improving yourself should be to look beyond those weaknesses that are stopping you from achieving greatness. Accept your weaknesses, identify where they stem from and be determined to overcome them. It's not easy, but it's certainly not impossible.

Let your journey of self-improvement turn every weakness into a strength and only take you upward. By nurturing and playing on your strengths, you are more likely to attain success and move towards shaping a happier and more productive life.

Final Thoughts

If you are still reading this book, then I want to congratulate you for your commitment and desire to become a better version of yourself. Facing our demons and shortcomings is not an easy or pleasant task. By opening yourself up and acknowledging your true inner self, you have set into motion your subconscious mind. It is the power of your subconscious mind that will then assist in helping you become the person you truly know you are and desire to be.

When I first set out to write this book, I wanted to provide you with the all the life-changing information I have discovered during my personal journey, including principles and tools I have learned from masters who have spent their lives researching and developing them. I know these principles and tools work because they have helped me totally redefine how I think, my decision process and the actions I have taken.

As I began transforming this information into written words, I at first became frustrated with the fact there was so much to tell you that I could not possibly write it all in one book. If I did, the book would be so large that it would discourage a reader from even starting it. Thus, I have done my best to highlight the main principles and tools in as detailed but tolerable manner as I could. I am confident the information I have provided will help you get started and well on your way towards becoming all you are destined to be.

When you faithfully implement the information and tools you have learned in this book into your life, I am confident that you are well on your way to constant and never-ending improvement. You are on the path towards living a purposeful, happy and fulfilling life and achieving all your dreams and desires. At the beginning, the progress may not be so obvious or the results as quick as you want. But rest assured that if you are working with these principles and tools, then improvement is taking place.

To help you understand this process better, I would like to tell you one more story. It is about the Chinese bamboo tree. Like any plant, growth of the Chinese bamboo tree requires nurturing with water, fertile soil and sunshine. In its first year, we see no visible signs of activity. In the second year, again, there is no growth above the soil. The third, the fourth, still nothing. Our patience is tested and we begin to wonder if our efforts of caring for and watering it will ever be rewarded.

And finally in the fifth year—behold, a miracle! We experience growth. And what growth it is! The Chinese bamboo tree grows 80 feet in just six weeks!

But let's be serious, does the Chinese bamboo tree really grow 80 feet in six weeks? Did the Chinese bamboo tree lie dormant for four years only to grow exponentially in the fifth? Or was the little tree growing underground, developing a root system strong enough to support its potential for outward growth in the fifth year and beyond? The answer is, of course, obvious. Had the tree not developed a strong unseen foundation it could not have sustained its life as it grew. The same principle is true for people. People who patiently toil towards worthwhile dreams and goals, building strong character while overcoming adversity and challenge, grow the strong internal foundation to handle success.

People are like the bamboo tree. They need nurturing, feeding and care to develop into the best version of yourself. Though each person develops at different rates, they all are required to build a solid root foundation before they can sprout to become the towering success they were meant to be. Have patience and let your foundation grow. Tend to yourself daily and nurture yourself to become the person you are capable of becoming.

Please take this book and read it over and over again. Every time you do reread it, I assure you that you will discover something that will help you progress towards your goal of becoming the best version of yourself possible. Go over the exercises and compare them to your earlier attempts. This is one way that you will notice the improvements that have already transpired.

Also, I encourage you to start reading books or listening to audios from some of the great self-improvement masters. People like Tony Robbins, Jack Canfield, Norman Vincent Peal, Dale Carnegie, Napoleon Hill and others have dedicated their lives to helping others become the best they can be. Also watch for more books and workshops from me. I am developing detailed workshops around the principles and tools I have introduced in this book. Visit my website Lifemastery.ca where you will find resources to help you along your journey to living a life with purpose, happiness and fulfillment.

I would like to close by thanking all those people who have helped me turn a directionless life of pain, misery and suffering into one of meaning, purpose and direction. I now have a life of happiness and fulfillment. I pray and believe that you too will also achieve your dreams and live the life you have always desired and deserve.

Remember

You are a child of the universe,
no less than the trees and the stars;
you have a right to be here.
And whether or not it is clear to you,
no doubt the universe is unfolding as it should.

Therefore be at peace with God
whatever you conceive Him to be,
and whatever your labors and aspirations,
in the noisy confusion of life keep peace with your soul.

With all its sham, drudgery, and broken dreams,
it is still a beautiful world.
Be cheerful.
Strive to be happy.

Now go out and **Achieve Your Dreams** like I know you can.

May God Bless you, keep you safe and guide
you to never-ending happiness and peace.

About the Author

Gary Haney was born in 1957, the second youngest in a family of six children. His father was an officer in the Canadian Army and was away on missions for most of the first 10 years of Gary's life. Because of army demands, the family moved many times until 1966 when they settled in Calgary, Alberta.

As a child and into his youth, Gary was always in search of attention. His attention-seeking often got him in trouble and in a few cases involved the police. Because of his father's standing in the army, Gary often got off with little or no consequences for his actions. Eventually, he developed an attitude towards life of "I can do what I want."

At sixteen, Gary met a girl and was married against the advice of both of their parents. Within five years, they had four children. Within the first year of their marriage, they moved to Sparwood, British Columbia, and Gary took a job with a coal company and purchased a home. Gary was not mature enough to handle the pressures of being a husband, father, homeowner and worker. He became irresponsible and spent most of his time finding things to do with friends for personal enjoyment.

In 1979 he quit his job, left his house and moved his family back to Calgary, where he drifted from job to job and was rarely there for his family. As the years transpired, there were several family breakups and Gary was in and out of prison four times. While he was in prison, he was introduced to Christianity. The Salvation Army had a Friday night service in which they had women, cookies and coffee. For those reasons and to get out of his dorm, Gary gladly attended while proudly proclaiming that religion was for the weak-minded (although while attending the service he acted like he had been a devoted Christian all his life). He said that there was no way he was falling victim to the religious brainwashing.

As he served his last sentence, he and his wife separated for the last time and she moved back to B.C. with the children. While incarcerated, Gary's father passed away from cancer. Gary was able to see him on one last occasion in the hospital and then attend his funeral, both times with guards and in handcuffs.

After his release from prison, Gary again had periods of short employment and unemployment. He moved from one place to another, even becoming homeless for a short period of time because he was locked out of his apartment for nonpayment of rent. He began smoking pot and hash oil for the first time.

Finally, on a summer afternoon in July 1986, he was lying in his bed broke and depressed. He had hit rock bottom and was eating a Fudgesicle he had bought at the corner store with the last pennies he was able to scrape up. He had no job, money or motivation and his rent was due in two weeks. It was then he decided, "No more. I am better than this." He called a friend whom he had worked for several times in the past and had taken advantage of on more than one occasion. He put his pride aside and begged for another chance. To his surprise, his friend agreed to help him get a job.

This new motivation empowered Gary for several months. He had purpose and a plan. Gary even connected with and started visiting with his children. Around this time, he met Linda, his future wife, at a hockey game. Gary had no desire to be in a relationship at the time but went out with her on several occasions. Linda was a strong Catholic and responsible girl. She treated his children from his first marriage as if they were her own when they came to visit. Gary now refers to meeting Linda as his angel sent to him from somewhere up above, as sung in the Alabama song. Linda became a positive influence in his life and inspired Gary to become more open to others' feelings and needs. In 1988 Gary, who had found true love, proposed to Linda after saying he would never get married again. Linda agreed, but first Gary had to deal with his first marriage and get a divorce. It was six months later that Linda unexpectedly lost all of her eyesight because of diabetes.

Against all medical odds, Linda became pregnant in 1989 to the joy of both of them. The wedding had to wait because Gary had not yet received his divorce. They had a daughter on January 1, 1990. The divorce finally came through in April 1991 so Gary and Linda were married on April 14th. They had an addition to the family in 1995 with the birth of a son.

As life started to look a little better, in 1992 Gary received a book during sales training that began a positive change in his life. The book was *The Success System That Never Fails* by W. Clement Stone. Though Gary was living more responsibly, he still had many negative habits and issues in his life. After reading the book, he found a desire to learn more about himself and why he acted the way he did.

It was at this point that Gary was introduced to crack cocaine by some friends and instantly became an addict. In just six months, he managed to embezzle over $50,000 from his friend's company and spent it all on feeding his addiction. He was able to hide the addiction for about four months until it completely overtook him. In desperation, Gary was sent to an addiction program in Santa Monica, California.

While there, his friend found out about the missing money; when he confronted Gary on the phone, Gary admitted what he had done. After meeting with Linda about what had happened, Gary's friend—in a show of concern and compassion—chose not to press charges and allowed Gary to work off the money he took when he got back.

Gary spent six weeks in the program before prematurely pulling himself out, thinking he no longer required help. When he arrived home, he began working and ordered Tony Robbins's taped program called *Personal Power* that he saw on an infomercial.

About the same time, Gary was driving Linda to Sunday Mass each week because of her blindness. Though he had no part in what was transpiring, he was drawn to find out what the church was all about. He started to attend the church's Rite of Christian Initiation for Adults program (RCIA). This was a program that explained what the Catholic Church was, what it believed and how they lived their faith.

Gary also joined a community service group, the Lions Club. For the first time in his life, he became involved in helping others in need without concern for personal gain. After the first year of service and to his surprise, he was named Lion of the Year. Gary had won many awards in the past but they were always calculated and an end goal for him. He said that this was the best compliment he had ever received because he had no part in arranging it, and for the first time in his life he felt truly proud of himself. Now he believed that he did have good in him.

While Gary was studying the Personal Power program, he had a few setbacks again using crack but without the costly results. He was not yet cured of the drug's addicting pull. It was what he learned in the taped program that finally gave him the tools to completely overcome his addiction and get his life on track.

Now that Gary had life tools to help him improve his life, he was still having a problem figuring out what his purpose and mission in life were. As he continued his RCIA lessons, he finally decided to give his life to the Lord. He made a promise to God: "Lord, I do not really believe You exist. But I do believe from what I have learned that if You do exist and I turn my life over to You and do what You ask of me even if I do not understand it, that You will help me come to believe."

Gary was accepted into the church and became completely involved with volunteering. He became a fourth-degree member of the Knights of Columbus, helping whenever needed.

Shortly thereafter, Gary had a premonition from God telling him to go and serve the prisoners in jail. After years of being in prison as a prisoner, he wanted no part of this, but he remembered the promise he made earlier. "Tell me what to do and I will do it even if it does not make sense to me." He started volunteering in a few prisons, helping with faith services and programs. He eventually went on to become the full-time chaplain at the Drumheller Federal Penitentiary where he served for over 11 years and finally retired in 2017.

Not long after Gary's first premonition, again he had a calling from God to become a deacon in the church. Gary had no idea what a deacon was or what a deacon did so he read a pamphlet on the diaconate. After reading it, he laughed and exclaimed, "Good joke, Lord. A deacon is everything I am not." But remembering his promise, he spoke to the pastor and after six years of discernment and education, he was ordained a deacon in the Catholic Diocese of Calgary on June 8, 2008. Gary chose prison ministry as his focus as a serving deacon and continues his ministry today.

Not long after starting as a volunteer in the prisons, Gary witnessed many prisoners who had attended the chapel programs and made life-changing improvement in their attitude and actions but ended up back in prison after they were released. It did not take long to learn that upon release most prisoners had no support and ended up back in the negative environment they had originally come from. It was the lack of programs, support, resources and mentorship that contributed to their reverting back to their old beliefs and behaviours.

Gary decided to correct this problem, and in 2005 he created an organization called the St. Dismas Prison Ministry Society, which provides prisoner reintegration and aftercare programs, support, resources and mentorship. It begins in the prison and continues during and after release. In a true sense of co-operation, he brought together many organizations that were already providing theses service. Since its inception, they have assisted over 250 prisoners reintegrate back into the community as happy and contributing members of society.

After retiring from prison chaplaincy, Gary continues to direct the St. Dismas Prison Ministry Society and its prisoner reintegration and aftercare mandate. He has also developed the Life Mastery Solutions organization, which provides resources, workshops, training and coaching to prisoners both in the institution and in the community after release. Life Mastery's programs are also designed for people in the community who struggle with addiction and life issues. This includes youth for whom the goal is to provide help before they become an addict or criminal.

Gary wrote this book for anyone who needs it and for it to be placed in prisons. This book will become the basis for several workshops and self-help programs provided in the future.

Though his children have moved out, Gary is now happily living his purpose and mission with Linda's loving support. He is now achieving his dreams and personally improving each day while helping others to improve and achieve their dreams by living a purposeful, happy and fulfilling life.